From Naming to Saying

D1219431

*With my affection and with gratitude, I dedicate this book to
my mother and father
Mary Olga Cothern and Nelson Eugene Gibson
and to my favorite philosopher
Dennis Wilson Stampe*

From Naming to Saying

The Unity of the Proposition

Martha I. Gibson

WITHDRAWN

Blackwell
Publishing

BOWLING GREEN STATE
UNIVERSITY LIBRARIES

© 2004 by Blackwell Publishing Ltd

350 Main Street, Malden, MA 02148-5020, USA
108 Cowley Road, Oxford OX4 1JF, UK
550 Swanston Street, Carlton, Victoria 3053, Australia

The right of Martha I. Gibson to be identified as the Author of this Work has been asserted in accordance with the UK Copyright, Designs, and Patents Act 1988.

All rights reserved. No part of this publication may be reproduced, stored in a retrieval system, or transmitted, in any form or by any means, electronic, mechanical, photocopying, recording or otherwise, except as permitted by the UK Copyright, Designs, and Patents Act 1988, without the prior permission of the publisher.

First published 2004 by Blackwell Publishing Ltd

Library of Congress Cataloging-in-Publication Data

Gibson, Martha I.
  From naming to saying : the unity of the proposition / Martha I. Gibson.
    p. cm.
Includes bibliographical references and index.
  ISBN 0-631-22655-9 (alk. paper) — ISBN 0-631-22656-7 (pbk. : alk. paper)
  1. Proposition (Logic)   2. Grammar, Comparative and general—Sentences.
I. Title

  BC181.G46 2004
  160—dc21

               2003013378

A catalogue record for this title is available from the British Library.

Set in 10/12.5pt Palatino
by SNP Best-set Typesetter Ltd., Hong Kong
Printed and bound in the United Kingdom
by MPG Books Ltd, Bodmin, Cornwall

For further information on
Blackwell Publishing, visit our website:
http://www.blackwellpublishing.com

Contents

Preface

Words which, when spoken in succession, signify something, do fit together, while those which mean nothing when they are strung together, do not. . . . For example, "walks runs sleeps," and so on with all the other verbs signifying actions – you may utter them all one after another, but that does not make a statement. . . . And again, if you say "lion stag horse" and any other names given to the things that perform actions, such a string never makes up a statement. Neither, in this example, nor in the other do the sounds uttered signify any action performed or not performed or the nature of anything that exists or does not exist, until you combine verbs with names. The moment you do that, they fit together and the simplest combination becomes a statement of what might be called the simplest and briefest kind. . . . [I]t does not merely name something but gets you somewhere by weaving together verbs with names.

Plato, The Sophist[1]

Plato suggests that for a string of words to say something, it must be composed of two different kinds of words – a noun and a verb. Taken by themselves, the words only name things. The noun "Theaetetus" names a boy and the verb "flies" an act. Neither says anything. But string the words together, one of each kind, and you have a *sentence*, "Theaetetus flies." It *says of* Theaetetus that he *does* that act. Now they represent Theaetetus *as* flying. This is "the unity of the sentence."

This phenomenon lies at the center of our capacity to speak and even to think. We combine this word with another and in so doing we represent the world as being some way. Thoughts too seem to have constituents that can be combined and recombined in endless ways, the thought of the cat and the thought of the mat into the thought that the cat is on the mat or the mat on the cat. By putting this word or concept together with another one, we produce a sentence or a thought: a representation, which, as Plato says, "gets you somewhere," that is, which does not merely list things, but represents something as being the case.

1 In *The Collected Dialogues of Plato*, 15th edn., eds. E. Hamilton and H. Cairns, (Princeton: NJ, Princeton University Press, 1994), tr. F. M. Cornford, pp. 957–1117. See 261–2, pp. 1008–9.

It is important that this power to combine one word with another is not constrained by what the facts are with regard to what the words name. Our powers of imagination too outrun what facts are present to us. So even if our states of mind are determined by the experiences we have had and the facts we have witnessed, those states of mind are not simply records of those experiences and facts. The natural world surely impresses itself upon us, but the representations that arise in this way do not exhaust the representations we are capable of generating. We represent the world in ways it is not, in stories and poems and plans and lies and counterfactual conditionals and idealizations and in countless other ways.

The power of representation does not belong to us alone. Inanimate Nature is replete with representations: shadows, impressions, tracks and paw prints, stratified deposits of minerals and ice, the growth of tree rings. All of these have a kind of meaning or content. Given the way they were produced and their structure, they contain information about their causes. The paw print tells us about the size and shape of the paw. The stratified deposit is a record of the region's geological history. Each of these is a record of some past fact, and what they mean is what they can tell us about the facts and events that produced them. They represent what was the case.

Because our thoughts and language, by contrast, often represent things as being the case that are not the case, their meaning cannot be identified with the fact that they represent. My utterance "George McGovern was elected President" means George McGovern was elected President, even though, in point of fact, he was not. There is no fact with which to identify its meaning. Nor can its meaning be identified with the information it carries owing to the way it was caused to occur.

That is not to say that our representations are totally cut off from the facts. A representation will be true or false just in case it is a representation of something actual. The representation must be anchored to the world, and it is anchored by its parts. Language and thought then are "compositional." The meaning or content of a sentence or thought is a composition from its parts. From a finite stock of words and finite ways of combining them we can produce an infinite number of sentences and thoughts.

But compositional content is not unique to mental and linguistic representations. The stratified deposit is composed of parts arranged in certain ways. It may contain a layer of limestone that is the remains of an ancient sea below a layer of coal that is the remains of an ancient forest. These parts represent, respectively, the sea and the forest. Here the arrangement of the parts of the deposits is determined *by* the actual arrangement of the things designated by the parts: the temporal relation between sea and forest (together with the forces of gravity and geological processes) *governs* the spatial relation between limestone and coal. (Thus, the spatial relation of coal to limestone contains information about the temporal relation of forest and sea.) By contrast, in language and thought, the arrangement of things denoted by the parts does not necessarily govern the arrangement of names. The compositional rules or laws of language and thought allow deviation from the way things actually are. So it is not *that* our representations are compositional but *the way* in which they are compositional that distinguish them from other representations in nature.

Nature does not dictate how our representations are composed. It is up to us to put the words or mental symbols together in this way or another. But, as Plato points out, not every way of putting together the parts will work. And even when we do put together the right parts in the right order, there remain difficult questions about why they combine in such a way as to represent something as being the case.

In the sentence "Snow is white," the fact that "snow" names snow and "white" names the property of being white does not explain why the sentence represents these two things as related – the one as *exemplifying* the other. Even if the relation said to obtain were itself named by some further expression, the string of words would still "be just a list" – snow, being white, exemplification. What is it about the way in which the words of the sentence are combined that makes a sentence different from a list of words?

Some philosophers believe that the question is answered by recognizing that in addition to the parts of the sentence listing or naming certain things, the parts have functions. The parts of the sentence combine in the required way because their functions *differ* so as together to make a complete statement. But this explains nothing until the relevant functions are identified, and without begging the question. (Obviously, to identify the function of the verb as that of *predicating* what it designates to what the noun names merely redescribes the phenomenon.) The words in a list, for example "lion, stag, horse," each likewise has a function that relates their designata and explains what might be called "the unity of the list." The items in the simplest of lists, however, all have the *same* function and stand in a symmetrical relation to one another, whereas, in the simplest sentence, the items have distinct functions: one plays the role of saying something about what another item designates. There is a crucial *asymmetry* between subject and predicate.

The parts of sentences have certain syntactic functions and are combined according to syntactic rules. So if the question is what kind of linguistic unity a sentence is (e.g., how it is distinguished grammatically from a phrase), one can appeal to the distinctive syntactic structure of sentences. But to identify syntactic structure and function does not further the question of how the parts of the sentence combine in such a way that their utterance represents something as being the case. For what could the relevant difference between a noun and a verb be, but that the noun may be the grammatical subject of the sentence and the verb the grammatical predicate? And what is it to "be the grammatical predicate," but to be the element that normally functions to make a predication, that is, to say something about the thing the subject names. Now we've gone in a circle. The concept of saying something about something is the concept we want explicated.

In the context of questions about the unity of the sentence, Frege's comment "Only in a proposition do the words really have meaning" is often admiringly quoted, and some philosophers think an appreciation of this somehow undercuts the problem.[2] One of the many things that might be meant by the aphorism is that a specification of the meaning of words is a kind of abstraction from their contribution to the meaning of the sentences in which they occur. But this does not undercut the question of unity; it turns it upside down. Now we have the question "How is it that the many sentences in which a word may occur have a meaning to which the word makes a single semantic contribution?" The central question may be framed as a question about the *unity* of the sentence: how do the words combine to make up a sentence. Or it may be framed as a question about the *multiplicity* of the sentence: how does a sentence have a unitary meaning when the sentence decomposes into words which outside that context, by hypothesis, do not "really" have a meaning, or decomposes into words which reoccur in other sentences that then have something of the meaning of the first sentence?

I will consider the question cast as a question about unity. Even so, there are many distinguishable questions about what is called "the unity of the sentence." The phenomenon is also sometimes called "the unity of the proposition" to distinguish that what is at issue is how

2   Gottlob Frege, *The Foundation of Arithmetic, The Frege Reader*, ed. M. Beaney (Oxford: Blackwell, 1997), §60, pp. 84–129. See p. 108.

the sentence expresses a proposition, not what kind of syntactic unit a sentence is. One speaks of the unity of the sentence, however, in reference to the capacity of a sentence (that one thing made from many) to give expression to a proposition, and the question is what is it about that combination that makes it do so. In any case, I will focus throughout on what classic descriptions of the problem (Plato's) and accounts of it (Frege's and Wittgenstein's) have taken the phenomenon to be: that in a subject–predicate sentence, the elements combine to represent something as being the case, express a proposition, or predicate a property to the object of reference. I will call this phenomenon "the unity of the sentence" even though there are other phenomena that might bear that name and even though constructions that are not of subject–predicate form may be, and have the unity of, sentences.[3]

This book is a study of the unity of the sentence. Part I presents and criticizes three classical theories: Frege's doctrine of concept and object, Russell's analysis of the sentence, and Wittgenstein's picture theory of meaning. Part II focuses on the relation between the semantic distinction between subject and predicate (referring vs. predicating) and the grammatical, logical, and metaphysical distinctions that are drawn between subjects and predicates. P. F. Strawson has elaborately defended the view that the difference in the kind of thing that is designated by subjects and predicates – the difference between particulars and universals – lies at the basis of the grammatical, semantic, and logical distinctions. I question whether a unified theory of predication can explain these various phenomena, and whether the metaphysical difference between particulars and universals does, in fact, explain the semantic function of subjects and predicates.

In Part III, I develop a pragmatic explanation of the unity of the sentence, arguing that the utterance of a sentence expresses a proposition because of certain unity in the causal explanations of the constituent utterances that comprise the complex act of uttering a sentence. In particular, I argue that the differing functional role of subject and predicate in virtue of which the sentence expresses a proposition can be traced to a distinctive, asymmetrical causal explanation of the tokening of the expression serving one role or another in the speech act. I propose that there is an interconnection and interdependence of the cause of the utterance of the predicate on the cause of the utterance of the subject that explains the unity of the sentence. The unity of the sen-

---

3 Throughout I will use "unity of the sentence" and "unity of the proposition" interchangeably, unless otherwise noted.

tence is explained in terms of the unity of the act of the utterance and the pragmatic character of the expressions rather than by the ontology of what those expressions denote. The account has it roots in the pragmatic distinction between subject and predicate set out by John Cook Wilson and F. P. Ramsey, and in the idea, worked out in different ways in the writing of J. L. Austin and H. P. Grice, that the meaning of sentences is a function of what a speaker is doing in uttering words. The account I provide was conceived within the framework of the kind of causal or information-based theories of meaning that have been developed by Dennis Stampe and Fred Dretske, among others. In the end, however, the view I propose does not depend upon an acceptance of those views of meaning.

Acknowledgments

This book grew out of an idea I presented in a paper called "The Unity of the Sentence and the Connection of Causes" (1998). I taught much of this material in graduate seminars at Wisconsin (Madison), and I want to thank the students in those seminars for their suggestions, criticisms, and assistance. In particular, I want to thank Madeleine Arseneault, Chris Baush, Brian Brost, Sara Chant, Paul Dunn, Ken Harris, Michael Humiston, and Greg Novack.

I have also benefited greatly from discussions and instruction at one time or another from Mike Byrd, Fred Dretske, Ellery Eells, Berent Enç, Terry Penner, and Antonio Rauti. I wish also to thank the philosophers who read the manuscript for Blackwell for their comments and criticisms, and Norma Sober for invaluable editing work. There are three people to whom I owe special thanks: Greg Mougin whose discussions were of great help to me when I was working out the nuts and bolts of the account, Alan Sidelle whose astute and helpful comments on a draft very much improved the final product, and Dennis Stampe to whom I owe my conception of the problem as well the general framework of my attempted solution to it.

Part I

Classical Theories of the Unity of the Proposition

1

Frege's Account of the Unity of the Sentence

1 Introduction to Frege's View

Frege held that the parts of the sentence "would not hold together" to express a thought unless they referred to things of appropriately different kinds. One part (at least) has to refer to what he called an *object*, and another part to what he called a *concept*. The subject expression refers to an object, the predicate expression refers to a concept. The different role of the subject and predicate expression is explained by their referring to these things of different kinds. And it is in virtue of the fact that the role of the one expression is the complement of the other that the subject and predicate fit together so as to say something:

> Statements in general just like equations or inequalities or expressions in Analysis, can be imagined to be split up into two parts; one complete in itself, and the other in need of supplementation, or "unsaturated". Thus, e.g., we split up the sentence
>   "Caesar conquered Gaul"
> into "Caesar" and "conquered Gaul". The second part is "unsaturated" – it contains an empty place; only when this place is filled up with a proper name, or with an expression that replaces a proper name, does a complete sense appear.[1]

The expression referring to the concept, the predicate, has an empty place that is filled or completed by a name referring to an object:

1 G. Frege, "Function and Concept," in *Translations from the Philosophical Writings of Gottlob Frege*, tr. P. Geach and M. Black (New York: Philosophical Library, 1952), p. 31.

predicates are "incomplete," "unsaturated," or "gappy," and expressions referring to objects are just the sorts of things that complete the predicate, that fill the gap. Frege recognizes that these characterizations are merely metaphorical: " 'Complete' and 'unsaturated' are of course only figures of speech."[2] But his significant contribution to this intuitive or metaphorical line of thinking – that predicates are somehow incomplete – is his idea that the reference of a predicate, a concept, is to be understood in terms of the mathematician's notion of a function, that is, of a rule that yields a definite value for each argument it is given. Just as the "+" function takes the argument 2 and 2 to the value 4, so the predicate "conquered Gaul" takes the object Caesar to the value true and Brutus to the value false.

A mathematical expression may be split up into a "constant component" that designates a relation and "a symbol which can be thought of as replaceable by others and which denotes the objects" which will stand in the relation.[3] For example, the expression "2 + 3," "3 + 5," and "1 + 4" may be split up into $(x) + (x)$ and (2, 3, 4, and 5). The constant component stands for a function; the replaceable components stand for arguments of the function.[4] Frege says:

> But the argument is not to be counted as belonging to the function, and so the letter "x" is not to be counted as belonging to the name of the function either. Consequently, one can always speak of the name of a function as having empty places, since what fills them does not, strictly speaking, belong to them. Accordingly I call the function itself unsaturated, or in need of supplementation, because its name has first to be completed with the sign of an argument if we are to obtain a *Bedeutung* [reference] that is complete in itself.[5]

The function itself is incomplete in that it requires supplementation by a certain number of arguments in order to produce a value. The name of the function is correspondingly incomplete, because the representation of the function contains empty places indicating the number of arguments the function requires to produce a value.

2 G. Frege, "On Concept and Object," in *Translations from the Philosophical Writings of Gottlob Frege*, tr. P. Geach and M. Black (New York: Philosophical Library, 1952), p. 55.
3 G. Frege, *Begriffschrift*, in *The Frege Reader*, ed. M. Beaney (Oxford: Blackwell, 1997), p. 66.
4 Ibid.
5 G. Frege, "Comments on *Sinn* and *Bedeutung*," *Frege Reader*, p. 174.

Frege thinks that concepts themselves are functions,[6] functions that map objects onto truth values: "Now with a concept we have the special case that the value is always a truth-value. That is to say, if we complete the name of a concept with a proper name, we obtain a sentence whose sense is a thought; and this sentence has a truth-value as its *Bedeutung*."[7] Given that functions require supplementation by arguments, the proper characterization of the expression naming a concept would contain an empty place(s) indicating where the sign(s) of the argument must go: for example, the proper characterization of "is a dog" in "Fido is a dog," "Rover is a dog," "Spot is a dog" would be "( ) is a dog." This corresponds to the fact that the concept of being a dog requires supplementation by an argument, an object, Fido or Rover or Whiskers, in order to produce the value true or false. Other concepts require supplementation by more than one object to produce a value: the concept "( ) loves ( )" requires supplementation by two arguments, "( ) is between ( ) and ( )" requires three, and so on. The incompleteness of the concept is just its need to be supplemented with objects in order to produce a value true or false.

As so far developed, Frege's account does not yet fully explain how the parts of the sentence combine to express a thought. David Wiggins characterizes its inadequacy in this way:

> Even if there really exists the incomplete sort of thing which Frege wants, it is still unclear how it can help to distinguish a sentence from a list to say that a sentence is unlike a list in mentioning something complete

---

6 Frege's view of concepts should remind us of Kant's, for Kant too thought that concepts were functions, and that concepts without objects were "empty" (*Critique of Pure Reason*, tr. Kemp Smith [New York: St. Martin's Press, 1965], A51/B75). According to Kant, in order for a representation to comprise a judgment, i.e., a representation that represents something as being the case, it must have two complementary parts, an intuition and a concept. Kant understood the difference between intuition and concept in terms of the complementary role of the sensibility and the understanding in cognition and thought. The sensibility provides us access to objects and explains the judgment's being about an object. But the object is represented as being some way in the judgment, because we categorize or classify it according to certain rules or concepts of the understanding. A concept brings together "various representations under one common representation," as when the various intuitions of Fido are classified under the concept "dog" (A68/B93). They are "predicates of possible judgments," and "relate to some representation of a not yet determined object" (A69/B94). Considered in abstraction from its employment in an actual judgment, a concept is something that could serve as a predicate of judgment, if it were supplied with an object by the intuition. Lacking an object, the concept is empty.
7 "Comments on *Sinn* and *Bedeutung*," *Frege Reader*, p. 174. *Sinn* and *Bedeutung* are often translated respectively as "sense" and "reference."

and then something incomplete. How is it that he who mentions something complete and then something incomplete thereby gets to say something.[8]

Wiggins thinks that Frege needs to tell us how the designation of the parts, the complete and incomplete objects, "combine to constitute a subject matter that can be judged or asserted as a truth."[9]

An additional problem is this: the fact that the concept referred to by the predicate maps the object referred to by the subject onto a truth-value does not explain why, when the sentence expresses a thought, it expresses the *particular* thought it does. Two sentences whose subjects and predicates refer to the same object and concept may express different thoughts. "The third US president liked gardening" and "The second husband of Martha Skelton liked gardening" express different thoughts, though in each sentence, the subject and predicate expressions refer, respectively, to the same object and concept.

Frege's proposed answer to both of these questions relies on the distinction he drew between the reference of an expression and what he called its "sense" (*Sinn*). An expression has a sense. A sense contains a particular mode of referring to its referent.[10] For example, the sense of the phrase "The third US president" differs from the sense of "The second husband of Martha Skelton," but both phrases refer to Thomas Jefferson. The difference in the sense of the expressions is illustrated in the different ways Jefferson is presented, by means of one property or another. The sense of an expression is not to be confused with the subjective idea associated with the referent, for the sense is objective in that grasping it "may be common property of many and is therefore not a part of a mode of the individual mind."[11] Frege identifies an "idea," in contrast to a sense, with a psychological experience or mental particu-

---

8   D. Wiggins, "The Sense and Reference of Predicates: A Running Repair to Frege's Doctrine and a Plea for the Copula," *Philosophical Quarterly*, 34 (136) (1984), pp. 311–28. See p. 324. See also Donald Davidson, "Truth and Meaning," *Synthese*, 17 (1967), pp. 304–23. Davidson says that the doctrine of completeness and incompleteness "seems to label a difficulty rather than solve it" (p. 304). Or Mark Sainsbury, "How Can we Say Something," in *Russell and the Origins of Analytical Philosophy*, ed. R. Monk and A. Palmer (Bristol: Thoemmes Press, 1996), pp. 137–51. Sainsbury says, the question "is of essentially the same kind as our original question. Argument-function unity is of a piece with propositional unity" (pp. 145–6).

9   Wiggins, "Sense and Reference of Predicates," p. 324.

10 Frege, "On Sense and Reference," Geach and Black, p. 57.

11 Ibid., p. 59.

lar in some person's mind: and so "one man's idea is not that of another."[12] The senses of the expressions that make up the sentence (not the ideas associated with the expressions or their referents) determine what thought is expressed. The two sentences above thus express different thoughts, because their subject expressions have different senses.

On Frege's view, we must distinguish three different levels. There is the level of *expressions* that combine in a sentence to express a thought. But the thought that they express is determined by the *senses* of the expressions. And the senses themselves contain ways of presenting the *referents* of the expressions. Frege seems to think that on each level – that of sentences, thoughts and referents – a complete and an incomplete element are fitted together. We've seen already that he thinks that the name of the function or concept is incomplete in a way that the name of an object is not, because the name of the function has an empty place. The name of the function fits together with the name of an object to express a thought. The referents of the names, the object and concept, are correspondingly complete and incomplete. The concept must be completed by an object to itself produce something complete, a value. Finally, the senses, like the things they are modes of referring to, have distinct and complementary natures that make them fit together:

> For example, the sense of the phrase "the number 2" does not hold together with that of the expression "the concept prime number" without a link. We apply such a link in the sentence "the number 2 falls under the concept prime number"; it is contained in the words "falls under," which needs to be completed in two ways by a subject and an accusative; and only because their sense is thus "unsaturated" are they capable of serving as a link. Only when they have been supplemented in this twofold respect do we get a complete sense, a thought.[13]

Frege apparently holds that the senses of the expressions determine both *what* thought is expressed and *that* a thought is expressed. Regarding the latter, the words do not merely list two things, object and concept, but fit together to express a thought because the senses of the expressions are respectively saturated or unsaturated.

12   Ibid.
13   Frege, "On Concept and Object," Geach and Black, p. 54.

2　A First Interpretation of the View

Peter Carruthers suggests that we think of the sense of the predicate as a rule or law correlating objects with truth values:

> If the semantic role of a functional expression consists in a rule mapping objects onto objects, then the semantic role of a predicate, for Frege, will consist in a rule mapping objects onto truth-values . . . the force of a predicative expression consists in a rule for determining, with respect to the objects referred to in any atomic sentence in which it occurs, whether or not that sentence is a truth about those objects. Or what comes to the same thing: the semantic role of a predicate consists in a rule for determining, of any given object, whether or not that predicate correctly applies to it.[14]

This might be interpreted as follows: the sense of the predicate "x is a bachelor" consists in a rule which says that any given object is a bachelor just in case x is an unmarried man. When supplied with the name of a particular object, the predicate generates a truth-condition, something we can compare to the way the world is.

Carruthers thinks that Frege can then provide an account of the unity of the sentence:

> The reason why a string of names does not constitute a sentence is that there is no general *rule* for determining whether that arrangement of names does correctly represent the relations between their referents. In the absence of such a rule we do not know how to *compare* that arrangement of names with reality. And the reason why a combination of relational expressions with a predicate does not constitute a sentence is that the sense of a relational expression consists in a rule for determining, of any given ordered pair of objects, whether or not that expression correctly applies – whereas here, of course, no object has been given.[15]

If a predicate expression expressed a rule, then sentences would differ from strings of names and strings of relational expressions, because the sentence would contain reference to an object and a rule for determining with regard to any object whether the relational expression correctly applies to the object.

14　P. Carruthers, "On Concept and Object," *Theoria*, 49 (1983), part 2, pp. 49–86. See p. 66.
15　Ibid.

While what Carruthers says may be true, it does not fully address the depth of the problem. The original problem was that the sentence does not just represent two things that fit together; it represents those things *as* fitting together or *as related* in the relevant way. And one might produce a *list* of the words in a sentence – "Theaetetus," "flies" – where those words referred to things of the required two types, but the utterance of this list would not be *saying* anything, because the things referred to have not been represented as fitting together. This problem is not fundamentally changed by postulating a saturated and unsaturated sense. In a list of the words of the sentence "Theaetetus flies," "Theaetetus" may have a complete sense and "flies" an incomplete one, expressing a rule for when it correctly applies to some object, but even so the two expressions remain just a list, and do not express a thought: for there is nothing about the rule that indicates that it is to be applied to *this object*, Theaetetus, the one referred to by the referring expression. The fact that one expression "Theaetetus" refers to the person Theaetetus and another expression "flies" expresses the rule that "x flies" is true if and only if x flies does not make it the case that Theaetetus is the object being said to fly. And while the sentence may be true if and only if Theaetetus flies, what the sentence says is not that Theaetetus flies if and only if Theaetetus flies.

I offer this criticism of (this aspect of) Carruther's view because his view is an example of a certain approach to the unity of the sentence in which sentential unity is explained by identifying the meaning of one of the expressions with a rule that determines a truth-condition, and that general approach may be subject to the criticism. For example, David Wiggins suggests that a sentence would differ from a list if a part of the sentence expressed a rule about when the sentence would be true. He proposes recognizing, in addition to the sense of the subject and sense of the predicate, a distinctive sense of the copula which can be characterized by a schematic rule of truth: "for any sentence of the form 't + copula + Pred,' where t is a term and Pred is a verb or adjective, or 'a' + substantive, that sentence is true if and only if 'Pred is true of the designation of t.' "[16] The sense of the copula links the subject and predicate together in such a way that the whole sentence represents the referents (of the subject and predicate) as related (to assert that that condition holds).

---

16 Wiggins, "Sense and Reference of Predicates," p. 318. Wiggins suggests that such a repair be made so that Frege's paradox – the expression "the concept 'horse'" does not refer to a concept – can be avoided.

Suppose that Wiggins is right that the sense of "is" is characterized by such a schematic rule of truth. Then "is" has that sense in isolation, when, as it were, it is floating out in space. But in isolation "is" does not express a proposition. Why should anything change when it is put together with other words? Why is it that when one puts "is" together with other words the string that results sometimes expresses a proposition? That is not explained by the fact that the string of words satisfies the condition stated in the rule which characterizes the sense of "is" – that the string is comprised by "t + copula + p." Because, again, take the words in the sentence "Theaetetus is running" and make a list. That list is formally, phonologically, and semantically (i.e., as regards the senses of the expressions) identical to the string of words that comprises a sentence which says something. It is true of that string of words that *if* it expresses a proposition, it is true if and only if Theaetetus flies. But that string of words might or might not express a proposition: it doesn't do so when it lists the words in the sentence. There is nothing about the rule that identifies the sense of "is" that makes one but not another identical string of words fall under the rule. So long as the string of words does not fall under the rule, there is no reason to think that it expresses a proposition. While there may be many reasons, on Frege's view, for regarding the sense of the copula or the concept word as a rule, doing so does not suffice for explaining how a string of words expresses a proposition.

There are, however, other approaches to try. In particular, in what follows I will sketch how a Fregean might supply an "externalist" account of the unity of the sentence, deriving the unity of the sentence from a unity found in the world external to the language, in particular from the object's saturating the concept. Finally, I will consider whether Frege would want to reject questions about how the senses or the words fit together to comprise a thought and so can avoid the issue about unity.

3   An Externalist Conception of Frege's Account

In recent years, it has been useful in various areas of philosophy to cast certain issues in terms of a choice between "internalist" and "externalist" accounts of this or that phenomenon, concerning whether some crucial factor is contributed from within the mind or instead by the external world. Epistemologists debate whether true belief is converted into knowledge by some factor internal to the mind (e.g., by the possession of something like a proof) or instead by an external factor (such as some natural law connecting the belief with the fact that makes it true). Theorists of meaning debate whether what determines the extension of some predicate is something internal to the mind (like a standard definition) or instead the nature of the external object referred to in an authoritative ostensive definition. The issue of what makes a string of words express a proposition has in some respects a similar dialectic. Is that factor internal to the mind, like Kant's act of combination in a unified consciousness,[17] or is it instead something external?

Consider some simple sign such as a paw print in the sand. The parts of the print are fitted together, and their being fitted together in the way that they are is explained by the fitting together of what is represented by the parts of the print, that is, by the fitting together of parts of the paw itself. That is why the way that the parts of the prints are fitted together, for example, why the spatial relation between the pad prints and nail prints, represents a relation as obtaining between the pads and nails themselves. The parts of the paw print stand related in such a way as to represent the paw, because the parts of the paw stand related in such a way as to comprise a paw and because the paw being pressed into the sand explains the paw print. The unity of the representation is derived from the unity of something external to it, that of the paw itself.

Applying this simple analogy to the sentence will not work. The parts of the sentence "The cat is fat" combine to represent the cat as fat. But the cat's being fat cannot explain how the sentence has this property, for the simple reason that the cat may not *be* fat. When the sentence is false, there is no relevant relation between the cat and the property of being fat that explains why the sentence represents the cat as fat. The unity of the sentence, apparently, cannot be derived in this way from a unity external to it, in the property and object represented – from the object's *instantiating* the property or from an object's *falling under* the concept. This motivates "internalist" accounts, where the unity of the sentence is derived, as it is by Kant, from a psychological act wherein the constituents of the representation are combined in the mind of judger or speaker.

Notice that on Frege's view, an object O saturates a concept F whether the sentence "O is F" is true or *false*. An object O saturates a

---

17 Kant thinks the unity of the parts of the judgment, intuition, and concept, in virtue of which it represents something as being the case is owing to an act of the mind (*Critique of Pure Reason*, B135).

concept F whether or not O instantiates the property F or falls under that concept. Where the saturation relation is neutral between the truth and falsity of the sentence, the "instantiation" and the "falling under" relations are not. The object Milwaukee saturates the concept "is the capital of Wisconsin," producing the false value, but Milwaukee does not instantiate the property of being capital of Wisconsin or fall under that concept, because Milwaukee is not the capital.

This puts Frege in a unique position to supply an externalist account of the unity of the sentence. The referents of the parts of the sentence fit together in the same way whether the sentence is true or false. Thus, the object's saturating the concept may explain the relation holding between the expressions composing the sentence wherein the sense of the subject expression saturates the sense of the predicate. The relation between those expressions, the saturation of the predicate by the subject, may then represent the saturation of the concept named by the object named. The unity in the sentence may derive from a unity in the world, that of the saturation of concept by object. (Concept and object are not, in Frege, internal or psychological entities.)

Frege himself does not sketch any such externalist account as this. But he can formulate a simple version of an externalist theory of representation, because he has found a relation – the saturation relation – that the referents of the sentence can stand in whether the sentence is true or false, which can explain the crucial relation between the parts of the sentence. And Frege does seem to think that the relation between concept and object is in some way mirrored in or reiterated at the level of senses and expressions. Each sentence must contain a complete and an incomplete sense, a complete expression combined with an incomplete one. The completeness or incompleteness of the sense and of the expression even seems to be derived from or dependent upon or, at least, correspondent with the completeness or incompleteness of its referent. That is evident in Frege's claim that the name of a function must contain empty places indicating how the function itself must be saturated by an object in order to produce a value. The name of the function must be completed by exactly the number of names of objects as the function must be completed by objects or arguments.

Frege's argument that a subject expression cannot refer to a concept but must always refer to an object provides further evidence he thought that the completeness and incompleteness at one level corresponds to that of the other. Of the sentence "The concept 'horse' is a concept easily attained" Frege says, "one would expect that the reference of the grammatical subject would be the concept; but the concept as such cannot play this part, in view of its predicative nature; it must first be converted into an object, or speaking more precisely, be represented by an object."[18] He thinks that if the expression in the subject position referred to a concept, there would be no way to explain how the sentence expresses a complete thought: "For not all the parts of a thought can be complete; at least one must be unsaturated, or predicative otherwise they would not hold together."[19]

His reasoning here seems to be this. If both the subject and predicate expression referred to concepts, then the parts of the thought, the senses, would not fit together to express a complete thought because they would not be of different natures, the one saturated and the other unsaturated. The implication is that if the subject expression referred to a concept, an unsaturated entity, the *sense* of the subject expression would *itself* have to be unsaturated. If the senses of both of the expressions were unsaturated, they would not "hold together" to produce a complete thought. This argument depends on the premise that the sense of an expression has the same saturated or unsaturated character as that thing to which it is a mode of referring.

In the thought expressed by a sentence, the object and concept are represented as fitting together. If the fitting together of senses and expressions is analogous to the fitting together of their referents, as Frege indicates, then, perhaps the fitting together of two expressions (where the sense of the one saturates the sense of the other) *represents* the fitting together of saturated object with unsaturated concept. And if the saturated or unsaturated nature of a sense (or expression) is a reflection of the nature of its referent, then the fitting together of senses (expressions) may be a consequence of the fitting together of concept and object.[20] In that way, Frege's account can be construed as an externalist account, deriving the unity of the sentence from the unity of nonpsychological entities, concept and object.

What is missing from the account I have sketched is any compelling argument for the idea that an expression has to be like its referent or that a sense has to be like that to which it is a mode of referring.

18   Frege, "On Concept and Object," Geach and Black, p. 46.
19   Ibid., p. 54.
20   To allow for the unity of sentences with vacuous referring expressions (e.g., "the greatest number is a big one"), one would have to say the following: an expression that has a saturated sense, *if it refers*, refers to a saturated thing, and an expression that has an unsaturated sense, if it refers, refers to an unsaturated thing. An expression's having the kind of sense it has may be derived from the ontological character the referent would have if it existed.

Generally, a representation does not have to share the features of what it represents: a word does not have to be red to represent a red thing or square to represent a square thing. Perhaps Frege's view contains the seeds of the idea that Wittgenstein later develops in the *Tractatus* – that the words in a sentence represent something as being the case because there is a structural isomorphism between the relation between the words and the relation between the things represented.[21] That structural identity might consist in the saturated and unsaturated nature of the expressions and senses, on the one hand, and of the referents on the other. The saturation of the incomplete name of the concept by the complete name of the object represents the saturation of incomplete concept by complete object. In that way, the fact that words are related as they are, the one saturating the other, represents the things named as correspondingly related.

The chief difficulty with this externalist interpretation is that it does not seem to properly identify the thought expressed by the sentence. Frege characterizes the thought expressed by "Opposite magnetic poles attract one another" as follows: is it the thought "of the mutual attraction of the poles" or the "circumstance that" the poles attract one another?[22] Generalizing, the thought expressed by "A is F" would be the thought of A as F or the circumstance that A is F. If the externalist view outlined above worked, the saturation of one expression by the other would express the thought of the object *saturating* the concept. The issue is whether that *is* the thought expressed by the sentence. The question is whether thinking of an object A as saturating the concept F is equivalent to thinking of the circumstance that A is F or thinking of A as F.

To argue that it is or isn't, we've got to have some idea what saturation consists in – what it would be for a sentence to express the thought of the object saturating the concept. We know that saturation is supposed to be neutral between truth and falsity, for an object A saturates a concept F whether the sentence "A is F" is true or false. So suppose that "S expresses the thought of O as saturating F" means S determines a condition under which S is either true or false. And "S determines a condition under which S is true or false" means S identifies a condition C such that, if C holds then S has a truth-value. Thus,

21   See especially Wittgenstein's 3.1412 in the *Tractatus Logico-Philosophicus*, tr. D. F. Pears and B. F. McGuiness (London: Routledge & Kegan Paul, 1961).
22   Frege, *Begriffschrift*, §2, p. 53, *Frege Reader*. He thinks that such a thought is what is common to the assertion, interrogative, command, and so on. See also p. 329 of "Thought," *Frege Reader*, pp. 325–45.

"S expresses the thought of O as saturating F" is neutral between the condition (1) O is F and (2) O is not F. However, "S expresses the thought of O as F" is not neutral between condition 1 and 2. "S expresses the thought of O as F" entails S identifies the C as one in which O is F. It appears then that the externalist interpretation of Frege's view of sentential unity would wrongly identify the thought that Frege thinks is expressed by the sentence.

Interestingly, the very thing that would enable Frege to give an externalist account seems to be what prevents such an account from working satisfactorily. There is a relation – the saturation of concept by object – that the referents of the parts of the sentence can stand in whether the sentence is true or false, and this relation may correspond to and explain the saturation of the predicate by the subject. The sentence may then be said to express the thought of the object as saturating the concept. But the thought expressed by the sentence is not that the object saturates the concept. It appears, rather, to be the thought of the object as falling under or instantiating the concept. In finding a relation between concept and object that can explain the relation between expressions whether the sentence is true or false, Frege seems to be cut off from a correct account of the thought expressed by the sentence.

We've now examined two views about how a Fregean theory might account for sentential unity. The first suggested that the sentence is unified because the sense of the predicate contains a rule determining when the predicate correctly applies to an object (or when a sentence would be true). I argued that the fact that the predicate expresses such a rule does not entail that the collection of words in which it occurs actually falls under that rule. It fails to provide an account of why a collection of words expresses a thought. The second approach derived the unity of the sentence from a unity in the world outside the sentence wherein the object saturates the concept. This seems to fail to explain what thought the sentence expresses. I will conclude this discussion of Frege's view by considering whether he might avoid altogether questions about the unity of the sentence.

4 Resisting Questions about the Fitting Together of Parts

The senses of the words of a sentence determine which thought is expressed. But the senses themselves do not combine to "express" a thought. Rather the words of the sentence express a thought, though the words express the thought they do because they have the senses they do. What is the relation between the saturated and unsaturated sense and the thought (expressed by words with those senses)? The obvious answer might seem to be that the senses of the words fit together to *constitute* a thought, the one as it were "saturating" the other. If so, then the thought is composed of certain senses. In that case, Frege's account would be incomplete, awaiting an explanation of what fits the saturated and unsaturated sense together in such a way as to constitute a thought.

The problem with that obvious answer is that Frege denies that a thought is composed of senses. And if the senses of the expressions do not combine to make up a thought, perhaps there just is no question about how a saturated and unsaturated sense "fit together." Perhaps the question how they fit together is misguided, and so no account of the unity of the sentence is needed. In what follows, I examine Frege's arguments that thoughts are not composed of senses, for they shed light on what the relation is between the senses and the thought expressed by words with those senses. I argue that even if the question about how senses are fitted together can be avoided (and I don't think it is clear that it can be), the question about how words with those senses combine to express a thought cannot be avoided.

Frege's remarks in several places support the view that thoughts are not constituted by senses. Throughout his writing on this subject he asserts, with increasing emphasis, that there is no unique way to analyze a thought into semantic constituents.

In the earlier *Begriffschrift*, Frege points out that sentences with different grammatical subject and predicate expressions may express the same thought. He cites as an example, a sentence in the active voice and the synonymous sentence in the passive voice: "At Plataea the Greeks defeated the Persians" and "At Plataea the Persians were defeated by the Greeks." Frege calls it "that part of the content that is the same in both the conceptual content."[23] This is the thought or judgment.

Of the subject–predicate distinction, Frege says that which expression functions as subject or predicate depends upon facts about the interaction of the speaker and listener.

> The linguistic significance of the position of the subject in the word-order lies in its *marking* the place where what one particularly wants to draw the attention of the listener to is put. This can have the purpose, for

23   Ibid., §3, p. 53.

example of indicating a relation between this judgement and others, thereby facilitating the listener's grasp of all the interconnections.[24]

Such factors regarding the interaction of speaker and listener are not relevant to the judgment made or thought expressed: "the only thing that is relevant in a judgement is that which influences its *possible consequences*."[25]

Frege identifies the subject of a sentence with its principal argument, and the predicate with a function. The sentence "splits up into a constant component, which represents the totality of relations, and a symbol which can be thought of as replaceable by others and which denotes the object that stands in these relations. The former component I call a function, the latter its argument."[26] Frege then argues that there is no unique way of analyzing simple sentences into a saturated and an unsaturated part. He gives the example of the sentence "Cato killed Cato." We might think of "Cato" in the subject position as being the replaceable element, in which case the function would be represented by "x killed Cato." Or we might think of "Cato" in the predicate as being replaceable, in which case the function would be represented by "Cato killed x" Finally, we might think of "Cato" as being replaceable in both of its occurrences, in which case the function, killing oneself, would be represented by "x killed x."[27] Frege says, "For us the different ways in which the same conceptual content can be taken as a function of this or that argument has no importance so long as the function and argument are fully determined."[28]

Frege's point is not just that different sentences with parts that have the same senses (the active and passive voice sentences) may express the same thought, but that, in one and the same sentence, there is no unique way of analyzing it into subject or predicate, concept or object,

24   Ibid., p. 54.
25   Ibid.
26   He then says that the distinction between function and argument (concept and object) is not a distinction in the thought, but only with our way of grasping the thought: "This distinction has nothing to do with the conceptual content, but only with our way of grasping it" (*Begriffschrift*, §9, pp. 65–6). By the time of "On Concept and Object," Frege seems to have changed his view, for there the distinction between concept and object is a distinction in ontological kinds, not a distinction in how we come to grasp the thought.
27   *Begriffschrift*, §9, p. 66, *Frege Reader*.
28   In the *Begriffschrift*, Frege says that the only time a sentence must be analyzed in a certain way regarding concept and object is when a part of the sentence is indeterminate, for then "the whole splits up into function and argument according to its content and not merely according to our way of grasping it" (§9, p. 66).

or saturated and unsaturated sense. It is a consequence of this that the thought is not composed of senses which are its parts. It cannot be said to be made up of the complete sense of "Cato" and the incomplete sense of "x killed x," any more than of the complete sense of the "Cato" and the incomplete sense of "x killed Cato" or the complete sense of "Cato" and the incomplete sense of "Cato killed x."

In the later "On Concept and Object," Frege goes further. There, he says that two sentences may express the same thought even if the expressions in the respective sentences make reference to distinct concepts and objects. In the sentence "There is at least one square root of 4," we may say (or assert) something of a *concept* – the square root of 4 – namely, that it is not empty. The thought that is expressed by that sentence may also be expressed by the different sentence "The concept square root of 4 is realized." In this sentence, "the first six words form the proper name of an *object*, and it is about this object that something is being asserted."[29] He adds, "But notice carefully that what is asserted here is not the same thing as was asserted about the concept."[30] There is also the sentence "There is something that has the property of giving the result 4 when multiplied by itself."

Frege uses these examples to argue that what the sentence is about and what is said by the sentences may be different, but the thought expressed may be same: "This will be surprising only to somebody who fails to see that a thought can be split up in many ways, so that now one thing, now another appears as subject or predicate. The thought itself does not yet determine what is to be regarded as the subject."[31]

Different sentences composed of words with different senses and different referents may all express the same thought. In the three sentences "There is at least one square root of 4," "The concept square root of 4 is realized," and "There is something that has the property of giving the result 4 when multiplied by itself," the words in each case refer to different things and have different senses, yet they all express the same thought. Therefore, the thought cannot be composed of the senses of the words of one of the sentences rather than those of another.

29   Frege, "On Concept and Object," Geach and Black, p. 49
30   Ibid.
31   Ibid. Yet Frege thinks that only certain things can be said of things of a given kind (p. 50), for what is said of an object cannot be said of a concept. Only certain concepts apply to an object of a given kind, while other concepts must themselves have application only to other concepts. For example, the object Dobbin cannot fall under the concept "is frequently instantiated" – only certain "lower level" concepts, such as "being a horse" or "being blue," fall under the concept of being frequently instantiated.

This finding makes the thought like a *value* in one respect. Just as the value 8 is not composed of the numerals 4 and 4 or 1 and 7 – they are not its parts – so the thought that there is at least one square root of 4 is not composed of the senses of the words of one of the sentences that expresses that thought rather than those of another. The arguments 4 and 4 are arguments/objects from which the addition function can produce the value 8. The analogy should be that the saturated sense of "the concept square root of 4" (the argument) provides something from which the unsaturated sense of "is realized" (the function) produces the thought that the concept square root of 4 is realized. But there are other functions that produce that same thought from different arguments (as there are different functions and arguments that might produce the value 8; e.g., 2×4, or $4 + 4$, or $16/2$). Thoughts are abstract objects, and various functions and objects may go together to produce the thought.[32]

Do these considerations allow us to avoid questions about how the saturated and unsaturated sense fit together to produce a thought? Perhaps. Certain saturated senses *can* go together with certain other unsaturated senses to produce a thought. If one asks, "When *does* the sense of 'the earth' go together with the sense of 'has a moon' to produce the thought the earth has a moon?" that question makes no sense. What is true is just that those senses can go together to produce the thought the earth has a moon. The sense of "Millie" and "is dead" cannot go together to produce the thought the earth has a moon. There are facts about which senses can and which cannot go together to produce a thought, but no facts about when they do do so and when they do not. That is a possible view.

But this concerns the relations among senses, and all it tells us about the words that express those senses is that they express senses that can combine in such ways. It does not say, for instance, that *when* those words are combined in an actual utterance of them, then those senses *do* combine in the way that they can, and then a thought *is* actually *expressed*. And indeed, it is not necessary that they do, as we have seen. For an utterance of such a string of words may be merely a list of words

---

32   This view need not be inconsistent with what Frege said elsewhere about thoughts. In "Sense and Reference" he holds that (1) a sentence expresses the thought it does, and not a different one, because of the senses of its parts. And in the later "Thought," he says that (2) "thoughts are senses of sentences" (p. 328). But 1 and 2 are consistent with (3) sentences with parts that have different senses may express the same thought. I take 3 to imply that, strictly, thoughts are not composed of senses, which, again, is consistent with 1 and 2.

that would make a sentence, but in this occurrence do not do so. It can be a list of the words in the sentence "The Earth has a moon," that is, a string of words that can go together to make a sentence, but in this occurrence do not do so. And it is clear that an adequate account must address the question "When is a thought actually expressed by a string of words that could do so, or by a string of words that express senses that can combine to yield a thought?" It is not obvious how Frege's account explains that.

2

Russell on the Analysis of the Sentence: Three Views

Bertrand Russell's analysis of the sentence, of how it expresses what it does, changed several times. The problems in earlier accounts gave rise to new theories, the new theory incorporating solutions to the old problems. In this way, his account became increasingly sophisticated: it could account for more of the things it ought to and had fewer of the implications it ought not to have. A study of the development of Russell's views is a lesson in what an adequate theory needs to be able to account for and what it had better not imply. Russell, in rejecting various of his own attempts, both defines the conditions of adequacy on any account and develops a positive account that, in many respects, is still very much with us today. Here I will focus on three different periods of Russell's thinking about this issue. The first is the early theory given in 1903 in *The Principles of Mathematics*. By 1910, this is rejected and begins to be replaced by what is called the "Multiple Relation" theory. Influenced by Wittgenstein's criticisms, Russell later abandoned certain features of the Multiple Relation theory and provided a new account in his 1918 lectures on logical atomism.

1 The *Principles of Mathematics* View

In *The Principles of Mathematics*, Russell talks throughout of the propositions of mathematics and logic. He says, "A proposition, we may say, is anything that is true or that is false."[1] So while propositions are the

1 B. Russell, *The Principles of Mathematics*, 2nd edn. (London: George Allen & Unwin, 1937), §13, pp. 12–13.

kinds of things that can be given "linguistic expression," they are also the kinds of things that can be judged or believed. Speakers may assert propositions, and judgers judge them true or false. Propositions can be proved or disproved; generalizations can be formed from them.[2]

In chapter 4 of *Principles*, Russell undertakes a philosophical analysis of the grammar of the sentence that he expects to provide insight into how the sentence expresses a proposition. His use of "proposition" here can be confusing. Sometimes, he seems to mean by "proposition" just sentence, because in talking about the parts of the proposition, he talks about its grammatical parts – noun, verb, predicate adjective. But strictly, Russell, at this time thinks that propositions are distinct from sentences and are unitary entities composed of parts. The parts of the proposition are the things designated by the parts of the sentence, which he takes to be objects, relations, and class concepts: "*Words* all have meaning, in the simple sense that they are symbols which stand for something other than themselves. But a proposition, unless it happens to be linguistic, does not itself contain words: it contains the entities indicated by words."[3] Thus, when Russell talks about "the unity of the proposition," it is not clear whether he is talking about a unity of expressions in a sentence or a unity of object, relation and concept in a proposition. Eventually, we'll have to make sense of his different uses of "proposition," but I will begin by just looking at what he says.

In analyzing the sentence, Russell first distinguishes three major parts of speech: substantives, adjectives, and verbs. There are two kinds of substantives: *primary* and *derivative*. Primary substantives can only occur as substantives, and include proper names.[4] Other substantives, such as "humanity," "triangularity," "pointedness" are according to Russell derived from adjectives – "humanity" from "human," "triangularity" from "triangular," "pointedness" from "pointed" – and can figure as either subjects or predicates of propositions.[5] Primary substantives name things. Adjectives and verbs name concepts. Adjectives are "predicates" and designate class-concepts such as human, canine, triangular. Verbs also designate concepts, but they designate relational concepts.[6]

2   Ibid., p. viii.
3   Ibid., §51, p. 47.
4   Ibid., §46, p. 42.
5   Ibid., pp. 42–3.
6   Ibid., §48, p. 44.

Russell recognizes that the analysis of a sentence and its correspon-ding proposition in terms of the different parts of speech and their cor-responding designata – object, relational concept, class concept – is not complete.

> Consider, for example, the proposition "A differs from B." The con-stituents of this proposition, if we analyze it, appear to be only A, dif-ference, B. Yet these constituents, thus placed side by side, do not reconstitute the proposition. The difference which occurs in the pro-position actually relates A and B, whereas the difference after analysis is a notion which has no connection with A and B. . . . A proposition, in fact, is essentially a unity, and when analysis has destroyed the unity, no enumeration of constituents will restore the proposition. The verb, when used as a verb, embodies the unity of the proposition, and is thus distinguishable from the verb considered as a term, though I do not know how to give a clear account of the precise nature of the distinction.[7]

The verb embodies the unity of the proposition because it does not simply *designate* a relational concept; it actually *relates* the constituents of the sentence: the verb is "a relation actually relating" rather than "a relation in itself."[8] Verbs, Russell says, "are distinguished by a special kind of connection, exceedingly hard to define, with truth and false-hood, in virtue of which they distinguish an asserted proposition from an unasserted one, *e.g.*, 'Caesar dies' from 'the death of Caesar.' "[9]

In *Principles*, Russell also provides an analysis of the proposition in terms of the *function* of the parts of speech. In the proposition, one may distinguish between what is asserted and "something about which the assertion is made."[10] He calls that about which something is asserted a "term": and a term is "whatever may be the object of thought."[11] Both objects and concepts may be the objects of thought.[12] Whatever is the term of a proposition – that which it is about – is its subject. What is asserted about it is its predicate. According to Russell, the advantage of the analysis of the proposition into a subject and an assertion, is that while "less complete," it "does much less to destroy the proposition"

7   Ibid., §54, pp. 49–50.
8   Ibid., p. 49.
9   Ibid., §46, p. 43.
10   Ibid.
11   Ibid., §48, p. 45.
12   Ibid., §§47–8, pp. 43–4.

than an analysis in terms of the simple constituents of the proposition
– substantive, verb, adjective.[13]

> A subject and an assertion, if simply juxtaposed, do not, it is true, con-
> stitute a proposition; but as soon as the assertion is actually asserted of
> the subject, the proposition reappears. The assertion is everything that
> remains of the proposition when the subject is omitted: the verb remains
> an asserted verb, and is not turned into a verbal noun; or at any rate the
> verb retains that curious indefinable intricate relation to the other terms
> of the proposition which distinguishes a relating relation from the same
> relation abstractly considered.[14]

In chapter 7 of *Principles*, Russell introduces the notion of a "propositional function," and he identifies the propositional function with the
part of the proposition that makes an assertion. What is asserted of one
subject might be asserted about another subject. The sentence "Socrates
is a man" may be used to assert of Socrates that he is human, but the
same thing might be said of any number of people: "Thus we can consider a class of propositions containing this assertion, and this will be
the class of which a typical number is represented by 'x is a man'."[15]
'X is a man' is a propositional function, something which is not yet
true or false, because it contains an undetermined constituent x. The
propositional function, considered as a single entity, combines the role
of the verb as relating relation and the adjective. As Russell conceives
of it, if we do not allow the verb and adjective to be considered as separate constituents but consider them as one together, they will represent a propositional function which already embodies the unity of the
proposition.

In the case of many propositions, there is more than one way of distinguishing what they are about, the term, from what they assert, the
propositional function. Of the sentence "A is greater than B," Russell
says that A might be regarded as the subject and "is greater than B" as
the assertion or B might be thought to be the subject and "A is greater
than" as the assertion. The only thing that must remain constant is that
what is asserted contains a verb.[16] However, in the case of subject–predicate sentences, Russell thinks there is only a single way of analyzing
them: the grammatical subject identifies what the subject is about, the

13   Ibid., §81, p. 83.
14   Ibid., pp. 83–4.
15   Ibid., p. 84.
16   Ibid., §48, p. 44.

predicate what is asserted. Russell seems to regard the verb and predicate adjective as a fused unit, so that the propositional function in such a sentence must be 'x is human,' not 'Socrates is F.'[17]

Throughout the analysis, Russell makes no pretense of having an account of how the parts of the sentence combine to express a proposition. He clearly thinks that it is the verb which "embodies" the unity of the proposition: "Owing to the way in which the verb actually relates the terms of a proposition, every proposition has a unity which renders it distinct from the sum of its constituents."[18] But when it comes to explaining how the verb relates the various constituents, he says that the verb as relating relation is "exceedingly hard to define," or it is something such that "I do not know how to give a clear account of the precise nature of the distinction."[19] We have seen him say that in the propositional function the verb "retains that curious indefinable intricate relation" that accounts for propositional unity.[20]

Russell was right to think that the notion of a propositional function did not solve the problem of sentential or propositional unity. For, on the one hand, if the propositional function were taken to be a constituent of either the sentence or of a separate entity, the proposition, there would still remain a question about unity: how are the parts of the sentence – "Socrates" and the propositional function "x is human" – combined in such a way as to represent Socrates as human? Or if, instead, the propositional function is what is designated by the predicate, the question would be how what is designated by "Socrates" combines with the propositional function 'x is human' to comprise the proposition 'Socrates is human.' The only difference the introduction of the propositional function makes in the question about unity is that now there are only two constituents to be unified (the propositional function and its argument) where before there were three (Socrates, is, and human).

Of course, it is probably quite wrong to think of the propositional function as a constituent either of the sentence or of the proposition. The role of the propositional function in Russell's analysis might rather be that it is a representation of what is asserted by the sentence: the propositional function 'x is human' represents what we assert of

17 Russell does not argue for this view, and he realizes it has odd consequences, such as that the proposition expressed by "Socrates is wise" is different from the one expressed by "Humanity is instantiated in Socrates." See §48, pp. 44–5; and §53, p. 49.
18 Ibid., §55, p. 52.
19 Ibid., §54, p. 50.
20 Ibid., §81, p. 84.

Socrates when we say "Socrates is human." But then a different problem arises. If the propositional function represents what is asserted by the sentence, it does not explain how the parts of the sentence are combined to assert something. Either way, as a constituent of the proposition or as a representation of what is asserted, the notion of a propositional function provides no solution to the question about the unity of the sentence.

If we keep in mind that Russell thinks that there are two sorts of entities, both unities, sentences composed of words and propositions composed of the things designated by the words of a sentence, his view seems to be this. The sentence "Socrates is human" can be analyzed into certain grammatical parts, noun, verb, predicate adjective (or more simply, into subject and predicate). These parts designate things of a certain kind, an object, relation, and attribute (or more simply an object and propositional function). The things designated, the man Socrates, the instantiation relation, and the attribute of being human, are the constituents of the proposition. In the sentence, the verb functions somehow to relate the other parts so that together they comprise a unitary entity. By analogy, the relation in the proposition functions to relate the other constituents of the proposition. In the proposition 'Socrates is human,' the instantiation relation functions to unify the object and attribute. Russell does not attempt to explain how the verb functions to unify the sentence or how the relation functions to unify the proposition. Nor does he discuss the relation between the unity of the sentence and that of the proposition.

Russell soon came to reject the view that the constituents of the proposition are the things designated by the symbols. While he may have been right to reject it, there are considerations that make the view seem reasonable. The term "proposition" is introduced as a name for the thing that various sentences or beliefs may have in common. The sentences "John is a bachelor" and "John is an unmarried man" both express the same proposition. If I believe John is a bachelor and you believe John is an unmarried man, then we believe the same proposition. That is the *object*, the *single* thing, to which we are both related. To know what the constituents of the proposition are, we have to know what the single thing is to which various people may be thereby related when they have the same belief or make the same statement. It is not the words, for sentences that comprise different words may express the same proposition. Russell seems only to consider two possibilities: that we are related to a combination of words or else to a combination of nonrepresentational things. There are other alternatives, most obviously a collection of mental symbols. An act can occur in my mind that is of the same kind as the one that occurs in your mind, because mental symbols of the same kind are combined in the same way. What we are both related to when we have the belief is a certain kind of structured mental symbol. Of such a structured mental symbol, one can then legitimately ask, "What makes the symbol occurring in my head and your head be symbols of the same type?" Part of the answer has to be that it is the relation of the symbols to objects, properties, and relations in the world. So Russell can justifiably say that, ultimately, what is common to what we believe are the objects, relations, and properties the belief is a belief about.

2   The Multiple Relation Theory

By 1910, Russell rejects his earlier view that what we are related to when we make a judgment is a proposition and that a proposition is a unitary entity comprising the things designated by the symbols in the judgment or sentence that expresses it. In "On the Nature of Truth and Falsehood" Russell poses the question of whether the judging relation is a relation between the judger and some single thing (e.g., the fact or proposition that Charles I died on the scaffold), or a relation between the judger and various things (such as Charles I, dying, and the scaffold). Russell argues that it must be the latter. Suppose the opposite – that there are unitary objects comprising the relevant objects, relations, and properties – for example, Charles, dying, and the scaffold. Following Meinong, these unitary objects might be called "Objectives." When we make a true judgment we will be related to a true objective, and when we make a false judgment we will be related to a false objective.

This works fine for true judgments, since the object to which we may be related when we judge that Charles I died on the scaffold may be that fact itself. That fact is a unitary thing comprising Charles I, the relation of dying on, and the scaffold. But when we judge something falsely, for example that Charles I died in his bed, there is no such fact or event, no unitary thing wherein Charles I stands in the dying relation to his bed. Russell says, "To say that there ever was such a thing as 'Charles I's death in his bed' is merely another way of saying that Charles I died in his bed."[21] A theory that held that there are such objec-

---

21   B. Russell, "On the Nature of Truth and Falsehood," in *Philosophical Essays* (New York: Simon & Schuster, 1966), pp. 147–59. See p. 151.

tives would imply what is false – that there were such events as these. It would also entail that all sentences are true, for corresponding to every sentence, would be an objective comprising the object standing in the relation said to obtain.[22] Consequently, Russell rejects the view that, when we make a judgment, the object of the judgment is a proposition.

So far, Russell's argument should make us doubt only that the constituents of propositions are objects, properties, and relations, not that what we believe when we believe something is a proposition, a single unitary thing. Propositions might be things designated by the clause 'that . . .' – for instance, 'that Charles died in his bed' or 'that the cat is on the mat.' But Russell gives two objections to such a view. First, he finds it "difficult to believe that there are such objects as 'that Charles I died in his bed,' or even 'that Charles I died on the scaffold.'"[23] 'That such and such is the case' doesn't plausibly denote any object. Second, "If we allow that all judgments have objectives, we shall have to allow that there are objectives which are false. Thus, there will be in the world entities, not dependent upon the existence of judgments, which can be described as objective falsehoods."[24] This he thinks too incredible, because "we feel that there could be no falsehood if there were no minds to make mistakes."[25]

Philosophers distinguish between a particular sentence or judgment "token" and its content – what is said or judged to be so. Sometimes the content of what is said or judged is called a "proposition." But it is not obvious that "what a sentence says" or "what is judged to be so" designates an entity of any kind. The view that Russell is criticizing supposes that a proposition is an entity distinct from the sentence or judgment. Russell argues that this supposition runs contrary to a correct account of truth and falsity. On a correct account, truth and falsity are properties of representations, mental or linguistic; the truth or falsity of the representation is a relational property determined by whether the representation corresponds with the way the world is. If there were no representations, there would be no such things as truth or falsehood. Whereas, if the propositions of this theory exist and are

---

22 According to Russell, Meinong said that when the sentence is false, the objective merely "subsisted," but did not exist, whereas when the sentence is true, the objective "exists" ("On Denoting," p. 45 in *Logic and Knowledge*, ed. Robert C. Marsh [London: Unwin Hyman, 1956], pp. 41–56). But this is a sham explanation.

23 Ibid., p. 151.

24 Ibid., p. 152.

25 Ibid.

the objects of true and false judgments, then corresponding to every possible false judgment will be a unitary entity, a thing like 'that Charles I died in his bed.' These would be the objects of false statements or judgments to which the judger is related in making the judgment. These entities would exist whether or not the false statement or judgment is made. This would seem to imply what Russell thinks we do not believe, that falsehood does not depend on our making mistakes.

Whether that is implied depends upon how falsehood is to be defined, but attempts to do that give rise to new problems. The explicable difference between a true and false judgment is supposed to be that "when we judge truly that some entity 'corresponding' in some way to our judgment is to be found outside our judgment, while when we judge falsely there is no such 'corresponding' entity."[26] The falsehood of statements and judgment should arise from there being no such thing corresponding to the sentence. If propositions exist, there *is* something corresponding to the whole false sentence, namely the proposition. So Russell asks, what is the difference between the truth or falsity of the judgment? One can *say* the one "objective" is false and the other true, but that does not *explain* the difference between truth and falsity.

Perhaps Russell's criticism may be avoided by defining truth and falsity at another level. Since every true and false sentence corresponds to a proposition, truth and falsity would be a matter of whether the proposition in turn corresponds to the facts. This would raise a new issue about what constitutes the correspondence of the proposition with the fact. In the case of the sentence or judgment, it is that the world is the way it is represented as being by the judgment. But the propositions of the theory are not representations; they are abstract, nonpsychological entities. Still, the fact has got to match the proposition for it to be true. It is mysterious what this matching is if the proposition does not represent something as being the case. (And if the propositions were representational, the view would be that sentences and judgments are representations that represent propositions which are themselves representations. But this makes the introduction of propositions seem pointless.)

Russell thinks that the difficulty in giving an adequate account of truth and falsity might be avoided by simply assuming that when we make judgments, we are not thereby related to any single unitary object:

26   Ibid.

> The way out of the difficulty consists in maintaining that, whether we
> judge truly or whether we judge falsely, there is no one thing that we are
> judging. . . . [W]hen we judge that Charles I died in his bed, we have
> before us the objects, Charles I, dying, and his bed. These objects are not
> fictions: they are just as good as the objects of the true judgment.[27]

The objects of the judgment are Charles I, dying, and his bed, and these
things exist whether the judgment is true or false. And while it does
not seem necessary for the judgment to exist that there be, in reality,
such a thing as Charles dying in his bed or that Charles died in his bed,
it does seem necessary for the existence of the judgment that there be
such a things as Charles, and dying, and a bed.[28] Russell thinks that in
making a judgment a person relates the separate objects of the judgment to the mind: "judgment is not a dual relation of the mind to a
single objective, but a *multiple relation* of the mind to the various other
terms with which the judgment is concerned."[29] The judgment relates
the judger (the subject) to the objects of the judgment. The constituents
of the judgment then include both the judger and the objects of the
judgment.

Such a view of judgment allows for an adequate account of truth
and falsity. If a person judges that A loves B, that is a relation between
the judger, A, loves, and B. The making of the judgment does not neces-
sitate that there is an object, 'A's love for B,' as would be necessary if
judgment were a dual relation between the person and the proposition
'A's love for B'. It does not entail that A stands in the loving relation to
B: "When the judgment is taken as a relation between me and A and
love and B, the mere fact that the judgment occurs does not involve
any relation between its objects A and love and B: thus the possibility
of false judgments is fully allowed for."[30] Russell then can define truth
and falsity as follows: "Every judgment is a relation of a mind to several
objects, one of which is a relation; the judgment is *true* when the rela-

---

27   Russell, "On the Nature of Truth and Falsehood," p. 153.
28   Russell thinks that the things to which we are related when we make a judgment
must be real (or reduce to something real). So even in the judgment "Charles I died
on a unicorn," Russell will suppose that the judger is related to Charles, dying, and
the concept of being horned, white, and horse-like. If such concepts did not exist,
the judger couldn't make the judgment. (Following Russell's views in "On Denoting,"
such a judgment would not be a subject–predicate sentence, but a disguised existence
claim: There exists an x such that x is horned, white, horse-like, and Charles died
on x.)
29   Ibid., p. 155 (my emphasis).
30   Ibid.

tion which is one of the objects relates the other objects, otherwise it is false."[31] The judgment that A loves B, for instance, is true if the relation loves, which is one of the objects of the judgment, actually relates the other objects of the judgment, A and B. If it is false, then A will not stand in the loving relation to B. What is required for the judgment to exist, whether it be true or false, is that the *judging* relation relates the constituents of the judgment (the judger, A, the loving relation, and B), not that the *loving* relation relates A and B. So 'loves' does not function in the judgment to unify any constituents of the judgment: in terms of Russell's earlier way of thinking about it, 'loves' does not function as a "relating relation" in the judgment. Rather, the judging relation relates the judger to A, the loving relation, and B in such a way that A is represented as loving B.[32]

It should be emphasized that when Russell characterizes judgment as involving a multiple relation, more is built into this than simply that there are three or more constituents of the judgment. First, judgment is "not several instances of a relation between two terms, but one instance of a relation between more than two terms."[33] This may be illustrated as follows. When someone judges that Charles I died on the scaffold, he is thinking of Charles I, dying, and the scaffold. But the relation 'thinking of' that holds between him and those objects is not the relation that characterizes the making of a judgment, for a person might think of those things without making the judgment that Charles died on the scaffold. When the person thinks of those things, this is an example of *several instances* of the *same* relation existing between two terms: he thinks of Charles I (one instance), he thinks of dying (second instance), he thinks of the scaffold (third instance). By contrast, when someone makes a judgment, judging must be a relation wherein, in *one* instance of relating, all of the constituents of the judgment – judger, Charles, dying, the scaffold – become related. Russell says, "we must have one single unity of the mind and Charles I and dying and the scaffold."[34]

31   Ibid., p. 156.
32   Russell thinks it is the judging relation which supplies that direction of the judgment: e.g., in judging that A loves B, the direction of the judgment is that A loves B, not that B loves A. See "On the Nature of Truth and Falsehood," p. 158; and *Problems of Philosophy*, p. 126. Originally published in Home University Library (New York: H. Holt, 1912), and published later (Buffalo, NY: Prometheus Books, 1988). All references are to the latter.
33   Ibid., p. 154.
34   Ibid.

The second feature essential to a relation's being a multiple relation is that the relation cannot be reduced from a relation between three or more relata to "dual relation"; that is, to a relation between two things, namely one of the relata and some *complex* of them. For example, in '(2 + 3) × 5', there are three constituents. Russell, however, would not consider this a multiple relation of constituents, for the parentheses indicate that one first forms a complex by adding 2 and 3, and then multiplication is applied to that sum. While there are more than two constituents, '(2 + 3) × 5' is not the multiple relation of three constituents but a dual relation between a unified complex, 2 + 3, and another constituent, 5. Russell thinks that in judging Charles died on the scaffold, the judger is not related to some already unified complex – the proposition that Charles died on the scaffold. Judgment is not the dual relation of a person to a proposition, but the multiple relation of the person to the objects of the judgment, Charles, dying, the scaffold. For there to be a multiple relation, it must be that in one instance of relating three or more relata are related, that relation not being reducible to a dual relation between one of the relata and some complex formed from the other relata.

Russell's multiple relation theory of judgment is incomplete, and many of the critics of the theory have focused on what he leaves unexplained. F. P. Ramsey, for example, wants Russell to have explained what relation it is that the mind stands in to the objects of judgment, when one makes a judgment.[35]

Russell does, however, say quite a bit about the relation. For example, he says that when one makes a judgment, the objects of the judgment are what the judgment is about. In making the judgment, that is, when the mind is multiply related to those objects, the judger must know what he is making a judgment about: "it seems scarcely possible to believe that we can make a judgment or entertain a supposition without knowing what it is that we are judging or supposing about."[36] This characterizes one feature of the relation.

It might be objected that this is not a very revealing feature of the multiple relation, because one cannot understand the judger's knowledge of the objects of the judgment independently of multiple relation

35 F. P. Ramsey, "Facts and Propositions," p. 142. Originally appeared in *Aristotelian Society Supplementary*, 7 (1927), pp. 153–70. Reprinted in *The Foundations of Mathematics*, ed. R. B. Braithwaite (Paterson, NJ: Littlefield, Adams, 1960), pp. 138–55. All references are to the latter.
36 B. Russell, "Knowledge by Acquaintance and Knowledge by Description," in *Mysticism and Logic* (New York: W.W. Norton, 1929), p. 219.

itself. But Russell thinks one can. Judgments are about only those things that we can have "acquaintance" with, and acquaintance is defined not circularly in terms of judgment, but independently:

> I say that I am *acquainted* with an object when I have a direct cognitive relation to that object, i.e. when I am directly aware of the object itself. When I speak of a cognitive relation here, I do not mean the sort of relation which constitutes judgment, but the sort which constitutes presentation.[37]

This, in a way, is a partial analysis of the multiple relation involved in judging. It is a relation which is such that when it obtains, the judger has immediate, noninferential knowledge of the objects that the judgment is about.

It is not a complete analysis of the relation, because one might be acquainted with the objects that could comprise a judgment, for example the dog Fido and the property of sleeping, without judging that Fido sleeps. Recently, Steward Candlish has argued that Russell does not explain how, in the act of judgment, the objects of the judgment are combined in such a way as to comprise a judgment rather than an ordered list of things.[38] (Part of Russell's answer to this would be that a judgment is one instance of things multiply related, whereas in making a list the person is separately related to various objects. The list involves several instances of a dual relation. But Candlish thinks this is more a description of the difference than an explanation of it.) While Russell's work continued to focus on the analysis of judgments and statements, it increasingly focused on how to analyze them into parts in such a way that we can be acquainted with their objects rather than in how to put the parts of the judgment back together again.

While Ramsey and Candlish make fair demands for a complete theory of judgment, Russell's account is aimed at giving an account of how the mind is related to reality in judgment and how judgment can be both truth and false. The theory, after all, is developed in a paper called "On the Nature of Truth and Falsity" and in a chapter called "Truth and Falsity." In those works, Russell provides a formal theory of judgment; that is, a structural description of the judging relation that identifies what must minimally exist in order for there to be true and

---

37 Ibid., p. 209.
38 S. Candlish, "The Unity of the Propositions and Russell's Theories of Judgement," in *Russell and the Origins of Analytical Philosophy*, ed. R. Monk and A. Palmer (Bristol: Thoemmes Press, 1996), pp. 110–18.

false judgment. And it is not so clear that anything that Russell has said about that is wrong. We talk of what is judged to be so, the proposition, as though there were a single thing – that being what is common to what different people may judge when they make the same judgment. Russell thinks that this way of talking, if taken quite seriously, is not consistent with the objectivity of judgment, the possibility of its being true or false, and with maintaining a "vivid sense of reality." If the theory of judgment is to entail that the judgment is about things out there in the world beyond the mind and that the judgment can be true or false, and if the theory does not postulate unreal entities, then there cannot be any *single* object of the judgment, what is judged to be so, or the "proposition." What this leaves, Russell thinks, is that the judger must be related in one instance to the various objects of the judgment.

Russell's work in these papers is important, not least because he so clearly identifies certain criteria that any adequate account of the unity of the sentence or judgment must meet. They are criteria that guide Wittgenstein's attempts to work on these same problems. Yet Wittgenstein thinks that Russell's multiple relation view violates another criterion on the adequacy of the theory, and Russell comes to agree. Of Wittgenstein's criticism, Russell said "I saw he was right . . ."[39]

3   The Lectures on Logical Atomism View

Russell's account of judgment and his analysis of the sentence continued to evolve. By the 1918 lectures, "The Philosophy of Logical Atomism," Russell has both combined and rejected certain features of the 1903 theory from *Principles* and the later Multiple Relation view. He also has a new view about the form and structure of the sentence that he owes, partly, to Wittgenstein, because part of what Russell says is an interpretation of certain ideas of Wittgenstein as well as a response to his criticism.

Before presenting Wittgenstein's criticism and Russell's response, it is necessary, to avoid confusion, to comment on how Russell uses the word "proposition" in these lectures. There, as in *Principles*, Russell is perfectly happy to talk about the composition, structure, and constituents of propositions, with these important differences: first, the constituents of propositions are symbols, not the earlier objects, rela-

---

39   This is from a letter Russell wrote to Lady Ottiline Morrell, March 14, 1916.

tions, and class concepts designated by the words; and second, a proposition is not in any sense the object of the belief or what is believed. Thus Russell continues to insist, as he did at the time of the Multiple Relation view, that when you believe something, what you believe – the object of the belief – is not a proposition in any sense of that word. When you believe that the cat is on the mat, you believe neither (1) a complex symbol, nor do you believe (2) a fact. And finally you aren't believing (3) some sort of entity designated by a 'that' clause, such as 'that the cat is on the mat.'

As against the view that what you believe when you believe p is a fact, he says, "Wherever it is facts alone that are involved, error is impossible. Therefore you cannot say you believe facts."[40] Nor does Russell think that what you believe is some entity designated by a 'that' clause. It may seem, as he says, that:

> You have to say that you believe propositions. The awkwardness of that is that obviously propositions are nothing. Therefore that cannot be the true account of the matter. When I say 'Obviously propositions are nothing' it is not perhaps quite obvious. Time was when I thought there were propositions, but it does not seem to me very plausible to say that in addition to facts there are also these curious shadowy things going about such as 'That to-day is Wednesday' when in fact it is Tuesday. I cannot believe they go about the real world. It is more than one can manage to believe, and I do think no person with a vivid sense of reality can imagine it.[41]

In view of Russell's point that it is implausible to posit such things as that 'snow is black' in the real world, perhaps a proposition should be identified with something that *does* exist – namely, a complex symbol. While Russell is perfectly happy to call these "propositions," he will insist that, when you believe something, what you believe is not a symbol. He concludes, "You cannot say when you believe, 'What is it that you believe?' There is no answer to that question, i.e., there is no single thing that you are believing."[42]

40   B. Russell, "The Philosophy of Logical Atomism," in *Logic and Knowledge* (London: Unwin Hyman, 1956), p. 223. Originally published in *Monist*, 1918.
41   Ibid.
42   Ibid., p. 224. Russell puts the point more clearly when he says that there is no answer to that question "What is it that you believe?" – for it is every bit as bad an answer to say you believe Charles and dying and his bed, as if what you believe were several things, as it is to say you believe a proposition.

When Russell does speak of propositions at this time, he uses "proposition" interchangeably with "sentence." Sentences or propositions are complex symbols, symbols composed of words which are themselves symbols. Sentences have a kind of complexity or structure or form. Part of this may simply be seen as a return to his view in *Principles* – that the sentence must be composed of certain grammatical parts (noun, verb, and predicate adjective) – standing in a certain relation to one another. But Russell's return to the notion of the structure of the proposition is motivated by Wittgenstein's criticism.

In 1913, Wittgenstein had written to Russell:

> I can now express my objection to your theory of judgment exactly: I believe it is obvious that, from the proposition "A judges that (say) *a* is in a relation R to *b*", if correctly analysed, the proposition "a R b.v.~a R b" must follow directly *without the use of any other premiss.* This condition is not fulfilled by your theory.[43]

Wittgenstein thinks that, for any judgment a person might make, what he judges either is the case or it is not the case. A person cannot judge 'that Socrates, Aristotle, and Plato.' Nor can he judge 'that runs, walks, sleeps': for what is judged has to either be the case or not. 'That Socrates, Aristotle, and Plato' and 'that runs, walks, sleeps' are not either the case or not the case, whereas 'that Socrates sleeps' is. This puts a clear constraint on what Russell calls the "objects" of the judgment. In making the judgment, the judger would have to be multiply relating things of certain determinate kinds, symbols that are subjects with symbols that are predicates, or things that are substances and attributes. Otherwise the judgment might be something that is neither true nor false.

But why did Russell find Wittgenstein's objection "paralyzing"? Why can't Russell just add to his Multiple Relation theory the constraint that, in making the judgment, the judger has to relate things that are of the required kinds, subjects and predicates or particulars and universals? The problem is that adding that clause to the theory would raise the question "*Why* must the things being related be of these certain kinds?" The answer seems to be because only things of those kinds combine to either be the case or not be the case. They combine in that way independently of and antecedently to anyone making the

---

43   L. Wittgenstein, Appendix 3: Extracts from Wittgenstein's Letters to Russell in *Notebooks 1914–1916*, 2nd edn., ed. G. H. von Wright and G. E. M. Anscombe (Chicago: University of Chicago Press, 1979), p. 121.

judgment. That certain things can or cannot combine so as either to be the case or not seems to constrain what we can judge a priori. This suggests, contrary to what Russell had been arguing, that the object of the judgment *is* a unity of constituents, and that judgment is the dual relation of a person to that unified complex (which may be called the "proposition").

The same point is made in another way by Wittgenstein's remark in the *Tractatus* that we cannot judge nonsense: "The correct explanation of the form of the proposition, 'A makes the judgment p', must show that it is impossible for a judgment to be a piece of nonsense. (Russell's theory does not satisfy this requirement.)"[44] When the judger relates the objects in the judgment, he can't put together just any jumble of objects, so judging something that is nonsense. This shows there are things that go together to form unities independently of the mind putting them together. Those unities are things the mind can judge, and if one can judge them, they have to be the kinds of things that either are the case or are not the case.

In the 1918 lectures, Russell does not discuss whether judgment is a multiple relation of the judger to many objects or the dual relation of judger to a complex symbol. But he does think that propositions are symbols combined in a certain form. Sentences or propositions have a kind of complexity or structure. The structure of the sentence, Russell thinks, is mirrored in the fact for which it is a symbol: "in a logically correct symbolism there will always be a certain fundamental identity of structure between a fact and the symbol for it; and that the complexity of the symbol corresponds very closely with the complexity of the facts symbolized by it."[45]

Russell says that his lectures "are very largely concerned with explaining certain ideas which I learnt from my friend and former pupil Ludwig Wittgenstein."[46] It is difficult at this point to know what in this view to attribute to Russell and what to attribute to Wittgenstein. It is certainly one of Wittgenstein's fundamental ideas in the *Tractatus* that it is this identity of structure between the symbol and what it symbolizes that explains the unity of the proposition. Russell, on the other hand, in these lectures makes no mention of the unity of the proposition or of the relation of that unity to the identity of

---

44   L. Wittgenstein, *Tractatus Logico-Philosophicus*, tr. D. F. Pears and B. F. McGuiness (London: Routledge & Kegan Paul, 1961), 5.5422, p. 54.

45   Russell, "Philosophy of Logical Atomism," p. 197.

46   Ibid., p. 177.

structure between the symbol and what it symbolizes. Accordingly, I will postpone discussion of Wittgenstein's idea.

The thought that a sentence has a certain complexity or structure that is mirrored in the facts is present already in Russell's *Principles*, and those ideas take new shape in the 1918 lectures and the 1924 essay "Logical Atomism." Russell here sorts out what he seemed to run together in *Principles*: the words and their structure, and the things designated and their structure. And while the trappings of Russell's theory may resemble Wittgenstein's, the substance of it does not.

Russell thinks that corresponding to the two different kinds of expressions, subjects and predicates, are two different kinds of things, substances and attributes. Substances and attributes differ in form. He argues that this difference in form is evidenced in the epistemological conditions required for having knowledge of the one or the other. It is also reflected in the difference of the form of the expressions that respectively name the substance or attribute.

> The essence of substance, from the symbolic point of view, is that it can only be named – in old-fashioned language, it never occurs in a proposition except as the subject or as one of the terms of a relation. . . .
>
> Attributes and relations, though they may be not susceptible of analysis, differ from substances by the fact that they suggest a structure, and that there can be no significant symbol which symbolizes them in isolation. All propositions in which an attribute or a relation *seems* to be the subject are only significant if they can be brought into a form in which the attribute or the relation relates. . . . Thus the proper symbol for 'yellow' (assuming for the sake of illustration that this is an attribute) is not the single word 'yellow', but the propositional function 'x is yellow', where the structure of the symbol shows the position which the words 'yellow' must have if it is to be significant.[47]

The form of the predicate contains the form of the proposition. The form of the proposition determines both the number and the kinds of names required to constitute a proposition involving that predicate. Only names that name certain kinds of things can be put into something of the form 'x is yellow.' Analogously, the form of an attribute contains the form of the fact, determining the number and kinds of things required to comprise a fact involving that attribute. Furthermore, the form of the predicate expression must reflect the form of the

47   Russell, "Logical Atomism," in *Logic and Knowledge* (London: Unwin Hyman, 1956), pp. 337–8.

attribute it designates. In this way, the structure of the proposition as a whole determines that what is expressed by the proposition will be of such a kind that it either is the case or is not the case.[48]

Russell's evidence that particulars and universals differ in form is that there is a difference between what is required to be acquainted with a particular and a universal: the latter, but not the former, requires understanding "the form of proposition." But what does this epistemological difference have to do with the metaphysical nature of particulars or universals or with the form of the proposition? Russell's reasoning runs through "provisional definitions" he gives. He says that the constituents of the proposition are the symbols we must understand to understand the proposition. The meaning (referent?) of the constituents of the proposition are the components of the facts, the particulars and universals, which would make the proposition true or false.[49] The meaning of a proper name is identified with a particular; the meaning of a predicate is identified with a universal. What you understand when you understand the meaning (referent) of the symbol is a particular or universal. If what you understand when you understand the meaning of the symbols differ and if what you understand when you understand the symbols is one a particular and the other a universal, then particulars and universal must differ in nature.

On Russell's view, understanding the meaning of the symbols is having an immediate, noninferential acquaintance with the particulars and universals that they designate. Understanding the meaning of a

48 Leonard Linsky argues that this view enables Russell to enforce his theory of types and so to avoid what is called "Russell's paradox." According to Linsky, if an expression naming a universal can function both to designate a relating relation and a relation in abstraction from its roles as relating relation, then Russell's paradox may be generated. Consider the sentence "The concept of being non-self applicable is not self applicable." If the concept of being non-self applicable has the concept of being non-self applicable, then it is self applicable. If it is not self-applicable, then it is. This is contradictory. Linsky argues that the problem, as Russell sees it, is in allowing the expression to designate the same thing but function differently in the very same sentence. The 1918 theory avoids this paradox. Wherever such expressions occur, they designate not just the universal but its structure; they preserve its nature as relating relation, having a form or structure that must be completed by things of certain types. When the expression occurs in what appears to be the subject-position, the expression still designates a relating relation, something with the structure of a propositional function. If that is right, then a universal of the form '____ is non-self is non-self applicable' cannot be completed by another universal of the form '____ is non-self is non-self applicable,' so we can't form the kinds of sentences that generate the paradox. Leonard Linsky, "The Unity of the Proposition," *Journal of the History of Philosophy* 30 (1992), pp. 243–73. See especially pp. 249–53.

49 Russell, "The Philosophy of Logical Atomism," p. 196.

predicate – a verb or adjective – requires understanding the form of the proposition.

> To understand 'red', for instance, is to understand what is meant by saying that a thing is red. You have to bring in the form of a proposition. You do not have to know, concerning any particular 'this', that 'This is red' but you have to know what is the meaning of saying that anything is red. You have to understand what one would call 'being red'.... When you understand 'red' it means that you understand propositions of the form that 'x is red'. So that the understanding of a predicate is something a little more complicated than the understanding of a name, just because of that. Exactly the same applies to relations, and in fact all those things that are not particulars. Take, e.g., 'before' in 'x is before y': you understand 'before' when you understand what that would mean if x and y were given. I do not mean you know whether it is true, but you understand the proposition.[50]

By contrast, understanding the meaning of the name, according to Russell, is simply a matter of our having a sensory experience of that particular: "in order to understand a name for a particular, the only thing necessary is to be acquainted with that particular. When you are acquainted with that particular, you have a full, adequate, and complete understanding of the name, and no further information is required."[51]

Russell overstates his claim. Acquaintance with what a name names is not the *only* thing necessary for understanding the meaning of a name. At the very least, one also has to know that the name is the name of that particular. And if one has to know of some name, for example "John," that it is the *name* of that particular, then one has to know something about the symbol, specifically that "John" *is* a name not a predicate or another part of speech. To know that, it seems, one must know that the word functions in the way names do in a sentence that expresses a proposition. Thus, one might say that to understand the name "John" is to understand who is referred to when one says that John has some property or stands in some relation. You have to understand, in the most general way, what it would be for John to have some property or stand in some relation or other, and that means that you understand propositions of the form "John is F." So it is not clear that Russell has here identified a genuine difference between subjects and predicates.

50   Ibid., p. 205.
51   Ibid., p. 202.

Russell thinks that understanding what some predicate "F" means involves understanding propositions of the form 'x is F,' but understanding a name does not. There is more than one way of interpreting his claim. He may mean that a person who understands the predicate "red" is actually acquainted with the propositional function 'x is red' or that she has it consciously in her mind. That is not terribly plausible. A more charitable way to interpret Russell's view is that we can best *represent* the understanding, the cognitive achievement, of a person when she understands the meaning of "red" in terms of a propositional function 'x is red.' Specifically, that understanding is best represented by saying that the subject knows something of the form, the propositional function 'x is red' is true if and only if such and such is the case. Reference to a propositional function provides a rich and well-articulated structural description of the ability to use general terms.

Russell might support this as follows. One cannot understand what it is to be F without a logically prior understanding of what *propositions* of the form 'x is F' mean. That is because understanding the meaning of some predicate "F" is a matter of understanding what it would be for something to be a *case* or *instance* of the property F:

> The notion of 'cases' or 'instances' depends upon propositional functions. Consider, for example, the kind of process suggested by what is called 'generalization', and let us take some very primitive example, say, 'lightning is followed by thunder'. We have a number of 'instances' of this, i.e. a number of propositions such as: 'this is a flash of lightning and is followed by thunder.' What are these occurrences 'instances' of? They are instances of the propositional function: 'if x is a flash of lightning, x is followed by thunder.'[52]

Understanding what a case or instance is implicitly involves the notion of *generalization* and *quantification*: that some x is F, or no x is F, or either some or no x is F. It is understanding, for any x, x is F if and only if such and such is the case. Russell says, "The only way of expressing a common property generally is to say that a common property of a number of objects is a propositional function which becomes true when any one of these objects is taken as the value of the variable."[53]

52 B. Russell, *Introduction to Mathematical Logic*, 2nd edn. (London: George Allen & Unwin, 1920), p. 156.
53 Russell, *Introduction to Mathematical Logic*, p. 156.

Russell's view may be characterized as follows. Seeing the color of a thing that is red is not sufficient for understanding what redness is. To understand what redness is, one must be able to understand what it would be for *any* thing to be red. Similarly, seeing the particular John does not suffice for understanding what John is either (one would have to be able to discriminate John from other things in the visual field, etc.). But by contrast, understanding what John is does *not* involve understanding what it would be for *anything* to *be* John. The idea of understanding what it would be for anything to be John makes no sense.

Is Russell's apparatus of propositional functions really necessary for these purposes? Might we not say instead that a person understands what "red" means so long as beyond having seen something red, she can reidentify the color when presented with it on other occasions. Or that the child grasps what it is for something to be red so long as she can discriminate red things from nonred things by their color when presented with them. This makes no reference to propositions or propositional functions.

But Russell could then argue that, while we could describe a person's understanding the meaning of the word in other terms, these descriptions will be informative only if reference to propositional functions lies at their basis. For example, this reidentification is essentially identifying other instances as instances of the same color, and the notion of an instance (as a "value" of the function) is what is crucial. For instance, 'There is red again' might not express a grasp of the meaning of "red," and would not, if the subject thought that in the same way that a particular like John might reappear in her view, red – the whole of it so to speak – had come into view again, and like John, could be found nowhere else.

Suppose that Russell is right that grasping the meaning of the predicate expression requires an understanding of the form of the proposition. The issue remains whether names and predicates differ on this point. One might argue, as was suggested above, that the understanding one has when one knows to whom the name refers is also best articulated with reference to propositional functions. Understanding what "John" names involves understanding that he is a particular, something that instantiates properties. And it might be urged that a structural description of what it is we grasp when we know who "John" refers to is an understanding of who makes propositions of the form 'John is F' true.

If, however, there is a genuine difference between subjects and predicates in this respect, then Russell would have an explanation of certain features of predicates: of why what we grasp, when we grasp the meaning of predicate is something that has general application or numerous instances. It is not clear, though, whether or how this difference might have application to the issues regarding the unity of the sentence.

Russell does not revisit the question of the unity of the sentence or proposition in his lectures on logical atomism. However, given his earlier views about the verb in its role as relating relation functioning to unify the proposition, perhaps the sentence quoted above expresses his view about the matter – "All propositions in which an attribute or a relation seems to be the subject are only significant if they can be brought into a form in which the attribute or the relation relates." He may think that there is a functional difference between subject and predicate, the predicate functioning to assert something about the referent of the subject. That functional difference must be reflected in the symbol that is the predicate, so that the proper symbol for the predicate "yellow," for instance, is 'x is yellow.' This is the proper symbol, because grasping what is designated by "yellow" involves an understanding of what it would be for propositions of the form 'x is yellow' to be true. (This because of what an attribute is: something that many distinct things may exemplify.) Finally, that symbol somehow functions as a "relating relation" because grasping the meaning of that symbol involves an understanding of propositions of the form 'x is yellow.'

Russell himself does not put together the various claims he does make in any such way. Even so, there does exist the idea (perhaps deriving from Russell, perhaps not), that because grasping – knowing – the meaning of a predicate is fundamentally different from grasping the meaning of a subject, and because grasping the meaning of the predicate somehow involves an understanding of the form of the proposition, that it is the predicate that functions to unify the proposition.[54] One rough doubt about this arises from the thought that the notion of a propositional function seems to be essentially an *abstraction* from the notion of a proposition. The symbolic form of the function 'x is yellow' abstracts from the concrete expression of propositions in sen-

54 P. F. Strawson, in his *Individuals: An Essay in Descriptive Metaphysics* (London: Methuen, 1959), develops a version of that idea. See pp. 183–7.

tences like "The Moon is yellow," which express a unitary proposition. One may question whether a notion abstracted in that way from the phenomenon to be explained could really explain the matter. There is also the question whether a fundamental account of how the string of words expresses a proposition can come from consideration of what is required to *understand* those words; that is, the question whether an epistemological matter provides a fundamental answer to a semantic question.

Let's examine the relationship between the claims that (1) grasping the meaning of a predicate F in "S is F" requires an understanding of propositions of the form 'x is F' and that (2) it is the predicate that functions to relate the words of the sentence in such a way that they express the proposition S is F.

How exactly might this account of what we grasp when we grasp the meaning of the predicate expression explain the predicate's functioning to unify the sentence? Suppose the meaning of an expression is identified with what one knows when one understands the meaning of the expression. Presumably, it is owing to the meanings of the words that they together express a proposition, if they do, and if we understand a string of words to express a proposition it is because of what we understand their various meanings to be. Perhaps the idea, then, is that if we put together their meanings, that is, what we grasp when we understand the separate words, then what we have will *be* a unitary proposition. Consider the sentence "John is a bachelor." What one knows when one knows the meaning of "bachelor" is, on the view being discussed, that the propositional function 'x is a bachelor' is true for some value of x, if and only x is an unmarried man. Now this may be what we understand when we understand its meaning, but it would be a mistake to conclude from that that what "bachelor" means is the propositional function 'x is a bachelor' is true for any value of x, if and only if x is an unmarried man. That, of course, is *not* its meaning (or its referent either, Russell's use of "meaning" being closer to our use of "referent"). Its meaning is unmarried man, not x is an unmarried man or anything of the sort. What one understands when one understands its meaning on this view is something more than what is identified by an expression that identifies its meaning.

The proposal cannot be, then, that if we juxtapose what is meant by the name with what is meant by the predicate, we get a structure like

John + x is an unmarried man

and that *that* is a proposition. In the first place it is not a proposition, or anything like a proposition, and in the second, 'x is an unmarried man' is not what is meant by the predicate. Nor can the idea be that "bachelor" means or designates being a bachelor, for it does not. And, even if it did, the juxtaposition of the designata of the words would be

John + being a bachelor

which again is not a proposition but just a sequence of categorially diverse things. We need an explanation of the fact that when you put together a word designating John and another in some sense "representing" (if not designating) being a bachelor or propositions of the form 'x is a bachelor', then one has a sentence and not just a list.

If we avoid the seemingly mistaken idea that the predicate means or designates a propositional function or a gappy entity or such a thing as being F, and attempt to state the position in terms of what one recognizes when one grasps its meaning, then how might the proposal be stated? (A) To understand "John" is to recognize that it is the name of John and to understand the meaning of "red" is to understand what it is for something to *be* red or for red to be *instanced*, that is, *by* something. And so (B) to understand the string of words "John is red" is to understand that *John* is what is being said to *be* red, or what is being represented as being red or as being an instance of red. Notice here that there are several gaps between A and B. The kind of understanding of what "red" means in A is understanding of a conditional form, for understanding what it would be or be like for something to be red is understanding of this form: x is red if and only if such and such is the case. How do we get from that fact to B, that understanding the string of words "John is red" is understanding that John is *said to be* red? If the understanding of "red" involves understanding a conditional, then understanding the meaning of the string "John is red" would be understanding that John is red if and only if such and such is the case. Or it is understanding what it would be like for John to be red, to have that attribute or be in that state. Understanding what it would be like for John to be in that state is not understanding that John has been *represented* as being (or been said to be) red. That is the first problem.

The second problem in the transition from A to B is that there remains the important question of what determines that (1) "John" is correctly understood, not just as naming John but that this token occurrence of the name is to identify what is being said to be red, and (2) what it is that determines that this token of the word "red" is correctly understood to be representing something as being red. For it does not follow just from the fact that to understand what "red" means is to understand what it is for something to be red that in this (or any other occurrence) it actually functions to represent some particular thing as being red. The fact that to understand the word "red" is to understand what it is for something, anything at all, to be red does not yet explain how it is that when "red" occurs in a particular sentence "John is red" it functions in such a way that some *particular* thing is being represented as red, much less that the particular is the thing named by the name "John." The fact that there is such a thing as one particular thing loving another, and that this is what is understood when we understand the general relational expression "loves" does not yet explain why that relational expression functions to "relate" the designata of the names "Desdemona" and "Othello" when it occurs in the string "Desdemona loves Othello." That is, that it functions to represent *that* particular thing as loving that other one. I conclude that the difference, if it exists, between the conditions required to understand the meaning of an expression designating a particular as opposed to an expression designating a universal does not in any obvious way explain the unity of the sentence: what we grasp when we grasp the meaning of a predicate expression does not explain how the sentence gets unified.

As one of Russell's views gives way to another, he defines what the puzzle about the unity of the sentence is and what criteria an account of it must meet. He thinks his own view in *Principles* fails because it cannot meet jointly three critieria on an adequate account. An account must explain the objectivity of our statements and judgments, allow for their truth and falsity, and postulate no unreal entities. The Multiple Relation meets those criteria, but apparently fails on another. (It was Wittgenstein who made him see this.) There are things that will go together to form unities that can be judged or stated and things that will not, and this should somehow follow from an account of judgment or sentence meaning. This motivates Russell's reintroduction of the structure and form of the sentence. The parts of the sentence designate things of such a kind as to form a unitary thing, and the form of the symbols in the sentence mirror the form of the things of those kinds. Here Russell makes no attempt to explain how the symbols' having such a form (or our grasping the meaning of symbols of such a form) makes the sentence represent something unitary – the particular instantiating the universal. I have argued it is not obvious how it would do so. Still, the dominant view, after Russell, is that the functional difference between subject and predicate in virtue of which the sentence expresses some unitary thing is somehow explained by the parts' naming things of distinct but complementary metaphysical kinds – particulars and universals. The idea that the predicate has a certain form, derived from its designating a universal, that allows it to effect propositional combination is still a standard part of philosophers' thinking about the question.

3

Wittgenstein's Picture Theory of the Unity of the Proposition

> *The reality that corresponds to the sense of the proposition can surely be nothing but its component parts, since we are surely* ignorant *of* everything *else.*
>
> *If the reality consists in anything else as well, this can at any rate neither be denoted nor expressed; for in the first case [the expression] would be a further component, in the second the expression would be a proposition, for which the same problem would exist in turn as for the original one.*
>
> Ludwig Wittgenstein, Notebooks 1914–1916[1]

In this entry in his notebooks, Wittgenstein identifies certain constraints that he thinks govern a theory of meaning. In explaining what is expressed by the sentence – that being "the reality that corresponds to the sense of the sentence" – one must make use only of the component parts of the sentence. This is because we understand the meaning of the sentence, being ignorant of everything except those parts.

The component parts merely name an object or a property, but in what is expressed by the sentence, the object is represented as instantiating the property. So Wittgenstein next reconsiders whether what is expressed might be owing to something more, and he argues that if there is something further, it cannot consist in some additional component denoting or expressing anything. If some further part of the sentence *denoted* some further constituent in the world – for example, the relation being said to obtain – this would simply compound the problem by adding yet another constituent that requires unification with the others in what is expressed.

And if one tries to explain the unity of the sentence in terms of something *expressed* by a part of the sentence, then the original question arises again. To say that the sentence expresses a proposition because there is an element of the sentence that expresses a proposition raises

---

1 All future references to the *Notebooks* will be made in the text by dates.

the corresponding question of how that element, which Wittgenstein thinks would itself be a sentence, expresses a proposition.

Thus, he wants to explain the unity of the sentence without postulating further constituents of the sentence (than the names that compose it) and without supposing that there is some constituent of the sentence that expresses what is expressed by the whole sentence. But he also thinks that he must be able to explain how the sentence means what it does with *just* its component parts – "off its own bat" (5.11.14). This would seem to tie his hands. How can the component parts of the sentence alone explain what the sentence expresses, when all the parts do is name one thing and another – like a list?

Wittgenstein recognizes that we are forgetting, so far, a feature the component parts have besides the fact that they name or denote what they do: there is the *fact* that the parts *stand related* one to the other in the way they do. That is just as much a property of the component parts as the fact that they name what they name. It is the fact that the words of the sentence stand related one to the other that represents the things named as standing related one to the other. This is a fundamental idea in the *Tractatus*, and from it emerges Wittgenstein's picture theory and the doctrine of showing. In its barest form, the idea is just this: "Instead of, 'The complex sign "*aRb*" says that *a* stands to *b* in the relation R', we ought to put, '*That* "a" stands to "b" in a certain relation says *that* a R b.'"[2] Earlier, in the *Notebooks*, he had written:

> In "aRb" it is not the complex that symbolizes but the fact that the symbol "a" stands in a certain relation to the symbol "b". Thus facts are symbolized by facts, or more correctly: that a certain thing is the case in the symbol says that a certain thing is the case in the world.
>
> Propositions [which are symbols having reference to facts] are themselves facts: that this inkpot is on this table may express that I sit in this chair.[3]

1 An Exposition of the Picture Theory

The crucial question then becomes, "How does the fact that one name stands in a certain relation to another name represent the things

2 L. Wittgenstein, *Tractatus Logico-Philosophicus*, tr. D. F. Pears and B. F. McGuiness (London: Routledge & Kegan Paul, 1961), 3.1432. All future references to the *Tractatus* will be made to this translation, by proposition number, in the text itself, unless otherwise indicated.

3 Wittgenstein, *Notebooks 1914–1916*, Appendix 1, pp. 96–7.

denoted as standing in a certain relation?" Wittgenstein's answer is that
the sentence is a kind of picture: "A proposition is a picture of reality"
(4.021). And "A picture is a fact" (2.141). In a picture, the fact that the
elements are related as they are *shows* the relation between things. (In
a picture of a cat on a mat, the spatial relation between the picture of
the cat and the picture of the mat shows the cat on the mat.) By analogy,
in the sentence, the fact that the elements of the sentence are related in
a certain way shows the things denoted related in a certain way: "The
proposition must shew what it is trying to say" (29.10.14). "A proposition *shows* its sense" (4.022).[4]

Wittgenstein's insight is that the sentence is a fact, just as what it
represents is a fact or possible fact. Because the sentence is itself a
fact comprising objects standing in a certain relation, Wittgenstein's
metaphysical views about the character of facts and objects apply
directly to sentences (facts) and names (objects) and are essential to
an understanding of his account of the unity of the sentence. A fact,
he says, is a combination of objects (2.01). Objects make up what he
calls "the substance of the world," but a list of all the things in
the world, standing alone, in isolation, does not determine the way
the world is. It is only when the objects are combined with one
another in determinate relations, when they are "structured" in states
of affairs, that the way the world is takes shape. Thus, "The world is
the totality of facts, not of things" (1.1), and "The world divides up into
facts" (1.2).

Nonetheless, objects "contain the possibility of all states of affairs"
(2.014), in the sense that the possible ways objects could combine determine the possible ways that the world could be: "If all objects are given,
then at the same time all *possible* states of affairs are also given" (2.0124).
While the object is independent of any state of affairs in which it occurs
precisely because that same object could recombine with other objects
in other relations, that independence connects it with other objects in
possible states of affairs.

2.0122   Things are independent in so far as they can occur in all *possible* situ-
         ations, but this form of independence is a form of connexion with
         states of affairs, a form of dependence. . . .

---

4 Wittgenstein identifies a proposition with "a perceptible sign" (3.11). In this chapter,
I will mean by "sentence" an uttered or written sign (so a perceptible one), and use "sentence" interchangeably with proposition, because a proposition is a propositional sign (a
perceptible one) in its projective relation to the world (3.12).

2.022 It is obvious that an imagined world, however different it may be from
the real one, must have *something* – a form – in common with the real
world.

2.023 Objects are just what constitute this unalterable form.

There are ways that objects can (and cannot) combine with other objects
to make up states of affairs. This is the basis for Wittgenstein's notion
of form: "The possibility of its occurring in states of affairs is the form
of the object" (2.0141). The form of objects determines what states of
affairs are possible and thus the form the world can take.

2.032 The determinate way in which objects are connected in a state of affairs
is the structure of the state of affairs.

2.33 Form is the possibility of the structure.

The actual world is determined by the way that objects are actually
structured in states of affairs. The form of any state of affairs is the possibility that things could stand related as they do in the state of affairs
– the possibility that things are structured as they are. This possibility
is contained in the form of the objects that make up the state of affairs.
The form of all objects determines what worlds are possible, that is, the
possible ways objects can be structured in states of affairs.

If we were to apply Wittgenstein's remarks about facts very literally
to sentences which are themselves facts and force an exact parallel
between language and the world, the parallel would be this. Sentences,
which are facts, are composed of objects, specifically names. If the
world comprises the actual combination of objects, then, by analogy,
language would comprise the actual combination of names, those
names standing in certain relations. The names determine all the
sentences that could be uttered. They determine the "form of language," since they determine what sentences are possible. The names
are independent of the sentences in which they occur, in that they can
occur in other possible sentences. In "The cat is on the mat," the name
"the cat" is independent of the other names, in that it can be separated
out and occur in other sentences, for example in "The cat is lost."
But that form of independence is a form of connection with the sentence, for the independence of the name is its ability to enter into other
combinations with other names in the other sentences in which it can
enter. A list of all the names delimits the possible sentences in the language. The form of a sentence is the possibility that the names can stand
in the determinate relation that they do – it is the possibility of the

structure of the sentence. And this possibility is written into the form of the names, into the possible ways they can combine with other names.

There are two parallel structures: the nonrepresentational fact in which objects stand in a determinate relation and the representational fact, the sentence, in which the objects are names standing in a determinate relation. So far, these two facts stand apart from one another just as any fact stands apart from any other. In each, there are objects structured in a certain way. However, in the case of the representation, that the objects are structured as they are represents things as correspondingly structured.

What distinguishes the relation between these two facts in which one is a representation of the other from the relation between two nonrepresentational facts? Why does the structure of elements of the representation *represent* things as correspondingly structured?

In the sentence, the names represent (i.e., name or stand for) the objects in some fact (actual or possible), but in nonrepresentational facts no constituent of the fact represents a corresponding constituent of another fact. That is one difference.

2.13   In a picture objects have the elements of the picture corresponding to them.
2.131   In a picture the elements of the picture are the representatives of objects.

However, this difference doesn't fully explain the matter, for lists are structures comprising names, but lists of names don't picture states of affairs.

Here Wittgenstein introduces a key feature of his account. What explains why certain structures of names represent states of affairs and others don't is that some but not other structures have a form in common with states of affairs. The structures of names that do picture states of affairs are ones that have a form in common with those states of affairs:

2.16   If a fact is to be a picture, it must have something in common with what it depicts.
2.161   There must be something identical in a picture and what it depicts, to enable the one to be a picture of the other at all.
2.17   What a picture must have in common with reality in order to be able to depict it – correctly or incorrectly – is its pictorial form.

The propositional fact must have the *same form* as that of what it pictures.

If the form of the sentence were construed on analogy with the form of any other fact, the form of the sentence would be the possibility that its names could stand in the relations that they do. But that would not *guarantee* that there is any form common to the sentence and what it represents, for there are many relations that words stand in that the things denoted by the words cannot stand in. The words, for example, are syntactically and phonologically related, but the things named, the cat and the mat, could not possibly stand in *those* relations. To guarantee that there is a form common to the representation and what is represented, we must consider the relations that the name can stand in, as James Griffin puts it, not as "a sign in its own right" but rather as "a representative of something, as a symbol" standing for some object.[5] The form of the sentence is determined by the form of what it represents.

2.15 The fact that the elements of a picture are related to one another in a determinate way represents that things are related to one another in the same way.

Let us call this connexion of its elements the structure of the picture, and let us call the possibility of this structure the pictorial form of the picture.

2.151 Pictorial form is the possibility that things are related to one another in the same way as the elements of the picture.

The *form* of the picture consists in this: its names can combine only in ways that are possible for the things denoted by the names to combine. It is not possible for a picture to have the structure that it does (for its elements to be related as they are) unless it is possible for the things represented by the parts of the picture to have the same structure, that is, be related in the same way.[6]

5 J. Griffin, *Wittgenstein's Logical Atomism* (Seattle: University of Washington Press, 1964), p. 90.

6 David Pears suggests that Wittgenstein thought we must construct our sentences in ways that "reflect the possibilities of combination inherent in things." See pp. 191–2, "The Relation between Wittgenstein's Picture Theory of Propositions and Russell's Theories of Judgement," *Philosophical Review* 86 (1977), pp. 177–96.

Sentences differ from lists because the words in a sentence do not merely designate certain things; they represent the things designated as combined in states of affairs. Wittgenstein accounts for this as follows. In the proposition, the determinate relation between the names represents a determinate relation of things in states of affairs because there is a form common to the structure of the names and that of the structure of objects in states of affairs. This common form is a constraint on the structure of the proposition: the elements of the proposition can stand structurally related only in ways that the objects designated can combine with each other in states of affairs. (No such constraint governs the occurrence of names in a list.) The structure of the names in a proposition shows a possible state of affairs, because the structure of the names *is* the structure of a possible state of affairs.

2   The Theoretical Role of Form and Structure

The notion of form and structure are the crux of Wittgenstein's account of the unity of the proposition, and the remainder of this chapter will focus on those two notions. The form of the representation enables the structure of the representation – the way the names are actually combined – to represent the things designated as combined. The form of the representation is "the possibility that things are related to one another in the same way as the elements of the picture" (2.151). That much is clear. But there are different ways to understand Wittgenstein's notion of common form – the notion that names can combine only in the *same* ways that the things designated can combine. There is also the question of how the fact that the representation has that form enables its structure to represent the things named as structured or related. I will examine two different conceptions of "sameness of form," the role that each would play in an account of the meaning of the sentence, and whether form together with structure adequately explains the unity of proposition. But first, I will trace Wittgenstein's development of the notion of form in the *1914–1916 Notebooks*, focusing on why Wittgenstein thinks that the form common to the representation and what it represents is one regarding the *possibility* of combination. His discussion in the *Notebooks* sheds light on the distinct role that form and structure play in the explanation of the unity of the proposition.

Development of Wittgenstein's notion of form

We have seen that, at the time of the *Notebooks*, Wittgenstein thought that the meaning of the sentence must be explained entirely in terms of the features of the component parts, by the fact that the names name what they do and the fact that the names stand in the relation to each other that they do. The fact that the names are related as they are represents the things as correspondingly related because of a form common to the sentence and the state of affairs represented. That form is something more than a one-to-one correlation of names with things named, for that one word names one thing and another word names another does not explain how the things named come to be represented as related. There must at least be, in addition, a correlation of relations too: not just a correlation of the *name* of a relation with a relation, but a correlation between the relation that the elements of the representation stand in and a relation that the things named stand in (25.9.14). Notice that, in this way of describing things, there is not yet any distinction between form and structure. There is the way the names are combined and that correlates with the way things are combined: that is why the relation between names represents things as being related to one another.

By the time of the *Tractatus*, this correlation of relations or common form concerns the way that the names and the things named can *possibly* combine, not the way that they are actually combined. The possible combinations of objects govern the possible combinations of names. Wittgenstein is led to this particular conception of form because it avoids the problems generated by other conceptions – only form as "possibility of combination" meets the various criteria required for an adequate theory. But once the notion of form concerns the possible combination of constituents of facts, he needs both the concept of form and structure to provide an explanation of the unity of the proposition.

Let us begin setting aside for a moment the notion of form that we know he comes to develop. Wittgenstein says, "The general concept of the proposition carries with it a quite general concept of the coordination of proposition and situation" (29.9.14). But then he begins to puzzle about what that correlation is, and part of the puzzle is about exactly what it is that the sentence has a form in common with. The representation has to have a form in common with "what it represents." Sometimes, he identifies what it represents with a fact.[7]

---

7   In the *Tractatus* 2.1, he says that pictures picture facts.

In that case, the representation should have a form in common with the fact it represents. The correlation is also to explain why the sentence represents the things as related in the way that it does. We should be looking for a correlation between the relation of the elements of the proposition and the relation of the constituents of the fact that can explain both why the proposition represents what it does and why it represents the things named as related in the way it does.

But can there be any correlation of the *actual* relation between the names, on the one hand, and the actual relations between things, on the other, that makes the sentence represent things as related in the way it does? Suppose the sentence is "The cat is on the mat," but the fact is that the cat is on the sofa. That the elements of the sentence are related in the way they are represents the things named as standing in a relation that the things do *not* stand in, in point of fact. There is apparently no form common to the way the names and the things named are actually combined. Even though the name "the cat" is actually combined with the name "the mat" – what they name, the cat and the mat, are not actually combined in the way depicted. On the other hand, the things that enter into the fact, the cat and the sofa, *are* actually combined, but the names that name those things are not actually combined, because the sentence in question is not "The cat is on the sofa" but "The cat is on the mat."

Wittgenstein says, "There must be something in the proposition that is identical with its reference, but the proposition cannot be identical with its reference and so there must be something in it that is *not* identical with the reference" (22.10.14). I interpret that remark as follows. There must be an identity in form between the proposition and what it represents, for it is the identity of form – the correlation of the relation between elements of the proposition with the relation between things named – that enables the proposition to represent something which is a fact or situation (as opposed to a mere jumble of things). But on the other hand, because the sentence may be false and the things may not actually be related in the way the sentence represents them as related, whatever identity there is between the relation between elements of the proposition and that of the things in states of affairs cannot entail the truth of the sentence. That leaves the question "What is the relevant correlation between the relation of names with the relation of things named?"

To find a form common to the representation and what it represents, Wittgenstein could deny that representations represent facts, and suppose, instead, that they represent possible facts or states of affairs. In the *Tractatus* he would write, "The picture represents a possible state of affairs in logical space" (2.202). But Wittgenstein had worried in the *Notebooks* about how a representation can have a form in common with a possible state of affairs when the possible state of affairs may not exist, that is, is not actual.

> The fact that in a certain sense the logical form of p must be present even if p is not the case, shews symbolically through the fact that "p" occurs in "~p."
> This is the difficulty: how can there be such a thing as the form of p if there is no situation of this form. And in that case, what does this form really consist in? (29.10.14)

He wrote, "A picture can present relations [between things] that do not exist! How is that possible?" (30.9.14)

He works through the puzzle at length in this passage:

> How does the picture present a situation?
> It is after all itself not the situation, which need not be the case at all.
> One name is a representation of one thing, another of another thing, and they themselves are connected: in this way – like a *tableau vivant* – the whole images the situation.
> The logical combination must, of course, be one that is possible as between the things that the names are representations of, and this will always be the case if the names really are representatives of the things. N.B. that connection is not a relation but only the *holding* of a relation.
> In this way the proposition represents the state of affairs as it were off its own bat.
> But when I say: the connexion of the propositional components must be possible for the represented things – does this not contain the whole problem? How can a nonexistent connexion between objects be possible, when it does not exist?
> "The connexion must be possible" means: the proposition and the components of the situation must stand in a particular relation.
> Then, in order for a proposition to present a situation it is only necessary for its component parts to represent those of the situation and for the former to stand in a connexion which is possible for the latter.

> The propositional sign guarantees the possibility of the fact which it
> presents (not, that this fact is actually the case). (4.11.14–5.11.14)

The question is, "How can there be a connection (a sameness in form)
between the proposition and the state of affairs, when the state of
affairs does not exist?"[8] The proposition must share a form in common
with something that *does* exist, and it represents that, something
real.

Many philosophers nowadays are perfectly happy to admit the
"existence" of possible but nonactual states of affairs. Wittgenstein was
not so willing to do so, perhaps because, like Russell, he thought that
it was both ontologically extravagant and compromised the account of
truth and falsity.[9] So Wittgenstein reduces the form of a possible state
of affairs to the form of its constituents. The form of a possible state of
affairs is the form of its objects, and the form of objects are the possible ways they can combine in states of affairs (2.0141). This postulates
nothing that does not exist. The objects are real and there really are facts
about the way that objects can combine in states of affairs.

This conception of form allows Wittgenstein to finesse rather nicely
the question of what the proposition represents. He has identified what
is represented alternately as a fact or a possible state of affairs. Facts
and possible states of affairs have exactly the same form, the form of
reality or actuality itself, namely, the way that objects can combine in
states of affairs. And the false sentence still represents something actual
(reality), but not an actual state of affairs.

Because the form of the sentence is derived from the form of the
objects named, Wittgenstein can give an account of meaning that is
both atomist and externalist. Form is not a similarity relation between
the proposition and some *complex* – an actual or possible state of affairs
– but between the elements of the proposition and the things named.
The things named do exist. The proposition has a form in common with
the bits – the *atoms* or *objects* – of reality. The form of the complexes,
the proposition, on the one hand, and the actual or possible states of
affairs, on the other, are reduced to the form of their respective atoms,

8 Wittgenstein's question about how a nonexistent connection can be possible when it
does not exist is puzzling if he is asking how a nonexistent connection can be possible
when the nonexistent connection does not exist. For the very idea of a nonexistent but
possible connection is of one that does not exist but *could* exist. "[W]hen it does not exist"
must mean when the state of affairs does not obtain.
9 Wittgenstein connects the question about how the sameness of form to what he calls
"the problem of truth" at 23.9.14–25.9.14.

names, and objects.[10] Thus, each name (considered as a symbol) can enter into a relation with another name only if its object can enter into that relation with that other object.

This atomism enables Wittgenstein to give an externalist account of the unity of the sentence. The sentence represents a state of affairs because it has a form in common with the state of affairs. The form of the sentences cannot be derived from that of actual states of affairs, since sentences might be false. Following Russell, he will not derive it from nonexistent possible states of affairs. All that appears to be left, for the externalist, is to reduce "the form of the state of affairs" – of both actual and possible states of affairs – to the form of the objects that comprise it, and understand the sameness in form between proposition and state of affairs in terms of an isomorphism between the possible ways that the names and objects named could combine. Then Wittgenstein can say:

> The knowledge of the representing relation must be founded only on the knowledge of the component parts of the situation. Then it would be possible to say: the knowledge of the subject-predicate proposition and of subject and predicate gives us the knowledge of an internal relation. (3.11.14)

This notion of form meets the following criteria: it is a form common to the representation and to what it represents, it allows for the truth or falsity of the representation, and it is a form common to the representation and something that really exists. Once form is defined in this way, Wittgenstein now has to distinguish (as he does by the time of the *Tractatus*) the form of the representation, the possible way that the names can combine, from its structure, the actual way that the names are combined.

In the end, Wittgenstein does not think that there is a single thing that explains both what is represented and the way it is represented as being. The role of the form of the representation is to explain what the representation represents, whether truly or falsely. What propositions represent is reality. More particularly, what is represented has the form of a state of affairs, because the proposition represents that with which it shares a common form and it shares a form with states of affairs. The

10 Griffin argues, "one cannot limit the form of a fact [a proposition], i.e. the possibility of the combination of its constituents, unless one limits the form of its constituents, i.e. the possibility of their combination in facts" (*Wittgenstein's Logical Atomism*, p. 91).

role of structure is to explain how the things named are represented as combined in a state of affairs. The structure of the picture or proposition shows things as combined in a state of affairs. The reason that the structure can show things as combined in a state of affairs is because the structure is a structure of a certain form, namely that of a state of affairs (or because the representation represents something that has the form of a state of affairs).

Evaluation of Wittgenstein's theory

The question is whether form together with structure adequately explain, the unity of the proposition. To understand how the form common to the proposition and what it represents enables the structure of the proposition to represent the things named as related in a state of affairs (actual or possible), we need to understand what Wittgenstein means when he says that form is "the possibility that things are related to one another in the same way as the elements of the picture" (2.151). Obviously, there are many relations the names stand in to one another that might be impossible for the things named to stand in (e.g., syntactic, phonological, or temporal or spatial relations). So the issue is what the constraint on combinations of names is supposed to be. In what follows, I will set out two alternative notions of form and then discuss whether, on either of those conceptions, form together with structure is sufficient to explain how the proposition represents something as being the case.

a. *First conception of form: the form of the name reflects the character of its object.* One interpretation of same form is this: combinations of names must reflect the categorial combination of the things named. One name can combine with another name only if the things named by those names could combine in a state of affairs. In combining the words "the dog" with the words "is dead," I say something meaningful, because even if the dog in question isn't dead, it is possible given what category dogs belong to – that they are living beings – that the dog is dead. But I cannot say something that is both impossible and meaningful, for example "Triangularity is dead." Such a sentence is nonsensical (in some views of sense and nonsense), because triangularity is an abstract object, not an organism, and so it cannot be alive *or* dead.

This interpretation may be supported by Wittgenstein's definition of the form of objects and of names. "The possibility of its occurring in states of affairs is the form of the object" (2.0141). He says, "If I know an object I also know all its possible occurrences in states of affairs" (2.0123). Knowing the form of the object is understanding its categorial character: it is knowing the kinds of properties and relations the object could enter into – it could fall from the sky or be colored or be located somewhere in space and time or have a square root. The form of the name is that of its object. Thus, the form of the name reflects the categorial classification of its object. If the form of the sentence is a function of the form of its names and the form of names reflects the categorial classification of its objects, then one name can be combined with another in a sentence only if the things named could combine in states of affairs.[11]

While this provides an interpretation of the claim in 2.151 that the form of the representation is the possibility that things combine in the same way as the names, it requires taking a nonliteral reading of "same relation." What is true is that if the names stand related in some way R, it has to be possible for the things to stand in some corresponding relation R*, the corresponding relation being the one represented as obtaining. His comments about rules for projecting the relation between the elements of the picture onto the relation represented as obtaining lend support to this view of the matter:

4.014   A gramophone record, the musical idea, the written notes, and the sound-waves, all stand to one another in the same internal relation of depicting that holds between language and the world. They are all constructed according to a common logical pattern. . . .

4.0141   There is a general rule by means of which the musician can obtain the symphony from the score, and which makes it possible to derive the symphony from the groove on the gramophone record, and, using the first rule, to derive the score again. That is what constitutes the inner similarity between these things which seem to be constructed in such entirely different ways. And that rule is the law of projection which projects the symphony into the language of musical notation. It is the rule for translating this language into the language of gramophone records.

If we combine the elements of the theory, a string of names would show a state of affairs as obtaining if and only if

---

11   This conception of sameness of form is also consistent with Wittgenstein's view that, owing to the form of representation, one cannot picture the impossible. See 2.202, 3, and 3.02.

1. The names name objects.
2. The names stand in some relation R to one another.
3. There are rules for projecting the relation R between names to some relation R* between things.
4. It is possible for the things named by the names to stand in the relation R*.

(If the rule in 3 just mapped one relation onto another with no regard to what the "terms of the relation" are (in particular with no regard for what is designated by the names), then there are relations the names could stand in which are such that the objects could not stand in the corresponding relation. So condition 4 is needed as a separate constraint.)[12]

Notice that on this conception of form, it is not clear it is a necessary condition of a proposition's having meaning that it have a form in common with what it represents. In the sentence "Triangularity is yellow," a property is predicated to something it could not possibly possess. Yet the sentence seems to have a meaning. It is because of what it means that it is, in one sense of the word, "nonsense." We can distinguish utterances of nonsense that do and do not represent something as being the case. "Brillig" does not and "Triangularity is yellow" does. (The latter example shows, we can say something that is nonsense, even when we cannot judge it.) If it is the fact that the words "Trian-

12 (I am indebted to Paul Dunn for that point) It might mistakenly be thought that, with these conditions in place, it straightaway follows that the representation represents a possible state of affairs rather than a list of objects. After all, if the names can enter into some relation R only when their objects can stand related by R* in a state of affairs, then whenever two names do stand in some relation R to one another, the mere fact that they do will *entail* that the objects named *could* stand in R*. Thus, the sentence may be said to represent or indicate (or mean "naturally" in Grice's sense) that this is a possible combination of objects.

Unfortunately, this interpretation does not correctly identify the *content* of the sentence. What one can infer from the fact that the names stand structured as they do – i.e., from the natural meaning of that fact – is that it is possible that the objects named could stand so related. But the sentence "The cat is on the mat," unlike the sentence "It is possible that the cat is on the mat," *says* nothing whatsoever about whether it is possible for the cat and the mat to comprise a state of affairs. The content of that sentence is not that it is possible that the cat is on the mat nor is it that the cat and the mat could combine in such a state of affairs. What is true of Wittgenstein's theory is this: regarding some state of affairs that is possible, the representation represents it. But Wittgenstein nowhere says, what is false, that the picture represents that situation *as possible* or that it represents *the possibility* of the situation.

gularity," "is," and "yellow" are related as they are that represents triangularity as yellow, then that, apparently, does not depend upon its being possible that triangularity is yellow.

It may be Wittgenstein's conception of the "laws of projection" that led him to think (if he did) that the structural relation between names could not express a proposition unless the objects named could constitute a genuine state of affairs. The laws of projection map one structure between things onto another structure between things. Where the musical score is mapped onto the gramophone record, the time lapse between notes is mapped onto the length of nonsmooth area in a groove of the record. The existence of the law presupposes that the things can stand in the relations mentioned in the law. If grooves in gramophone records could not have smooth areas, there would be no law that mapped the temporal lapse between notes onto the length of a smooth bit of the groove. The obtaining of the law depends upon the possibility of the things standing in the relations mentioned in the law. By analogy, if there are laws mapping the relation between the names in the sentence onto a relation between the things named, the things named must be able to stand in that relation. To evaluate whether such a notion of form is indeed a necessary condition of the structure showing a state of affairs, we would need to know more exactly what the laws of projection might be in the case of the proposition. As to whether the four conditions above are sufficient for a proposition to have meaning, I will postpone that question until I have presented the other conception of form.[13]

b. *A second hypothesis about the explanatory role of form: form as same polyadicity.* The second interpretation of form is more literal and takes seriously the claim that the relation between words is the *same* as that represented as obtaining between things. It begins in consideration of Wittgenstein's 4.04:

---

13 Anscombe cites Giancarlo Columbo's remark that sameness of form by itself is not sufficient to explain how the sentence represents what it does: one thing's being isomorphic with another is a symmetrical relation, but representation is asymmetric. So "that it was difficult to see why a described fact should not be regarded as itself a description of the proposition that would normally be said to describe it, rather than the other way around." Anscombe thinks that Wittgenstein requires also that the names are correlated with the objects (*An Introduction to Wittgenstein's Tractatus* [London: Hutchinson, 1959], pp. 67–9).

In a proposition there must be exactly as many distinguishable parts as in the situation that it represents.

The two must possess the same logical (mathematical) multiplicity. (Compare Hertz's *Mechanics* on dynamical models.)

In a picture, the parts of the picture are structured in a particular way. In a picture of a cat on a mat, the picture of the cat will be above (or fall within the space occupied by) the picture of the mat. But that structure – one thing's being above another – is a structure of a *general form* xRy shared by other structures. The relation 'being above' is a dyadic relation, requiring two relata, as are many other structures: being next to, below, the father of. Structures of other forms require a different number of relata: the relation of 'being in between' requires three relata – John is between Sally and Paul. A picture has the same form as the situation it represents only if the relation between the elements of the picture have the same number of relata – the same "polyadicity" – as the relation represented as obtaining in the state of affairs. Because the fact wherein "a" is related to "b" has a certain form, being a two-termed relation of elements, that fact will represent a situation of like form – a two-termed relation of things, the things designated by "a," "b." The form of the representational fact determines the form of the situation represented, and it does so by being a likeness of it.[14] This provides an interpretation of the otherwise mysterious 4.012:

14   While this is a possible interpretation, on its face, it seems false of sentences as opposed to pictures (and so, again, is not clearly a necessary condition of a sentence's expressing what it does). In a picture of a cat on a mat, one constituent represents the cat and another represents the mat, but no constituent of the picture represents the relation 'being on.' There is simply the fact that the picture of the cat stands in a spatial relation to the picture of the mat. Thus, there is the same multiplicity of elements in the picture and what it pictures. By contrast, in the sentence, an element of the representation, the segment "is on," does represent the relation said to obtain. The sentence does not have the same form as what it represents: it is a triadic relation of "the cat" "is on" and "the mat" representing a dyadic relation of things.

In "Naming and Saying," Wilfrid Sellars argues that Wittgenstein believes that the word(s) naming the relation would not appear in a perspicuous language: the sentence disguises the true logical form of the sentence, which really consists in names of particulars standing in relations, relations the polyadicity of which matches that of the relations represented as obtaining.

The other option, favored by Gustav Bergmann, is to say that in "The cat is on the mat" there are actually three things related, the words "The cat," "the mat," and "is on," which correspond to three things in the state of affairs. According to Sellars, at issue is whether Wittgenstein thought that only particulars exist (in which case Sellars'

"It is obvious that a proposition of the form 'aRb' strikes us as a picture. In this case, the sign is obviously a *likeness* of what is signified."

The view might be this: when "a" stands in some relation to "b," that *is* their fitting together in a certain form. The fact that the elements of the sentence are fitted together in a relation of that form (dyadic, triadic, etc.) then represents the things named as fitting together in a relation of that *same* form (dyadic, triadic, etc.). The particular relation is determined as before by "projection rules." It is the structure of the representation, "a" standing in relation to "b", that shows the object a and b as standing related in a certain form. That structure shows that because, when the names are so structured, the representatives of the objects have been fitted together in that form.

Regardless of whether form is interpreted as preserving the polyadicity of the relation represented as obtaining or the categorial classification of objects named, all of Wittgenstein's conditions above might be met by some collection of objects, without that collection of objects constituting a representation. Suppose two pennies are fitted together in a relation of a certain polyadicity, for example one penny is on top of the other, and it is stipulated that those two pennies represent two other pennies. For any relation that those two pennies might stand in, it is possible that two other pennies stand in that relation (form as categorical classification). There could be rules for projecting the relation between the original pennies onto the same or another relation between represented pennies. Still, it is not obvious that the fact that one penny is on top of the other thereby shows the one designated penny as if it were on top of the other designated penny. Notice that the original pennies are related in all sorts of ways: the one is on top of the other, may be slightly to the left of the other, its face against the face of the other, and so on. There might be rules for projecting all of these relations between the original pennies to ones between designated pennies. Does the fact that the original pennies are related in all of these ways represent the designated pennies as standing in all of these relations? That the elements fit together in various structures of

interpretation is favored) or that both particulars and universals exist (in which case Bergmann would be right).

W. Sellars, "Naming and Saying," *Philosophy of Science*, 29 (1962), pp. 7–26. Reprinted in *Essays on Wittgenstein*, ed. E. D. Klemke (Urbana: University of Illinois Press, 1971), pp. 78–103. See particularly pp. 80–7. Gustav Bergmann, "Ineffability, Ontology and Method," *Philosophical Review* 69 (1960), pp. 18–40. Reprinted in *Essays on Wittgenstein*, pp. 3–24.

various forms *could* represent the things named as fitting together in a structure of those forms, but is it necessary that they do so? It does not seem true that whenever one has things that designate other things fitted together in a relation of a certain form and they are fitted together in a relation that has a "translation" (where it is possible for the things named to stand in that relation), they thereby represent the designated things as standing in the relation that the translation would give. It seems to matter *why* the things are related in a structure of that form. We want some *explanation* of the fact that the original two pennies are related as they are. Is that random or by design? Wittgenstein's conditions may make the combination the kind of configuration that *could* represent a state of affairs. But there might be things that meet his conditions that are not representations.

This criticism of Wittgenstein's view is not decisive. First, one doesn't know exactly what intuition to have about such examples, because, one doesn't know, first, what is implicit in the stipulation that the one penny is a representative of the other, and second, one doesn't know sufficiently well what the projection rules are. They may flesh out the example sufficiently that we would have the intuition that the relation between pennies represents a relation as obtaining between the other pennies. The rule of projection for sentences may stipulate that when the words are related in a certain way, they say that the things are related in a corresponding way. This way of construing the law of projection would avoid the counterexample. But if this is the law of projection, Wittgenstein would have failed to *explain*, as he intended to do, why something is a representation or why the proposition says something. If the laws of projection stipulate that that is the case, no explanation is provided. The proposition is a representation simply by fiat.

Even if the counterexample is genuine, it is not clear that Wittgenstein thought such combinations were supposed to be representations, because he may not have thought the conditions in question were sufficient for representation. In the *Notebooks*, he says, "It is clear that the closest examination of the propositional sign cannot yield what it asserts – what it can yield is what it is capable of asserting" (18.3.15). And in the *Tractatus*, Wittgenstein distinguishes between a *Satz* (proposition or sentence), a *Satzzeichen* (a propositional sign) and a *sinnvolle Satze* (a significant sentence, or a sentence with sense). He says:

3.12   I call the sign with which we express a thought a propositional sign. And a proposition is a propositional sign in its projective relation to the world.

3.13   A proposition includes all that the projection includes, but not what is projected. Therefore, though what is projected is not itself included, its possibility is.

A proposition, therefore, does not actually contain the possibility of expressing it.

("The content of a proposition" means the content of a proposition that has sense.)

A proposition contains the form, but not the content, of its sense.

A proposition is a configuration of names together with the laws of projection: it contains the form of what is projected but not the content. That is to say, from the laws of projection and the fact that the names stand in a certain relation, one can derive the relation represented as obtaining between the objects, whatever the objects turn out to be.[15] The fact that the names are related as they are together with the laws of projection give the form of the state of affairs represented. But the sentence does not have a sense until the propositional sign is applied and thought out: "A propositional sign, applied and thought out, is a thought. A thought is a proposition with a sense" (3.5, 4).

Let us follow Wittgenstein's metaphor. The propositional sign is analogous to a photographic slide, and the projection analogous to the projection of the picture onto a screen by the light from the slide projector. In a way, the slide contains the state of affairs that is to be projected. But in another sense, it contains only the possibility of what is to be projected. For unless someone shines a light through the slide, the state of affairs encapsulated in the slide is not projected. From the slide and the laws of projection, given the method of projection (the light), one could know how things in the projection on the screen would stand related if it were projected. The laws of projection would describe how to derive the image on the screen from the slide, given the method of projection. And there can be various methods of and, hence, laws of projection. But until the light is shone through the slide, the state of affairs does not actually appear on the screen; it is kept in the slide. Nothing is actually given representation.

The propositional sign is like the slide. A propositional sign in its projective relation to the world is two or more signs fitted together in a structure of a certain form with rules for translating that structural relation into a relation between the things named. It is not yet a

15   Griffin, *Wittgenstein's Logical Atomism*, p. 131.

significant sentence, but only something such that it could comprise a significant representation. In a way, the state of affairs is present in the logical and syntactical form of the sentence. But in another sense, the propositional sign contains only the possibility of the state of affairs, because until one projects the propositional sign onto something – onto the world, perhaps? – the possible state of affairs encapsulated in the propositional sign remains unprojected and the sentence does not present a state of affairs. To have a significant sentence, the propositional sign must be "applied and thought out." Something has to function like the light shone through the slide. What functions like the light is our "thinking out" the sense of the propositions: "We use the perceptible sign of a proposition (spoken or written, etc.) as a projection of a possible situation. *The method of projection is to think out the sense of the proposition*" (3.11; my emphasis). When one thinks through the propositional sign, the thinking must take a certain form and the form it takes is determined by the propositional sign. (Compare: the light must acquire a certain form when it passes through the slide, the form being determined by the character of the slide.) The form that the thinking takes as a result of passing through the sign results in a particular thought being thought.

The question becomes, "What is this 'thinking through' the sign and how does it make something that could be a representation into something that *is* a representation?" Thinking through the sign is an act. Griffin suggests it is a matter of using the sign in a certain way. He compares Wittgenstein's distinction between a sentence and a significant sentence with Strawson's distinction in "On Referring" between a sentence and the use of a sentence. When the sentence is used on a particular occasion, "its names are used referringly."[16] So what transforms the proposition from "a combination of words along with their syntactical application" into a proposition with sense is someone using the proposition in such a way that the names in it make reference to things.[17]

Consider the shapes "The Lone Ranger is dead" found scratched in the sand on the beach. Suppose that a turtle meandering along the beach accidentally drew those letters with her tail. There are words

---

16 Ibid. Sainsbury, in "How Can we Say Something," suggests that the difficulties Russell and Wittgenstein had explaining how the proposition expresses something might be traced to their not attending sufficiently to the notion of the use of the words. See p. 151.

17 Ibid., pp. 130–1.

standing in a certain syntactic combination. But that inscription isn't a representation of the Lone Ranger. A person might come along and think this to be saying that the Lone Ranger is dead, attributing certain intentions to the author. That person's *thought* would be a representation of the Lone Ranger as dead. But the fact that he takes the turtle's inscription to be representing the Lone Ranger as dead does not make *it* such a representation. We can take things to be representations that are not.

The turtle was not "using the name referringly." But what is required in order for the names to be used referringly? Suppose the example were changed, so the words on the beach are words separately torn out of newspaper, where "The Lone Ranger" did refer to someone and "dead" did designate a property in the respective articles they came from. Now the wind blows together the words "The Lone Ranger is dead." This still isn't a representation of the Lone Ranger, and that may be because, in this context, "The Lone Ranger" does not any longer refer to someone.

But when *would* "the Lone Ranger" be a genuine referring expression? The obvious answer is if the expression were uttered or inscribed or placed in a given context and on that occasion functioned to pick out someone about which something were said or some property predicated. Perhaps there are semantically less rich ways of describing when something is a genuine referring expression. But if there is not, the notion supposed to be given an analysis – how the proposition says something or makes a predication – is being smuggled in under another notion – referring. The account is so far circular: the proposition says something or has a sense because the names are used referringly, and the names are used referringly because they occur in an instance of saying something. The concern, then, is that by adding a requirement that the name is being used referringly to Wittgenstein's account, one is presupposing the fact we want explained, namely that the sentence is predicating a property to some object.

So to sum up. There is the following dilemma. If the names stand for things but are just arbitrarily or by happenstance combined, their combination does not represent a state of affairs. There needs to be something that connects the fact that the names are combined as they are to their representing a state of affairs. That must be something more than Wittgenstein's structure and form. If, on the other hand, one says that the relevant fact is that the names must be used referringly – that that is the additional element needed – the account appears to be circular.

What is needed in Wittgenstein's account is some explanation of what makes things which are such that they *could* be representations really *be* representations. Clearly, his remarks about applying and thinking through the sign are addressed to that requirement. Applying and thinking through the sign may require that the names are not just arbitrarily combined, or that they have to be combined by some particular kind of act or be used in a particular way. But this has to be fleshed out and in a noncircular way, and the concepts of thinking through and (intentionally?) using expressions in a particular way seem very likely to presuppose, rather than to explain, the concept we wish to understand.

Part II

Subjects and Predicates and their Logical and Metaphysical Correlates

4

The Metaphysical Basis of the Subject–Predicate Distinction

1 Introduction

I want to begin by characterizing, rather roughly, a conception of subjects and predicates that emerges from some of the classical theories we have examined. It would not emerge from the careful exposition of any one of those philosopher's views in isolation, but is rather a broad-stroke, hodgepodge picture, which, for better or worse, comes to dominate philosophical thinking about predication. The conception is based on rather vague connections, associations, and "affinities" between subjects and predicates on the one hand, and objects and properties on the other. I will later flesh out and examine these connections critically.

The picture is this: the subject and predicate expressions in a sentence perform different functions, the subject referring to an object, the predicate predicating something of that object. In connection, somehow, with this difference in function, the subject expression is supposed to be a complete, independent sort of thing, while the predicate expression is incomplete and dependent. The completeness of subject expression is the required complement of the incompleteness of the predicate, so that together they produce a significant sentence. This difference in the function of the expressions is frequently associated with a metaphysical difference in the things named by the respective expressions. Aristotle associates the difference between subject and predicate with the difference between substance and attribute; Frege associates it with objects and concepts; Russell and Strawson, with particulars and universals.

This view of a "fundamental antithesis" between subject and predicate has its skeptics. F. P. Ramsey thinks that the difference has "only
to be questioned to be doubted."[1] He points out that "with a sufficiently
elastic language any proposition can be so expressed that any of its
terms is the subject."[2] The sentence "Socrates is wise" may express the
same proposition as the sentence "Wisdom is a characteristic of
Socrates." In the first sentence, "Socrates" is the subject expression, in
the second, "wisdom" is. Which expression may serve as subject or
predicate would seem to have nothing to do with the metaphysical
kinds that the words designate. Instead, according to Ramsey, the
expression that serves as the subject or predicate is a matter of "the
point of view from which we approach the fact" (were we initially discussing Socrates or wisdom) or on our "centre of interest" (do we want
to know something about Socrates or about wisdom).[3] Which is which
turns on what might be called "pragmatic" facts. Earlier, John Cook
Wilson had argued that the subject expression is the one that indicates
the topic of the sentence, that about which the predicate purports to
supply information. Both Cook Wilson and Ramsey warn against confusing what, in Cook Wilson's words, is a "subjective" distinction
regarding the order in which the objects are apprehended with
an objective distinction regarding the nature of the objects so
apprehended.[4]

Still, the association of the functional differences between subject
and predicate with the particular and universal distinction is not philo-
sophically unmotivated, and so neither is the traditional picture. If the
basic bits of the world are particulars and universals that combine in
facts, then, perhaps, our basic sentences and thoughts that represent
the simplest of such facts will have to be composed of two expressions,
one representing a particular, the other a universal. And just as there
must be some constituent in the sentence corresponding to each constituent of the fact, so there must be something in the sentence as a
whole – some unity of its constituents, subject and predicate – that
enables it to represent the unity of the particular and universal in a fact.
We should be able to read off the form of reality (the way that things

1 F. P. Ramsey, "Universals," *Mind*, 34 (136) (1925), pp. 401–17. Reprinted in *The
Foundations of Mathematics*, ed. R. B. Braithwaite (Paterson, NJ: Littlefield, Adams, 1960),
pp. 112–34. All references are to the latter.
2 Ibid., p. 116.
3 Ibid.
4 J. Cook Wilson, *Statement and Inference with Other Philosophical Papers*, 2 vols. (Oxford:
Oxford University Press, 1926), vol. 1, p. 141.

can be combined) from the form of the sentence (the way the words can be combined), for the form of the world determines that of the representations of it. It is mirrored in them. (While this idea may be owing to Wittgenstein, it is not, in his theory, associated with a difference in functional role of expressions or with the expressions' naming things of different kinds.)

The unity of the fact and of the corresponding sentence that represents the fact, however, is not unproblematic. F. H. Bradley argued that the notion of a fact as a unity of basic constituents is incoherent, because when the idea of a fact is thought through, it is seen to generate an infinite and absurd regress.[5] An object and property in isolation do not make a fact. The object and property need to be related in a certain way, for in the fact, the object *instantiates* the property. The simple fact must comprise at least three constituents: an object, a property, and the instantiation relation. But an object, property, and the instantiation relation, in isolation, still do not make up a fact, for in the fact, these three things are themselves related. The instantiation relation itself must be so related to the object and to the property that the object instantiates the property. These three things must, apparently, be related by some further relation. Even then, these terms in isolation do not constitute a fact, for there must be yet a further relation that relates them, and so on ad infinitum.

A parallel argument applied to the sentence reveals a requirement for an adequate account of sentence meaning. The fact that one part of the sentence designates an object and the other part designates a property does not explain how the sentence represents something as being the case with regard to the object and property. To suppose that there is a further expression – the copula, for instance – that specifies the instantiation relation does not solve the problem, for the fact that the three expressions designate, respectively, an object, the instantiation relation, and a property does not explain how the sentence represents something as being the case. In what is represented as being the case, the instantiation relation is represented as related to the object and property in such a way that the object instantiates the property. If this were fully expressed, a further expression would be required, but this would merely give one yet another thing that needs to be related to the others in what is expressed, and so the regress continues. Gilbert Ryle says:

---

5   F. H. Bradley, *Appearance and Reality*, 2nd edn. (London: Swan Sonnenschein, 1906), p. 28. Bradley makes the same sort of regress arguments regarding sentences in his *Principles of Logic*, 2nd edn. (London: Oxford Press, 1922), pp. 13–14.

So the words combined into a sentence at least do something jointly which is different from their severally naming the several things that they name if they do name any things. What a sentence means is not decomposable into the set of things which the words in it stand for, if they do stand for things. So the notion of *having meaning* is at least partly different from the notion of *standing for.*[6]

This "something" that the words do jointly may be understood in terms of a functional difference between the subject and predicate expression. Russell thought that the solution to such regress arguments for both facts and sentences lay in the recognition that the parts they have must be of different *types*, where the part of the one type functions to bring together the part of the other type. One of the parts of the sentence and of the fact is a relation that brings together all the constituents, thereby forming a single unitary thing. Frege also held that the two expressions have different functions, and he equated this with their naming things of different types. Both philosophers associated the explanation of the unity of the sentence with the unity of objects and properties (or concepts), and both thought that it is the universal or concept that effects the propositional combination. If the universal in the fact "relates" the constituents to form a fact – if it "brings them into" the instantiation relation – it is natural to think that it might be the expression that names that universal that analogously combines the constituent words to form a sentence. Perhaps the predicate somehow derives its function from the function of what it names, so that the function of the predicate is explained by what it designates.

The function of the universal is often thought to be the result of its being incomplete. Aristotle held that the universal is incomplete because it depends for existing on inhering in some object. The universal might be said to be an incomplete fact, containing the "form of the fact," for in being instantiated in the object, the universal determines the form the fact will take. By analogy, the predicate has a function that results from its being incomplete. The predicate is incomplete, for its existence in the sentence depends upon its having an object of which the predication may be made, and it is the predicate that determines what the sentence will say when supplied with that object. Russell thinks the predicate contains "the form of the proposition," in

6   G. Ryle, "The Theory of Meaning." Originally appeared in *British Philosophy in Mid-Century*, ed. C. A. Mace (London: George Allen & Unwin, 1957), pp. 239–64. Reprinted in *Philosophy of Ordinary Language*, ed. C. E. Caton (Urbana: University of Illinois Press, 1963), pp. 128–53. See p. 133.

the sense that it represents a propositional function which has only to be supplied with a name and it *"becomes* a proposition."[7] This incompleteness might be thought to enable the propositional function to effect the unity of the sentence.

Ramsey is skeptical of these ways of thinking. He says:

> The great difficulty with this theory lies in understanding how one sort of object can be specially incomplete. There is a sense in which any object is incomplete; namely that it can occur in a fact only by connection with an object or objects of suitable type; just as any name is incomplete, because to form a proposition we have to join to it certain other names of a suitable type.[8]

If "wise" contains the form of the proposition, then so does "Socrates," because it too has to be joined with other words in order to form a proposition. That, says Ramsey, is the point of W. E. Johnson's criticism of Russell: in the subject–predicate proposition "S is P," Russell does not treat S and P as on par, S and P representing two arguments of a function, but rather treats S as representing the argument of the function "x is P."[9] Johnson thinks that even if the parts of a sentence must be functionally distinct and that this involves one of the parts literally being a function, Russell's way of identifying the part that is the function is not the only option. The function might, as Russell says, be the grammatical predicate "___ is P," or the function might instead be the subject plus the copula "S is ___" or the copula by itself might be the function, as in "___ is ___."

Why should Russell's conception of what the function is be preferred? It is the larger demands of the theory of the proposition that makes Russell's view seem correct. The reason standardly given for treating the grammatical predicate as the propositional function is not that sentential unity requires it, but that an adequate account of *generalization* or *quantification* does. Analyzing such sentences as "Some birds are swans" or "Every bird is a swan" involves reference to the propositional function "x is a swan." Several things have the common property of being swans, if, when those things are values of "x" in the

7 B. Russell, *Introduction to Mathematical Logic*, 2nd edn. (London: George Allen & Unwin, 1920), p. 155 (my emphasis).

8 Russell, "On Relations of Universals and Particulars," in his *Logic and Knowledge* (London: Unwin Hyman, 1956), p. 121.

9 Ramsey, "Universals," p. 122; and W. E. Johnson, *Logic* (Cambridge: Cambridge University Press, 1921), part 1, p. 11.

propositional function "x is a swan," the resulting propositions are true. That conception of the predicate can also explain why certain logical properties accrue to predicates; for example, why "not wise" can be a predicate expression, but "not Tom" cannot be a subject expression. The theory of predication that takes the predicate to be such a propositional function has greater explanatory power and is more parsimonious. With a single conception of predication it can explain the unity of both atomic sentences and complex sentences, the logical properties of predicates, and it can provide an analysis of quantification. And so, despite the vagueness of the theory and despite the efforts of its critics, this picture survives from the classical accounts and continues to be found in one form or another.

P. F. Strawson, both in *Individuals* and in *Subject and Predicate in Logic and Grammar*, offers a contemporary defense of these views. His theory of predication gives concrete expression to the view found in classical accounts that the subject is complete and the predicate is essentially incomplete. He provides a novel interpretation of the view that the respective completeness and incompleteness of the subject and the predicate is grounded in the nature of the things they designate, particular and universal. Strawson shows how the nature of particulars and universals might also explain the logical properties of the expressions that designate things of such a metaphysical kind. The theory has impressive breadth and scope. He draws on work both from classical figures and that of many of his contemporaries – Peter Geach, Elizabeth Anscombe, and W. V. O. Quine. He argues against the skeptics of the metaphysical account of predicates, Cook Wilson and Ramsey, who think that the subject–predicate distinction is merely "pragmatic," determined by the context of the utterance of the sentence.

No serious study of predication can fail to consider these different features of predicates – grammatical, semantic, logical, pragmatic – and ask whether there is a unified explanation of them, and if so, whether that explanation is in fact metaphysical. Because Strawson's work is the most complete study available of the properties that distinguish subjects from predicates, much of the discussion in this part of the book will center on his work. In this chapter, I will examine his view in *Individuals* that grammatical and semantic asymmetries between subject and predicate are explained by the relation of the expressions to particulars and universals. I argue that his metaphysical explanation of the semantic function of the expressions fails to explain the unity of the sentence.

In chapter 5, I focus on Strawson's *Subject and Predicate in Logic and Grammar*, where he connects certain logical asymmetries between subjects and predicates with the referring and predicating function of the expressions and argues that an explanation of both can be given in terms, again, of the particular–universal distinction. I will argue that it is not clear that, if the logical asymmetries are real, they are explained in the way Strawson suggests, or that they are essentially tied to the referring or predicating functions of the expressions. Finally, in chapter 6, I discuss whether a certain kind of predicate is required by logical theory and, if so, what the relation of that sort of predicate is to the unity of basic sentences. I will set out an argument of Michael Dummett's that the kind of predicate required by logical theory is quite different from that required for the unity of the sentence, and will argue that we should not expect a unified theory of the various things that are called "predicates." Throughout, my aim in this part of the book is to examine the most comprehensive formulation – that provided by Strawson – of the traditional picture of the subject–predicate distinction. This, of course, will not show that it cannot be right, but only that other approaches to the question may be worth pursuing.

2 A General Description of Strawson's Project

In *Individuals*, Strawson describes his work as "descriptive metaphysics," which attempts to "lay bare the most general features of our conceptual structure."[10] In thinking about the world, we apply general concepts: we categorize this as that – Fido as a dog, the department meeting as maddening, the summer as cold. In doing so, we conceive of the world as made up of particular, discrete objects and events. We apply general concepts to these objects of experience. Concepts are "general" because they can, in principle, be applied to many particulars. Our ability to apply such concepts depends upon our ability to distinguish particulars while at the same time recognizing some common features in virtue of which they may be said to fall under the same concept. Thus, the applicability of general concepts and our recognition of their *being* concepts, being general, requires that we can distinguish particulars as distinct instances of the same concept. What is required for us to distinguish particulars? It requires the employ-

10 P. F. Strawson, *Individuals: An Essay in Descriptive Metaphysics* (London: Methuen, 1959), p. 9.

ment, Strawson says, of "the two great notions of Space and Time."[11]
We see two particulars that fall under the same concept when we see
two peas in the pod. Our ability to see *two* depends upon their spatial
distinction – one being here and the other there. Because it is in principle possible for the particulars to be qualitatively identical and still
be two, particulars must finally be distinguished in terms of their
spatial and temporal properties.

Our applying concepts to particulars further requires the ability to
distinguish the concept one is applying from other concepts and to distinguish the concept from the particular to which one is applying it.
How do concepts differ from particulars? One difference, according to
Strawson, is that a particular's instantiating one universal rules out its
instantiating certain other universals: Fido's being a dog rules out his
being human. But that a universal is instantiated in one particular does
not rule out its being instantiated in another particular: Fido's being a
dog does not rule out Rover's being a dog. Thus, Strawson says:

> Every general character competes for location, in any and every partic-
> ular individual it might belong to, with some other general character. But
> it is not the case that every particular individual competes for possession
> of any and every general character it might possess with some other par-
> ticular individual.[12]

Concepts themselves are partially individuated by such competition
relations, by the ranges they determine – as red competes with blue,
yellow, and green "for possession" of some particular, rather as pas-
sengers might compete for a seat on the bus. Once the seat is taken,
there is no more room at that location. Once the object is red, there is
no more room for green to occupy that space.

Even the most basic thought presupposes that our conceptual
scheme has the kind of features just described. To put a Kantian twist
on it, our having thoughts and making such judgments presupposes
that there exists a world of spatiotemporal objects and events to which
we can make reference, objects which themselves fall under certain
basic concepts. Having a thought presupposes the possibility of

11   P. F. Strawson, *Subject and Predicate in Logic and Grammar* (London: Methuen, 1974),
p. 15.
12   P. F. Strawson, "The Asymmetry of Subject and Predicates." Originally appeared in
Language, Belief and Metaphysics, ed. H. E. Kiefer and M. K. Munitz (Albany: State
University of New York Press, 1970). Reprinted in P. F. Strawson, *Logico-Linguistic Papers*
(London: Methuen, 1971), pp. 96–115. All references are to the latter, p. 102.

"applying" concepts to our experience of particulars, both because concepts are partially individuated by the way that they collect particulars, and because the experience of particulars is always *of* some general kind. The concepts

> which enter into our basic or least theoretical beliefs, into our fundamental judgments, are just those concepts which enter most intimately and immediately into our common experience of the world. They are what . . . we *experience* the world *as* exemplifying, what we *see* things and situations *as* cases of. Correlatively, experience is awareness of the world as exemplifying *them*.[13]

The application of such concepts is essential to our ability to experience a world of objects. The experience of the world of objects is essential to providing content to the concepts – to individuating the concepts in terms of their ranges of competition.

The basic constituents of thought are a reflection of the basic constituents of the world. They are reflected in the language we use to express our thoughts about the world and in the subject–predicate distinction itself. If a basic thought involves thinking of a particular as exemplifying a concept or property, then the sentence fully expressing that thought will presumably require an expression which functions to make *reference* to that particular, another which functions to *predicate* that property of the particular. The subject expression is a referring expression, and according to Strawson, it makes reference most fundamentally to particulars. Particulars are the basic bits to which our classificatory system of concepts is applied. Predicate expressions classify the particular referred to as falling under the concept designated by the predicate. Strawson wants to "help explain the traditional, persistent link in our philosophy between the particular–universal distinction and the subject–predicate (reference–predication) distinction."[14]

In *Individuals*, he distinguishes different conceptions – grammatical, pragmatic, and semantic – of the subject–predicate distinction and examines whether the difference between particulars and universals lies at the basis of the grammatical and semantic distinctions. Strawson offers several proposals about how what is referred to or designated by the subject and the predicate expressions can explain the semantic function of the expressions. In what follows, I will lay out those distinctions, examine the relation between them, and argue that

13 Strawson, *Subject and Predicate in Logic and Grammar*, p. 14.
14 Strawson, *Individuals*, p. 188.

his metaphysical account fails to explain a certain aspect of the semantic function of the expressions, namely how the expressions function together to say something or express a proposition.

3 Subject and Predicate in Strawson's Individuals

The grammatical distinction between subjects and predicates

We distinguish between the grammatical subject and the grammatical predicate of a sentence. The grammatical subject is the main noun-phrase. The grammatical predicate is the main verb-phrase. That verb-phrase contains both the verb and its complement, if it has one. These grammatical categories appear to be mutually exclusive. Subject expressions cannot be predicate expressions, and predicate expressions cannot be subject expressions. In a simple subject–predicate sentence such as "Socrates is wise," the subject expression of that sentence cannot be the predicate expression of another sentence: "Socrates" can only be part of a predicate expression, as in "Xantippe married Socrates." By the same token, the predicate expression "is wise" cannot be the subject expression of another sentence, but only a part of one, as in "The fact that Socrates is wise is no excuse for his drinking so much."

So far, this is a purely grammatical point, for the property attributed – wisdom – can certainly be named by the subject of a sentence, as in "Wisdom is rarely instantiated." The reason the grammatical categories of simple sentences exhibit this property – that the subject expression cannot be the predicate and vice versa – is because the grammatical predicate comprises *both* the verb and its complement. The grammatical predicate is "*is* wise" – that is, "be" + predicate adjective "wise" – so it cannot serve as the grammatical subject. And it is because the predicate is "*married* Socrates" that "Socrates" can be said to only be part of the predicate. The grammatical distinction does not have any obvious analog in semantics or ontology. From it, one cannot yet draw any conclusion about the semantic function of expressions – that the grammatical subject expression must be the referring expression, the grammatical predicate the predicating expression. Nor does the grammatical distinction entail that the expression that specifies a particular or a universal can only serve as the subject or the predicate respectively. On the contrary, expressions specifying both particulars and universals can be subjects (e.g., "Socrates" and "wisdom"), and expressions specifying particulars and universals can both serve as *parts* of predicates (e.g., "Socrates" and "wise").

The semantic asymmetry between subjects and predicates

Be that as it may, it is widely thought that the grammatical asymmetry between subject and predicate corresponds to a semantic asymmetry wherein the subject and predicate have different functional roles. The semantic function of referring and predicating are associated, respectively, with the grammatical categories of noun-phrase and verb-phrase. What performs one or the other of these functional roles may be tied to the sort of thing, particular or universal, the expression designates. Strawson characterizes several functional roles associated with subjects and predicates, and argues that the genuinely semantic role is explained by the particular–universal distinction.

a.   *The subject identifies what the sentence is about, the predicate says something of that object.* On one proposal, the parts of the sentence combine to represent something as being the case, because one part functions to pick out or identify what the statement is *about*, the other to *say something of* that object. John Cook Wilson describes the traditional definition of subject and predicate as follows: "the subject is what in the proposition or statement we are speaking about and the predicate is what we say of the subject"; "the subject is that about which something is asserted, and the predicate is that which is asserted about it."[15]

By this distinction, the functional role of the expression would not be identified exclusively with one kind of grammatical expression or metaphysical type designated by some expression. Cook Wilson's example, the sentence "Glass is elastic," could equally well be said to be *about* glass or elasticity.[16] Where one wants to know what properties glass has, the statement "Glass is *elastic*," will be about glass, a particular, and it will assert that it has the property of being elastic. Where instead one wants to know what substances are elastic, the same sentence may be used to make a statement about elasticity, a universal, and assert that it is found in glass. In different contexts, different grammatical parts of one and the same sentence may function to introduce what the statement is about and to say something of that thing.

15   Cook Wilson, *Statement and Inference with Other Philosophical Papers*, vol. 1, p. 114.
16   Ibid., p. 121.

Ramsey said that it seemed to him "as clear as anything can be in philosophy" that the sentences "Socrates is wise" and "Wisdom is a characteristic of Socrates" mean the same thing: "Which sentence we use is a matter either of literary style, or of the point of view from which we approach the fact."[17] He concluded that the subject–predicate distinction

> has nothing to do with the logical nature of Socrates or wisdom, but is a matter entirely for grammarians. Hence there is no essential distinction between the subject of a proposition and its predicate, and no fundamental classification of objects can be based upon such a distinction.[18]

These examples may show that *if* the semantic distinction between referring and predicating expressions is identified with the being-about versus saying-something-of distinction, then the semantic distinction is not tied to the grammatical distinction between subject and predicate. Nor would the semantic distinction seem to have a metaphysical basis, for in one instance, the statement is about the particular Socrates, in another, about the universal wisdom. Cook Wilson suggests that what differs from one context to the next in virtue of which an expression functions now as subject and now as predicate is which expression carries new and which carries old information. So in a context where one asks, "What properties does glass have?" and someone replies, "Glass is *elastic*," the word "glass" carries no new information or expresses no new fact. It simply indicates what we are speaking about; whereas, "elastic" supplies new information about the properties of glass. This is exactly what changes when, in answer to the question "What is elastic?" someone says, "*Glass* is elastic." In that context, "elastic" expresses no new information, but "glass" provides information about what is elastic. Cook Wilson concludes that the distinction between subject and predicate is contextually determined by our "subjective" order of apprehension, by what in the context we already know as opposed to what we have yet to learn, and is not to be confused with the objective distinction between the things named, particular and universal.[19]

17 Ramsey, "Universals," p. 116.
18 Ibid., p. 116.
19 Cook Wilson, *Statement and Inference with Other Philosophical Papers*, vol. 1, pp. 139–41.

Strawson agrees that the being-about versus saying-something-of distinction is contextually determined. It is a pragmatic distinction.[20] The issue is whether that pragmatic distinction underlies the semantic distinction between subjects and predicates. This, in turn, depends upon what the semantic distinction between subject and predicate is. The semantic distinction would seem to be that difference in function between the expressions in virtue of which they together combine to represent something as being the case, the one expression functioning to refer, the other to predicate. This is what Cook Wilson intended to characterize when he said that the subject expression functions to identify what the statement is about, and the predicate is that expression which functions to say something about that topic. Strawson is not prepared, as Cook Wilson was, to identify that pragmatic distinction with the semantic distinction between subjects and predicates. Strawson apparently thinks either that the semantic distinction between referring and predicating expressions is not pragmatically determined or that other properties, perhaps logical ones, are constitutive of the semantic distinction between subjects and predicates. He suggests that what is needed is some way to distinguish the semantic subject and predicate while granting Cook Wilson's point that in different contexts an assertion may be about either of the terms, particular or universal, that are designated or "introduced" by the expressions.

b.   *The semantic distinction between subjects and predicates consists in the different ways the expressions introduce what they do.* Strawson proposes that subjects and predicates may be distinguished in virtue of *the way in which* they introduce what they do – by their different "styles of introduction." Predicates introduce their terms in the "verb-like, coupling, propositional style," but subjects do not.[21] He initially describes the distinction as follows. A grammatical substantive such as "Socrates" might be completed into any kind of remark: an assertion ("Socrates is wise"), an exhortation ("Socrates, be wise"), a command ("Let Socrates be slain"), or an instruction ("Slay Socrates").[22] Thus,

20   When I speak of a 'pragmatic' distinction, in contrast to a semantic one, I mean a distinction having to do with what a speaker is doing in uttering the expression. Traditionally, a distinction is drawn between syntactic relations (expression to expression relations), semantic ones (expression to world relations), and pragmatic ones (speaker to expression to world relations).
21   Strawson, *Individuals*, p. 152.
22   Ibid., p. 149.

"the fact that the expression 'Socrates' occurs in a remark gives us no reason for expecting it to be one kind of remark rather than another."[23] By contrast, a predicate expression "demands a certain kind of completion, namely completion into a proposition or propositional clause."[24] For example, the fact that the words "is wise" occur in a remark signals that the remark will express an assertion, for those words have to be completed into an assertion or a clause, as in "Deny that Socrates is wise." The phrase "is wise" "does not merely introduce its term, or introduce it with merely such an indication of the style of introduction as is given by the case-ending of a noun. It introduces its term in a quite distinctive and important style, *viz.* the assertive or propositional style."[25] The propositional style is "a style appropriate to the case where the term is introduced into something which has a truth-value."[26] In the sentence "Socrates is wise," both "Socrates" and "wise" introduce terms: "But – to borrow a phrase of W. E. Johnson's – the expression 'is wise' not only introduces being wise, it also carries the assertive or propositional tie; or, in still older terminology, it not only introduces its term, it also copulates it."[27]

Given the way that Strawson characterizes the distinction, it is not clear how genuine it is. The rough idea is that "Socrates" can be completed into any kind of remark, an instruction, command, assertion, and so on; but "is wise" can only be completed into an *assertion*. But, as Strawson notes, that isn't *quite* true, since "is wise" can form parts of remarks that do not make assertions, as in "Who is wise?" and "If Socrates is wise, then Plato is wise." The first of those "invites us to complete and assert *propositions*," and the second "brings before us *propositions*, though without commitment as to their truth-value."[28] The idea of the predicate's introducing its term in the propositional style, then, is that it must be completed into a remark that brings before us a proposition, though without commitment to its truth-value. But if that is the criterion according to which something carries the assertive or propositional tie, why shouldn't we say that "Socrates" carries the propositional tie as well, for the different speech acts of exhortation, instruction, and command that "Socrates" can figure also "bring before us" propositions? After all, the command, instruction, or exhortation

23   Ibid.
24   Ibid., p. 153.
25   Ibid., p. 149.
26   Ibid., p. 150.
27   Ibid., p. 151.
28   Ibid., p. 150.

are such only if they do express propositions. The instruction "Socrates, be wise" tells Socrates that he is to be wise – it brings before him that proposition. The command "Slay, Socrates" tells someone that he is to slay Socrates, bringing before him that proposition, though without actually asserting the proposition and with no commitment to its truth. So "Socrates" too would introduce its term in the propositional style.

The issue as to whether Strawson is right about the distinction comes down to this: Are there speech acts that are not propositional in which subjects can figure but predicates cannot? If so, this would give us reason to say that the propositional style is essential to predicates but not to subjects. The speech acts of mentioning, listing, and calling out would seem to be nonpropositional. Strawson suggests that the substantival form "is the form we should naturally use if we merely wanted to make *lists* of terms."[29] But even in making lists, a proposition seems to be in the offing whether one is listing particulars or properties. After all, how are you to make the list? What do you list? You list things that have relevant properties. "List some Greek philosophers." "Socrates, Plato, Aristotle." The proposition in the offing is that Socrates was a Greek philosopher, Plato was a Greek philosopher, and Aristotle was a Greek philosopher. List what Socrates was – "wise, snub-nosed, stubborn." In listing objects or properties, the words in the list are taken from so many assertions or propositions.

The paradigm, nonpropositional speech act would seem to be "calling out to" someone or something. What is called out to is a particular, never a universal. You cannot call out to properties. You say, "Hey, John," but, when you say, "Hey, Stupid," "Stupid" is being used as if it were a nominal. While this is true, it is not true because words designating particulars are nonpropositional, whereas words designating universals are propositional. There are, after all, particulars that you can't call out to either. When we say, "Hey, Dog-Breath," we don't take that expression to name a particular dog's breath, but to name a person. One can only call out to things that can hear. Even in calling out to someone, we ordinarily utter a proposition: "Hey, fat head, move over," "Hey, stupid, be quiet." The only time one can purely call out the name, with no expectation of completion, is in greeting or acknowledging someone. Greeting someone is not referring to him. The long and short of this is that an examination of speech acts provides no

29   Ibid., p. 151.

compelling reason for thinking that predication is essentially propositional, where referring is not.

An additional worry about Strawson's description of the distinction is the assumption that what is introduced by "wise" is *being wise*.
We have a principled reason in syntax to take the "is" in "Socrates
is wise" as going with the "wise," forming a syntactic unit, a verb-
phrase. The issue is whether there is any principled semantic reason
for treating the simple sentence as having two semantic units corresponding to these two grammatical units: the main noun-phrase and
the main verb-phrase. The claim is that the whole grammatical predicate forms a semantic unit introducing its term in the propositional style. If, in arguing for that claim, it is assumed that what is
introduced by the term "wise" is "being wise," then that assumption
prejudices the issue. For being wise would seem to correspond not to
"wise" but to both the words "is" and "wise," that is, to the whole predicate, not just the predicate adjective "wise." And being wise would
seem to be what is asserted of something in a sentence, so making us
think that "wise" forms a unit with "is" and introduces its term in
the propositional or assertive style. But mightn't it be that semantically it is "wise," not "is wise," that introduces a term, plausibly,
'wisdom,' not 'being wise'? If what is introduced by "wise" is the
universal wisdom, then "wise" would seem to be much more on par
with "Socrates." "Socrates" introduces the particular Socrates, "wise"
the universal wisdom. Neither is more incomplete than the other;
neither by itself suggests some particular kind of completion into a
proposition.

Finally, we should not accept uncritically Strawson's notion of something's "carrying the assertive or propositional tie." What does that
alleged extra function of the predicate actually consist in? A distinction
should be made between that which *indicates* or *signals* that a string of
words expresses a proposition and that which *makes* the string of words
into something that expresses a proposition. The former is epistemological, the latter constitutive. It is not obvious that it is a *part* of a sentence that performs either of those functions. Is there some part of the
sentence that indicates that it expresses a proposition? Suppose there
were. If it were simply a matter of indicating this, any device might
work for doing so, and that function would seem to be purely conventional. Giving voice to Ramsey's skepticism, Strawson asks, "Could
we not undermine the whole distinction by merely making the propositional link something separate in the sentence, not a part of a term-

introducing expression?"[30] We might include a mark to indicate propositional combination, like Frege's assertion sign. If the question is how we mark that something expresses a proposition, then our preference for treating "is wise" as a semantic unit with that function is unprincipled because it is purely conventional.[31] If our convention for signaling that something is an assertion is located in some part of the verb-phrase, so be it. But that tells us nothing about whether there is some part of the sentence that functions to make the string of words into something that expresses a proposition. The predicate, we might grant, suggests a certain kind of completion, completion into something that will express a proposition. It in no way follows that it is the part of the sentence that makes the string of words into something which expresses a proposition. Compare "____ and ____" suggests a particular kind of completion. It does not follow from this that "and" then functions to make a conjunctive tie.

Strawson does not clearly distinguish the signaling from the constituting function. Sometimes when he talks about the predicate "carrying the assertive tie," it is in terms of its signaling that the combination is a sentence: the predicate "shows that we have a truth- or falsity-yielding combination."[32] Other times, when he says that the predicate "carries the assertive tie" or "propositional symbolism," he seems to suggest that the predicate functions to make the string of words into something that expresses a proposition. For example, he borrows Johnson's language to describe the function of the predicate where the copula not only introduces its term, "it copulates it" (with the other term).[33] This suggests that the predicate combines what it introduces with what the other expression introduces, thereby predicating a property to the object referred to.

In the discussions that follow, I will focus exclusively on the latter notion of predicates carrying the assertive tie. The former notion is of little apparent philosophical interest, since any convention for signaling that something expresses a proposition will work. What is of philosophical interest is, first, whether the verb-phrase goes together with its complement to form a semantic unit that functions to effect propositional combination: second, is that function somehow explained by

30   Ibid., p. 160.
31   Ibid., p. 163.
32   Strawson, *Subject and Predicate in Logic and Grammar*, p. 21.
33   Strawson, *Individuals*, p. 151.

the fact that the complement of the verb designates something of a certain metaphysical kind – a concept or universal.

c. *The explanation of the semantic distinction between subjects and predicates lies in the difference in epistemic conditions required for term introduction.* According to Strawson, we will not see what explains the grammatical predicate's effecting propositional combination until we look beyond the expressions themselves to differences in what is required for subjects and predicates to introduce terms of these different metaphysical kinds, particulars and universals. There is a difference between the epistemic conditions necessary for a subject expression to introduce a particular and for a predicate expression to introduce a universal. This difference provides the basis for Strawson's own account of predication.

In the case of a subject expression, "in order for an identifying reference to a particular to be made, there must be some true empirical proposition known, in some not too exacting sense of this word, to the speaker to the effect that there is just one particular which answers to a certain description."[34] For example, to know who is introduced by the referring expression "Socrates," one would have to know some empirical fact about Socrates that uniquely identifies that object, such as that he was Plato's teacher who died of hemlock poisoning. By contrast, to know what is introduced by the predicating expression "fat," one does not have to know any empirical fact to the effect that someone in particular is fat. Knowing what universal is introduced "merely entails knowing the language."[35] On Strawson's view, so long as one understands the meaning of a predicate word – "yellow," "fat," "tired" – one knows what property it introduces.

His point might be illustrated as follows. Assume linguistic competence of the language, and consider the sentence "The dog is red." One knows the meaning of "dog" and "red," and the function of "the." Knowing the meaning of "dog" and the function of "the" is not sufficient to know what is introduced by "the dog." The speaker and hearer must know some empirical fact unique to some particular dog that identifies it as the one referred to. By contrast, knowing the meaning of "red" does suffice for knowing what is introduced by "red."

Strawson thinks this difference in what is required for an expression to introduce what it does explains the functional role of the expression.

34 Ibid., p. 183.
35 Ibid., p. 186.

The grammatical subject expression functions as a *referring* expression, because it identifies its object by means of some empirical fact unique to that object. The grammatical predicate functions to *predicate* some property of that object, because it identifies its property simply in virtue of the meaning of the expression, without reference to any empirical fact unique to that property. Because of this difference, expressions that introduce particulars have a kind of completeness which expressions that introduce universals do not. He says:

> although they [subjects] do not explicitly state facts, they perform their role only because they present or represent facts, only because they presuppose, or embody, or covertly carry, propositions which they do not explicitly affirm. They necessarily carry a weight of fact in introducing their terms.[36]

By contrast universal-specifying expressions carry no such weight of fact when they introduce their terms. It is only when they are combined with subject expressions that they *"help* to carry a fact."[37] So "the manifest incompleteness of the assertive style of introduction – the demand to be completed into an assertion – answers exactly to the incompleteness of the predicate."[38] Strawson concludes:

> We have a contrast between something which in no sense presents a fact in its own right but is a candidate for being part of a statement of fact, and something which does already in a sense present a fact in its own right and is also a candidate for being part of a statement of fact. It is appropriate enough that in the explicit assertion constituted by both taken together, it should be the former which carries the propositional symbolism, the symbolism that demands completion into an assertion.[39]

4   A Criticism of Alleged Epistemic Asymmetry between Subjects and Predicates

Strawson's explanation is not entirely clear. Whatever the sense may be in which names of particulars are supposed to be complete, it does not seem that that completeness lies in their "presenting" facts, as he says they do. In the sentence "Socrates was snub-nosed," what the name "Socrates" presents is an object, not a fact. While knowledge of

36   Ibid., p. 187.
37   Ibid.
38   Ibid.
39   Ibid.

some fact, for example that Socrates was Plato's most famous teacher, may be necessary for the speaker to successfully identify or to refer to the man Socrates in using the name, the name does not in any obvious sense *present* this fact. And even if we were to grant what seems untrue, that there is a sense in which "Socrates" presents the fact that Socrates was Plato's teacher, it is not clear how this would help in explaining sentential unity. It is not as though the constituents to be unified are the *fact* that Socrates was Plato's most famous teacher and the property presented by the predicate "snub-nosedness".

Strawson thinks the sense in which the name "Socrates" presents this fact is this: "[T]he thought of the definitely identified particular is resolved into that of a proposition which *as a whole* individuates the particular, but contains no part introducing it."[40] Thinking of Socrates is thinking of a proposition or fact, and that is what makes "Socrates" complete. By contrast, the thought of a definitely identified universal is not the thought of a proposition that individuates that universal. That is why "the universal appears as still something incomplete for thought, a constituent of a fact."[41]

When it comes to cashing out how the respective completeness and incompleteness explain sentential unity, Strawson says, "the association of the symbolism of this assertion with the universal rather than the particular we see, in the end, as no more than a mark of the former's lack of that completeness which the latter possesses."[42] But far from explaining how the completeness and incompleteness of the expressions account for their different functional roles, Strawson's comments here seem deflationary. He seems to say, all there is corresponding to the association of propositional combination with the predicate rather than the subject is that introducing the universal into discourse requires thinking of a constituent of a fact, whereas introducing the particular into discourse requires thinking of a fact. Yet, Strawson's comments should not be deflationary. He rejects identifying the semantic distinction between subjects and predicates with the being-about versus saying-something-of distinction that Cook Wilson argued was pragmatic. What is the semantic distinction? It should be a distinction between the function of the two expressions in virtue of which they together express a proposition. Strawson seems to agree with that and takes the distinctive function of the predicate to be that of effecting propositional combination. He then proposes a way of differentiating

40   Ibid., p. 210.
41   Ibid., p. 212.
42   Ibid.

semantic subject and predicate in virtue of the epistemic requirements for introducing their terms (either of which the statement may be said to be about). If this is the basis of the semantic distinction, then this difference in subject and predicate should *constitute* their together expressing a proposition. But it does not seem to do so. That the thought of the particular involves the thought of a fact but the thought of the universal merely involves the thought of a constituent of a fact does not, on the face of it, make the word introducing the universal function to predicate the universal of the particular.[43]

In addition, there is the question of whether the epistemic asymmetry is itself genuine. Characterizating this asymmetry, Strawson seems to underestimate what is required to know what is introduced by a predicate relative to the subject. He thinks that knowing who "Socrates" introduces involves knowing "some reasonable proportion" of salient facts or properties associated with the man Socrates, such as that he was the teacher of Plato who drank hemlock and was married to Xantippe.[44] Even if Strawson is wrong about the sorts of empirical facts one must know to know who is named, he is still correct in saying that one must know some empirical fact about the person named in order to know that the name names him. To see that this is so, consider the view that the only property one needs to know about the man Socrates to know who is referred to by the name "Socrates" is that *he* is the person called "Socrates." That is a merely "linguistic property" of Socrates: the man Socrates is called or named "Socrates." But, notice, to know that the man has that linguistic property – to know of the man that *he*, rather than some other man, is the one called "Socrates" – one has to know some empirical fact about him.[45] These might be very minimal facts and tell us nothing much about who the man Socrates is. It would suffice, for example, to know that Socrates is the person my philosopher friends are always going on about.

43   It is a small step from Strawson's view that in order to introduce the universal F one must know what "F" means to saying that one must know what it would be for something to *be* F, and following Russell, that this is a matter of understanding propositions of the form "x is F." This would return us to the issue, discussed in connection with Russell's view, about how that understanding is related to the predicate's effecting propositional combination, if it does.

44   Strawson, *Individuals*, p. 191. Saul Kripke and others have argued that this view of names is false. See Kripke's *Naming and Necessity* (Cambridge, MA: Harvard University Press, 1972), pp. 70–90.

45   This is true even if one takes the most minimalist view about what you need to know. To know even that someone (however specified) is called Socrates, you must know that there is someone called Socrates, and this is an empirical fact about that person.

In order for the expression "Socrates" to successfully introduce Socrates, the speaker must have at least a piece of linguistic knowledge – know he is the man called "Socrates" – and the speaker will have that linguistic knowledge, just in case he or she knows an empirical fact about Socrates that connects the name "Socrates" to some nonlinguistic property of the man Socrates.

The question is whether there is an asymmetry in what is required for a predicate expression to successfully introduce a universal. Strawson thinks that the speaker can successfully introduce a universal into discourse if the speaker has a relevant piece of linguistic knowledge (knowing the meaning of the term). That is true, but the kind of linguistic knowledge one must have seems to be analogous to that required to know what particular is introduced, and like that knowledge, it involves further knowledge of some empirical fact. Just as to know who "Socrates" introduces requires knowing of some man that *he* is the one called "Socrates," so knowing what universal "red" introduces requires knowing of some universal that *it* is the one called "red" or that it is the one that would be predicated by the word "red." But how do we identify which property it is that is the one called "red"? (Compare: how do we identify what man it is that is called "Socrates"?) Seemingly, only by knowing some empirical fact about redness. To know what "red" means, one has to be able to distinguish the property of being red from other relevant properties such as being blue or green or yellow. There must be relevant facts that one knows about redness that would allow one to identify that property as opposed to those other ones. For complex predicates, that will not involve an empirical fact – they can be broken down into their component properties (e.g., bachelor – unmarried, adult male). But knowing what is introduced by a simple predicate does seem to involve knowledge of some empirical fact. One cannot differentiate the property of being red from being blue, yellow, and purple unless one knows some empirical fact about redness – that red is the property that looks a certain way, or reflects waves of a certain length, or that it is the color of your bike.[46]

---

46 Examples such as Hume's missing shade of blue might pose counterexamples to my claim that introducing any simple property requires knowing some empirical fact about it. I don't find this worry compelling. First, because it is not clear that the kinds of things one would have to know about the missing shade aren't empirical facts: it is the shade of blue that would be between this lighter one and that darker one. Second, because Strawson can't want his claims to depend on such cases. He is surely intending to describe what is generally true of what is required for subject and predicate expressions to introduce what they do.

Knowing what "red" introduces involves having a piece of linguistic knowledge, that *this* is the universal that "red" would predicate, and knowing *that* involves knowing some empirical fact about redness that connects the word "red" with some nonlinguistic property of redness. So Strawson's claim that knowing what particular is introduced involves knowing an empirical fact but knowing what property is introduced does not appears to be false. I therefore see no asymmetry between conditions required for the successful introduction into discourse of a particular rather than for a universal. And, as I've argued, even if there were such an asymmetry, it is not at all clear how that asymmetry would explain the difference in function between referring and predicating expressions in virtue of which they together express a proposition. The fact that knowing what particular is introduced by a subject expression involves knowing an empirical fact but knowing what property is introduced by a predicate only involves knowing a constituent of a fact does not obviously explain how the one expression functions to predicate that property to the object referred to by the other. Thus, I do not think Strawson has supplied us with a metaphysical account of the referring or predicating function of expressions, or a satisfactory account of the unity of the sentence.

5

Negation, Propositional Combination, and the Nature of Concepts

Strawson's view might be best characterized as follows. No single piece of data forces us to treat predicates as essentially different from subjects. Data from a variety of sources – from the theory of meaning, logical theory, metaphysics – suggest there are asymmetries between subjects and predicates. And it is a single, comprehensive explanation of all the data that makes unquestionable a real difference between subject and predicate and provides us with a unified account of predication.

For our purposes, it is essential to consider this other data, particularly the logical asymmetries between subjects and predicates and their relation to the unity of the sentence. Here, I will focus mainly, but not exclusively, on the alleged logical asymmetry regarding negation (that negation attaches to predicates but not subjects), because Strawson places particular emphasis on what he regards as an essential connection of negation to propositional combination. He thinks that if negation is essentially linked to propositional combination, then what explains why negation attaches to predicates may also explain the predicate's functioning to effect propositional combination. According to Strawson, what explains why negation attaches to predicates is that predicates refer to concepts. Hence, the predicate's referring to a concept may explain propositional combination.

I will argue that Strawson fails to link negation to propositional combination in the right way. So even if the facts about negation are explained by the predicate's referring to a concept, that gives us no reason to believe that propositional combination is explained in the same way. In addition, I do not think that it is clear that the logical asymmetry between subjects and predicates regarding negation is explained by the predicate's introducing a concept in the way Strawson suggests it is. I conclude that we should be skeptical of the metaphysical explanation of certain of the logical asymmetries and of their relation to the unity of the sentence.

1   Strawson's Characterization and Explanation of Certain Logical Asymmetries

The logical asymmetries consist, in part, in the fact that logical theory provides for negative, compound, and disjunctive predicates but not for negative, compound, or disjunctive subjects. Consider negative predicates first. Elizabeth Anscombe suggests that what distinguishes names from predicate expressions is that while "expressions for predicates can be negated, names cannot. I mean that negation, attached to a predicate, yields a new predicate, but when attached to a name it does not yield any name."[1] Attaching the word "not" to the predicate "is wise" yields a new predicate "is not wise." Attaching it to the name "Socrates" does not make a new name. "Not Socrates" is not an expression that names some object. Similarly, Peter Geach says, "when a proposition is negated, the negation may be taken as going with the predicate in a way in which it cannot be taken to go with the subject."[2] He suggests the reason for this is that "predicables always occur in contradictory pairs; and by attaching such a pair to a common subject, we get a contradictory pair of propositions."[3]

It is argued that just as there can be negative predicates but not negative subjects, so there can be compound and disjunctive predicates, for example "bald and tall" or "bald or tall," but not such subjects, for example "Tom and Jerry" or "Tom or Jerry." In each case, the arguments take the following form. Standard logical transformations work in sentences comprising negative, compound, and disjunctive predicates, but do work not in sentences that appear to have negative, compound, or disjunctive subjects. If these expressions formed genuine subjects, certain logical equivalencies would hold; since they do not hold, the combining of the expressions into a subject is merely apparent and really just stands for what can only be understood as a

1   E. Anscombe, "Retractation," *Analysis*, 26 (1965), p. 33.
2   P. Geach, *Reference and Generality* (Ithaca, NY: Cornell University Press, 1962), p. 32.
3   Ibid.

combining of sentences. "Tom and Jerry are bald" really just abbreviates "Tom is bald and Jerry is bald," but "Tom is bald and tall" contains a genuine compound predicate. Strawson provides several examples of arguments that show that logical equivalencies will not hold if subjects are treated as negative, compound, or disjunctive. For example, this is his argument regarding negative names:

> (1) Fa and Ga
> Then, by double negation, this is equivalent to
> (2) ~ (~(Fa and Ga))
> which, by the introduction of a conjunctive predicate, is equivalent to
> (3) ~ (~((F and G)a)).
> If we can frame negative subjects, (3) is equivalent to
> (4) ~ ((F and G)~a)
> and (4) can be expanded into
> (5) ~ (F~a and G~a)
> which will be equivalent to
> (6) ~ (~(Fa) and ~(Ga)
> Now (6) is equivalent to
> (7) Fa or Ga.
> But evidently (1) is not equivalent to (7).[4]

He concludes that we cannot sanction negative names. Arguments with similar results can be produced for conjunctive and disjunctive subjects. By contrast, whatever logical operations can be performed on negative, compound, or disjunctive propositions can also be performed on predicates, so that "the internal logic of *predicate*-composition is exactly analogous to that of *propositional* logic."[5]

In "Names and Predicables," R. H. Grimm argues there cannot be a logic that sanctions *both* negative, compound, and disjunctive subjects *and* such predicates.[6] According to Grimm, the fallacies present in arguments such as the one above emerge only if one's logic contains both compound, disjunctive, and negative subjects and compound, disjunctive, and negative predicates. But he thinks such arguments by themselves give us no reason for preferring the logic with compound, disjunctive, and negative predicates to the logic with such subjects.[7] Strawson does not disagree with Grimm's conclusion, but thinks there is a principled reason for preferring the logic with negative, compound,

4 Strawson, *Subject and Predicate in Logic and Grammar* (London: Methuen, 1974), p. 7.
5 Ibid., p. 6 (my emphasis).
6 R. H. Grimm, "Names and Predicables," *Analysis*, 26 (1966), pp. 138–46.
7 Strawson, *Subject and Predicate in Logic and Grammar*, p. 7.

and disjunctive predicates. That principled reason lies in the nature of particulars and universals (or concepts).[8] His argument begins from a discussion about the nature of concepts. General concepts are both "principles of collection" and "principles of distinction."[9] Being general, the concept may collect or be exemplified by many particulars. But concepts come in ranges. The concepts lion, tiger, panther, for instance, belong to one range, the feline animal species range; red, yellow, blue occupy another range, the color range.

> What ultimately differentiates one concept from another in the range is just the space that it occupies in the range. . . . What is meant is that the concepts of a range are principles of distinction among the particulars that come within the range, and are in logical competition with other members of the range throughout their field of application to particulars. If any particular (fairly and squarely) exemplifies one member of the concept-range, then there are other members of the range (or at least one other member) which that particular is thereby logically excluded from exemplifying.[10]

A particular's falling under one concept will rule out its falling under certain *other concepts* – Mini's being a cat rules out her being a dog. But that a particular falls under one concept does not generally rule out that *another particular* falls under that same or some other concept – Minnie's being a cat does not rule out Sweet Pea's or Boston's being a cat. Thus, particulars are not in logical competition with one another for places under concepts.

This leads to other differences between particulars and universals. Since the logical space occupied by one concept, scarlet, might be included in that occupied by another concept, red, but be excluded from some third concept, blue, we can say that being scarlet entails being red and is incompatible with being blue. The fact that concepts are included under or excluded from other concepts means that concepts carry with them certain entailment relations. These entailment relations can be expressed in terms of necessary and sufficient conditions: an animal's falling under the concept leopard would be sufficient for its falling under the concept feline, but not necessary. That a particular falls under the concept feline is a necessary condition of its

8 Ibid., pp. 7–8.
9 Ibid., p. 17.
10 Ibid., p. 18.

falling under the concept leopard. Particulars are not related in this way. The fact that one particular falls under a concept does not rule in or out that another particular falls under that concept. Thus, particulars do not stand in entailment relations to one another. Strawson says, "We can find no particulars so related that, whatever concept was in question, the fact that one of those particulars exemplified that concept would be either a necessary or a sufficient condition of the others doing so too (though not conversely)."[11]

Strawson uses these features of concepts to account for why there are negative, compound, and disjunctive predicates, but no such subjects. Because concepts are defined by such involvement and incompatibility relations to other concepts, new concepts can be created that are complements of the original concepts, involving all that the original did not involve. Such are the negative concepts – nonblue, nonwise, illegal. We can also form new more complex concepts where the constituent concepts stand in certain relations to each other, conjunctive relations such as "hot and thirsty" or disjunctive ones as in "mean or surly." These new complex concepts will be genuine concepts because, like the concepts they form, they carve out a portion of logical space and have their own involvement and entailment relations vis-à-vis other concepts.

Now consider negative predicates. Strawson says:

> So there is no theoretical reason why we shouldn't define, for any concept, its complementary concept: one which covers the whole of the logical space left unoccupied by the concept of which it is the complement . . . And there is every practical reason why, if we do introduce such a concept, we should represent it linguistically in a way which displays its logical character, i.e. by affixing a negation sign to the expression specifying the original concept. The resulting complex expression, when propositionally combined with a particular-specifying expression is, on our hypothesis, a predicate. And the propositional combination of this predicate with a given subject is equivalent to the negation of the propositional combination of the predicate specifying the original concept with the given subject. So, in introducing such a term, we have introduced a negative predicate.[12]

We cannot similarly create new names of particulars by attaching "not" to the name of a particular: we can't form not-Bill or non-Bill from

---

11 Ibid., p. 19. See also Strawson, "The Asymmetry of Subject and Predicates," p. 102.
12 Strawson, *Subject and Predicate in Logic and Grammar*, p. 24.

Bill. That is because "particulars do not stand to other particulars in such relations as concepts stand to other concepts."[13] For example, they don't stand in entailment relations to one another: Bill's being a person does not exclude Tom's being a person or entail that Jane is a person.

Why does negation always go with the predicate? Because predicates refer to concepts, and concepts are such that they have "complements," the complement including all of what was excluded by the original concept. Linguistically, one can designate that complementary concept by affixing the word "not" or "non" to the expression that designated the original concept. Why can't one negate a subject expression? Because the referent of the subject expression is a particular, and particulars do not have complements.

The same principles sanction complex concepts – compound or disjunctive – but not complex particulars; they sanction 'green and round' but not 'Tom and Jerry.' According to Strawson, we can create complex concepts because concepts are such that they can stand in necessary and sufficient condition relations to one another. Consider the complex conjunctive concept 'is a gray mare': it is necessary for being a gray mare both that the particular in question be gray and that it be a mare. That a particular fall under these two concepts is sufficient for its falling under the concept 'is a gray mare.'

Suppose we try to form a complex particular 'Tom and William.' Then we would have to say that Tom is necessary for being 'Tom and William' and William is necessary for being 'Tom and William,' and Tom together with William are sufficient for being the complex individual 'Tom and William.' Strawson thinks that this makes no sense.

> For this step could be taken only if we could speak of one particular individual being a necessary or sufficient condition of another in a sense which symmetrically corresponds to that in which we can speak of one general character being a necessary or sufficient condition of another. And as we have seen, there is here no such sense.[14]

It appears, then, that there are genuine compound, disjunctive and negative predicates, but not such subjects.

---

13   Ibid.
14   Strawson, "Asymmetry of Subject and Predicates," p. 109.

2 The Relation of Negation to
Propositional Combination

Strawson argues that the logical features of predicates, particularly that
negation goes with the predicate, is connected with the distinctive
semantic function of the predicate. While the subject and predicate
expression both introduce terms, particulars, and universals, the predicate expression has an additional function not shared by the subject
expression, which Strawson variously describes as carrying the
"assertive or propositional tie," as indicating propositional combination, as yielding something truth-evaluable.[15]

Strawson thinks that there can "scarcely be any doubt" that it is the
verb-phrase that has this function.[16] While the predicate expression
cannot perform its function without an expression of the right kind to
combine with – "The grappling machinery needs something to
grapple" – still "we locate that machinery on the side of the verb-phrase
rather than that of the noun-phrase."[17] If we take seriously this
metaphor of the machinery being located in the predicate, it suggests
that the predicate actually *effects* propositional combination. Strawson's
explanation of propositional combination is connected with that of
negation. Being the heart of the matter, I quote at length:

> The explanation proceeds by way of the notion of negation. Concepts
> and particulars being what they are, we know that, given our working
> hypothesis, we can have negative predicates but not negative subjects.
> So when it is a question of framing a formal contradictory for a propo-
> sition of our fundamental kind, we have two ways open to us: that of
> negating the sentence as a whole which expresses the proposition or that
> of negating the concept-specifying expression which is its predicate. . . .
> The symbolism of propositional combination serves to show that we
> have a certain sort of combination of the particular-specifying expression
> and the concept-specifying expression, *viz.* a combination which yields
> truth under one set of conditions and falsity under another. The effect of
> negating the proposition is simply to reverse (or exchange) the connec-
> tions between these truth-values and these conditions. *Nothing is more
> natural than to indicate this effect by, as it were, changing the sign of the propo-
> sitional indicator, or whatever indicates that we have a truth-or-falsity yielding*

15 Strawson, *Subject and Predicate in Logic and Grammar*, p. 34.
16 Ibid., p. 30.
17 Ibid.

combination. Thus, to modify a suggestion of Ramsey's, we might write "ass" [standing for assertion] upside down or backwards; or, as here, introduce an extra sign in association with it. So negation and the symbolism of propositional combination have a natural affinity for each other. But we have lately been engaged in demonstrating, among other things, the affinity of concept-specification and negation for each other. So here we have, as regards our basic class of subject-predicate sentences, a mediated or resultant affinity between the function of indicating propositional combination and the concept-specifying function; hence an explanation, or partial explanation, of why predicates have the form of the verb. We might put it like this: the "ass" function and negation are at home together; if negation can be absorbed into the predicate, conceived as that part of the combination which has the concept-specifying role, then the "ass" function can be absorbed into it too.[18]

You may negate a proposition "A is F" by saying, "It is not the case that A is F," or by saying, "A is not F." Strawson thinks that since one can negate "A is F" by negating the concept-specifying expression "F," by saying "A is not F," then it must be the concept-specifying expression that indicates propositional combination. Notice that if correct, this argument would establish that it is the concept-specifying expression that *indicates* or *signals* that the words express a proposition.

If Strawson is after the more ambitious conclusion that it is the concept-specifying expression that *effects* propositional combination making the form of words into something that is a proposition, then his reasoning might be characterized as follows. We negate such a proposition by denying that the particular instantiates the property. We may deny that the particular instantiates the property by negating the proposition as a whole, as in "It is not the case that Socrates is wise," or by negating the concept-specifying expression, as in "Socrates is not wise." Since negating the whole proposition is equivalent to negating the concept-specifying expression, it must be the case that it is the concept-specifying expression that effects propositional combination. Strawson does not put it as directly as this, but this seems to be his thinking. If negating a proposition is equivalent to negating the predicate, it must be because the predicate itself is the part of the sentence that makes the string of words into a proposition.

18   Ibid., pp. 30–1 (my emphasis).

3 Criticism of the Alleged Connection between Negation and Propositional Combination

I begin a critical assessment of Strawson's explanation of these asymmetries between subjects and predicates in consideration of the alleged "natural affinity" between negation and propositional combination. On Strawson's view, the effect of propositional combination is to produce something "which yields truth under one set of conditions and falsity under another."[19] "Snow is white" yields truth under the conditions that snow is white and falsity under the condition that snow is not white. Strawson suggests that we might indicate propositional combination by attaching the sign "ass" (standing for assertion) to words that introduce an individual and a concept respectively: "ass(i,c)" symbolizes that the individual, snow, is propositionally combined with the concept or property white. Snow then gets represented as white. The effect of negating the proposition snow is white is to reverse the relation between those conditions and those truth-values. The assertion "It is not the case that snow is white" is false under the condition that snow is white and true under the condition that snow is not white. He says that "Nothing is more natural than to indicate this effect, by, as it were, changing the sign of the propositional indicator, of whatever indicates that we have a truth-or-falsity-yielding combination."[20] Thus, we might introduce an additional sign to indicate that the relation between conditions and truth values is to be reversed, for example "~ ass" or "ass" written upside down.

Contrary to what Strawson says, on the face of it, it does not seem natural to indicate that effect – a reversal of relations between the conditions and the truth values – by attaching this additional sign *to the sign that indicates or effects propositional combination*. Consider some symbol "S is P," and suppose that the function of "ass" written next to it, as in "ass, (S is P)" is to indicate that S and P are combined (or are to be combined) in such a way as to express a proposition. What negating the "ass" function *should* symbolize, what it would be natural to take it as symbolizing, is that the expressions "S" and "P" are *not to be combined* or are not combined in fact into something that expresses a proposition. If "ass" functions to indicate that S and P are propositionally combined, then negating "ass" would be to deny that S and P are propositionally combined. But when one says, "~(S is P)" or "(S is

19   Ibid., p. 30.
20   Ibid., p. 31.

not P)" or "(S is non-P)," one does not deny that S and P are propositionally combined. Rather, one denies the proposition that S is P or affirms the proposition that S is non-P. In the denial ("It is not the case that Socrates is wise" or "Socrates is not wise"), the individual and concept remain propositionally combined. In the affirmation ("Socrates is nonwise"), the individual is propositionally combined with non-P, the complement of P.

So what is the affinity between negation and propositional combination? There is an affinity between negation and *propositions*. Whether the negation is attached to the proposition as a whole or to the copula "is," what is being denied is a proposition. If negation is instead attached to the predicate adjective forming "nonwise," we affirm a proposition. So throughout, what is being denied or affirmed by the use of negation, by attaching negation to one or another word, is a proposition.

However, this does not show any affinity between negation and whatever it is that functions to effect (or to indicate) propositional combination. Or, at least, we need to distinguish two senses of propositional combination. Strawson's argument feels compelling because he trades on those two senses.

Propositional combination:

1. combining the words in the sentence so that they express a proposition as opposed to their not expressing a proposition (and so yielding a combination regardless of whether that proposition is affirmed or denied).
2. combining words to yield an affirmation on the one hand and a denial on the other hand.

Negation has a natural affinity for propositional combination in the sense of 2, but not for that of 1. On the assumption that a string of words "S is P" expresses a proposition, attaching negation to the whole sentence or to the copula "is" will make that new combination of words a denial of the original proposition. It will have the effect, as Strawson says, of reversing the connections between truth-values and conditions from those associated with the affirmation of S is P.

When Strawson says that negating the proposition is equivalent to negating the predicate so we can associate the function of propositional combination with the predicate, what he should mean is that we can associate the function of *affirming* or *denying* a proposition with the predicate. If "It is not the case that Socrates is wise" is equivalent in meaning to "Socrates is not wise," then the "is not" in the predicate may indicate that we are denying the proposition that Socrates is wise. Or if denying that "Socrates is wise" is equivalent to affirming that he has the property of being nonwise, then the predicate "is nonwise" may indicate that we are affirming that Socrates falls under the concept complementary to 'wise,' namely 'nonwise.'

The problem for Strawson is that to draw the conclusion that he wants – that the predicate is the part of the sentence that makes the string of words into a proposition – he would need to show that negation has an affinity for propositional combination in the sense of 1 above. This he has not shown. If there were such an affinity, to negate the predicate would be to deny that the words are combined to express a proposition (to indicate that the words merely form a list). That, however, is not the case: to negate the predicate is not to deny that the words are propositionally combined. Thus, the facts seem to show that negation has no natural affinity for that part of the sentence that makes the string of words into something which expresses a proposition.

The main point I want to emphasize is that Strawson has not shown there to be any affinity between negation and what effects propositional combination. If that is right, then in the facts he has assembled about negation, we find no reason to believe that the grammatical predicate effects propositional combination or that the metaphysical facts that explain where negation attaches also explain propositional combination. Having said that, I do not think that Strawson's explanation of the relation between negation and those metaphysical facts should go entirely unchallenged.

4   Some Doubts about Strawson's View that the Nature of Properties is the Basis for the Facts about Negation

Contrary to what Strawson and Geach suggest, we can form the complement of a particular by attaching negation to a particular-specifying expression. Strawson denies this, because he thinks that particulars do not stand to particulars in the kinds of relations that concepts stand to concepts and it is the kind of relations that concepts stand in to other concepts that allows us to form complementary concepts.[21] Concepts, for example, compete with other concepts in their range for possession of particulars, but particulars don't compete with other particulars for

21   Ibid. See pp. 18 and 24.

possession of concepts. But if as he himself argues, particulars are individuated in terms of the space and time they occupy, then the principles whereby particulars are individuated, in distinction from the principles whereby concepts are individuated, must be brought into play. Particulars are not incompatible with one another because the one exemplifies a concept that the other does not. That one particular instantiates a concept does not rule out that another particulars does so, because particulars are not individuated by the concepts they collect but by the parts of space and time they occupy. That one particular occupies a part of space at a time *does* rule out that another particular occupies that exact region of space at that time.[22] Thus, we can form the complementary of the object introduced by "Tom" by affixing "not" to "Tom." "Not Tom" would then be all the people (things) who are not Tom, just as the complement of "nonblue" is all the colors (properties) not blue. That is, it will be all the occupants of space/time minus the region occupied by Tom. In that respect, there appears to be no asymmetry between subjects and predicates. This depends upon the assumption that spelling out (in)compatibility relations is connected to the principles by means of which the things in question are individuated. But Strawson's own explanation of the (in)compatibility of concepts is developed in terms of the individuation of concepts.

On the same theme, Geach says:

> An act of naming may be mistaken, and so may be contradicted or corrected: when a child says "Pussy" or "Jemima," I may say "Not pussy – dog" or "Not Jemima – another pussy." But "Not pussy" and "Not Jemima" are not themselves acts of naming. For as regards two uses of a single name in acts of naming we can always ask whether the same thing is named, the same Jemima or the same pussy. But it would be senseless to speak of the same non-Jemima or the same not-pussy. So the negation of an act of naming is never the use of a negated name as a name.[23]

It is true that in the example he gives we are not forming a negative name and using it to name an object. We can, however, attach a negation to a name and thereby form the complement of some object and

---

22 This might need qualification, for, arguably, the sock and the cloth it is made of can be at the same place at the same time. See David Wiggins, "On Being in the Same Place at the Same Time," *Philosophical Review*, 77 (1968), pp. 90–5. The qualification would have to be that one particular's being at a place at a time rules out other particulars not composed of that same matter being at that place at that time.

23 Geach, *Reference and Generality*, p. 33.

use that designator to name the object. I may introduce the complement of Tom by the use of the expression "Not Tom" and say of that
object, "Not Tom is a scattered object."[24] Here "Not Tom" designates
all the objects except Tom, and it forms a complement just as surely as
does "nonblue." Contrary to what Geach suggests, we can ask of two
uses of "Not Tom" whether the same thing was named. Whether "Not
Tom" is a proper name will depend on whether it is a rigid designator.
There is some case for saying it is not a rigid designator. In another
possible world in which there is a complement of Tom, the set of objects
that are not Tom may differ from the set of objects that are not Tom in
this world. So if we take the "not" as remaining a semantically significant component of the expression across possible worlds, then "Not
Tom" is not a name. It functions, instead, like a description. Of course,
we can form a name of a set of objects *in this world* by including all the
objects that are not Tom, and give this set of objects the name "Not
Tom." We might just as well have called it "GTom" or "Ztom." The
"not" simply indicates something about how the set of objects got
formed in the first place. (Compare "Erehwon" which is "nowhere"
spelled backwards and is the name for a Utopia which exists nowhere.
"Erehwon" is a name.) Whether one takes "Not Tom" as a proper name
or as a designator that functions like a description, it may function to
identify a set of particulars. And in the case where it functions as a designator identifying across possible worlds the set of objects that are not
Tom, it does so in part in virtue of the meaning of "not."

Ordinarily, when we attach a negating expression to a name, we do
not intend to pick out all the objects except the one that the name
names. Whether I am asked, "What is round?" and reply, "Not Tom"
or "What is Tom?" and reply, "Not round," in both cases I am denying
the proposition "Tom is round" and saying that Tom is not round. So
one correct point behind what Strawson and Geach say is that when
we do use a negated name as a description (e.g., "Not Tom is a scattered object"), that negation is in no way a denial of the original sentence. To deny the sentence "Tom is round" one does not say of another
object "Not Tom" that he is round: the denial of "Tom is round" is "Tom
is not round," not "Not Tom is round." In the denial, one attaches "not"
to the concept-specifying expression. That is the affinity between negation and concept-specification.

This works so long as there is only one concept-specifying expression in the sentence, but sentences can have concept-specifying words

24   I am indebted here to Antonio Rauti.

in both the subject and the predicate position: "The concept 'horse' is easily attained" or "Blue is my favorite color." We do not negate these sentences by applying "not" to the subject expression even though these subject expressions introduce concepts. The negation of "blue is my favorite color" is not "nonblue is my favorite color," but "Blue is not my favorite color." If negation necessarily goes with the predicate, it cannot then do so in virtue of the fact that the predicate introduces a concept.

Strawson thinks it is not the fact that a word introduces a concept per se that makes negation go with that word, but the fact that the concept-specifying word in the predicate will introduce a concept that competes with other concepts for possession of whatever is introduced by the subject expression, and not vice versa. Let us say that when X competes with other things of its kind for Y, but Y does not compete with other things of its kind for X, X is of a "higher" type than Y. Now consider Strawson's example "Happiness is found in all stations of life." The predicate, "found in all stations of life,"

> specifies a character of characters which has its own incompatibility and involvement ranges in relation to any and every character such that that character and it may be presented as assigned to each other. Thus being found in all stations of life is in this way incompatible with being found in few stations in life and entails (involves) being found in most stations of life.[25]

While *Bob's* being happy at time t is incompatible with his being in misery at that time, happiness' being found in all stations of life is not incompatible with *misery's* being found in all stations of life. So in the context in which one is talking about a property of the concept happiness, happiness is like a particular in that it is not competing with other things of its kind to occupy a certain region of logical space. Its occupying that region of logical space is compatible with other concepts occupying it. Just as John and Jane can both be happy, so misery and happiness can both be found in all stations of life.

This is important. It shows that it is not because an expression introduces a concept, and concepts have complements, that negation goes with that expression. There is no *necessary* connection between negation and concept specification. Rather, on Strawson's view, negation (and by its natural affinity propositional combination) is necessarily connected with the *higher-level* concept-specifying expression.

25 Strawson, "Asymmetry of Subject and Predicates," p. 113.

Strawson's explanation of why "not" attaches to the predicate is that the predicate introduces a concept that competes with other concepts for possession of what is introduced by the subject (but not vice versa), and so to negate the proposition as a whole, we simply attach "not" to the predicate word, thereby introducing the competing, incompatible concept – the complement of the original concept. Since what is introduced by the subject expression is not competing with other things of its type for possession of the predicate concept, the sentence cannot be negated by attaching "not" to the subject expression.

The problem with this explanation is that the same facts adduced in Strawson's explanation would also support an alternative explanation. It is true that there is no incompatibility between two particulars, but, by the same token, there is no incompatibility between two concepts or properties taken by themselves. The concept of being blue and being red are not by themselves incompatible. It is only in reference to their being instantiated in the same particular that two concepts may be incompatible: the car, for example, cannot be both blue all over and red all over. Even when we say such things as "Blue and red are incompatible," we mean that something's *being* blue and being red is incompatible. In fact, all the properties of concepts that Strawson emphasizes in his explanation – one concept's *collecting* particulars (or other concepts), their *competing*, their *compatibility–incompatibility* relations – are properties that concepts have only insofar as they are exemplified by some particular. If the concept red collects the particular the car, then the car cannot be blue, for red competes with blue for possession of particulars.

If Strawson is right to assert that the compatibility and competition relations explain where "not" attaches, then to what expression in the sentence should it attach? In the sorts of sentences under consideration, the predicate of the sentence consists of a *relation*-specifying word and a *property*-specifying word. In "Socrates is wise," "is" is the relation-specifying word, "wise" the property-specifying word. Both the relation and property-specifying words are "concept"-specifying words. So we need to distinguish which concept-specifying word negation attaches to. The notion of a concept's competing with or being compatible or incompatible with other concepts is defined by its relation to particulars (or lower-level concepts). The particular's *exemplifying* some concept, *instantiating* some property, makes for the competition of concepts (properties) and for their (in)compatibility with certain other concepts (properties). Suppose someone says that some particular exemplifies some concept (instantiates some property), and we deny that. What we deny when we deny the proposition is neither the object introduced by the subject nor the property introduced by the complement of the verb, but rather that the object and property stand in the relation said to obtain. One denies that the object and property are related in such a way that the object *exemplifies* the property. We do that by negating the expression that originally introduced the relation said to obtain between the particular and the property, not by negating the expression that designates the property. If Strawson is right that it is the fact that concepts (properties) stand in these competition and (in)compatibility relations that explains where negation is to attach, where it should and does attach is to the word that specifies the relation said to obtain. It attaches to the "is," not to the word that introduces the property.

Strawson might reply that negating the concept-specifying word that introduces the relation said to obtain is equivalent in meaning to negating the concept-specifying expression that introduces the property: "(The ball)([is *not*]blue)" is equivalent to "(The ball) (is [*non*blue])." For he thinks that "no theoretical reason" prevents us from defining for any concept, its complement which "covers the whole of the logical space left unoccupied by the concept of which it is the complement." When we do this we might "represent it linguistically in a way which displays its logical character, i.e. by affixing a negation sign to the expression specifying the original concept."[26] This would seem to show exactly what is wanted, that the relation-specifying word goes together with the property-specifying one to form a single semantic unit: "is wise" in "Socrates is wise" forms a unit of its own. This can be shown by the fact that the sentence "Socrates is not wise" is the same in meaning as "Socrates is nonwise."

But are these sentences in fact the same in meaning? The phrases "nonwise" and "nonblue" are not a part of natural language. They are philosophers' constructs. What do such phrases mean? When we say, "The car is nonblue," we may mean to say that the car has some color other than blue. The complement of blue would then be all the colors except blue. However, saying that something has some color besides blue is not equivalent to saying that the object is not blue. In saying "Abstract objects are not blue," I say they do not have the property of being blue, but this does not mean, what is false, that they have some other color.[27] On this account "not being blue" and "being nonblue" are

26   Strawson, *Subject and Predicate in Logic and Grammar*, p. 24.
27   I am indebted to Greg Novack for this point.

not extensionally equivalent. Abstract objects fall into the set of objects that are not blue but not into the set of objects that are nonblue. Thus, if the complement of "blue" is all the colors except blue, denying that something is blue is not the same as affirming that it is nonblue.

Strawson, however, suggests that the complement of a concept "covers the whole of logical space left unoccupied by the concept of which it is the complement."[28] So perhaps he is envisioning forming the concept of "nonblue," not by merely including all of logical space *in the color range* not occupied by blue, but by including every part of logical space not occupied by the concept of being blue. Then "not being blue" and "being nonblue" are extensionally equivalent. Any object that does not belong to the set of objects that are blue will belong to the set of objects that are not blue. Here, denying that some object is blue is more plausibly equivalent in meaning to affirming that some object is nonblue.

While one might define "nonblue" or "non-F" in that way, it would seem ultimately to undermine Strawson's view that the explanation of the semantic properties of predicates are found in the nature of what is named, the concept or property. Consider all the objects that fall outside of the extension of "blue." Those objects constitute an extension, but it is far from clear that there is a property common to all of them in virtue of which they instantiate the property (or fall under the concept) being nonblue. There is not plausibly a property for every extension. If saying that an object does not have a property is equivalent to saying that it has another negative property, then for every true sentence we utter, there must exist a property designated by the predicate that the object has. Admitting such properties seems to commit one to the principle that there is a property corresponding to every extension that can be formed.

Our only reason for postulating such properties as "nonblue" or "nonwise" is that there is a *name* for it in a true sentence which ascribes it, as in "The car is nonblue." But we can explain the truth of the sentence "The car is nonblue" in virtue of the car's having a property it actually has, that of being red, without having to postulate the property being nonblue which is to be a common property possessed by the set of things that fall outside of the extension of "blue." We might avoid a proliferation of properties by distinguishing those sentences whose truth implies that the object referred to instantiates the property introduced by the predicate from those sentences which are true even

28   Strawson, *Subject and Predicate in Logic and Grammar*, p. 24.

though their predicate does not introduce some property that the object referred does instantiate. The sentence "The car is red" and "The car is nonblue" may both be true because the car is red. "The car is red" is true by virtue of the car's having the very property predicated – by being red. The sentence "The car is nonblue" is true too, because the car is red: it is not true in virtue of the car's having another property that of being nonblue, where that is the common property of all the things that do not fall in the extension of "being blue."

While some philosophers are willing to be so liberal with properties, admitting into their ontology negative properties and facts, Strawson should not want to be so liberal. For if we are willing to admit such properties into our ontology, why not be correspondingly liberal in admitting objects? If there is a property corresponding to every extension, why isn't there, analogously, an object corresponding to every extension? And if we can form objects in that way, objects will have inclusion and exclusion relations and competition ranges: Tom's being at a certain place at a certain time will rule out Not Tom's being at that place and time; Tom's being there will exclude Not Tom's being there, and entail that all Tom parts are there. Then we will have lost the distinction that Strawson wants to maintain – that predicates, but not subjects, have certain logical properties and that this is explained by the fact that predicates introduce properties.

Of course it is not plausible that there are such objects. Just because there is an extension of things formed by excluding everything except Tom, it doesn't follow that there is an object Not Tom corresponding to this extension. But neither is it plausible that the extension of all the objects that exclude the blue objects have a common property in virtue of which they constitute that extension.

Strawson began by arguing that denying some proposition as in "It is not the case that Socrates is wise" is equivalent to negating the predicate, saying, "Socrates is not wise." This, he thinks, will explain why "not" goes with the grammatical predicate. But this so far gives us no reason to treat the entire grammatical predicate – the "is wise" – as a single semantic unit, rather than treating "is" as one semantic unit to which "not" attaches and "wise" as another. Strawson then needs to establish that the sentence "Socrates is not wise" wherein one denies that Socrates has a property is equivalent to the sentence "Socrates is nonwise" wherein one affirms that he has a negative property. Then we would have reason for taking the grammatical predicate to form a unit of its own to which certain logical properties accrue. And it could ultimately be the nature of the *property* specified by the predicate

adjective "wise" – that it has a complement – that explains why negation attaches to the predicate, and so why "is wise" forms a single
semantic unit. What is problematic about such an argument is that if
such sentences are equivalent, it is only because we are willing to be
promiscuous in admitting properties into our ontology. If we are
willing to be promiscuous about properties, we ought to be equally
promiscuous in postulating negative and conjunctive objects.[29] And
then we have no reason to think that logical properties accrue to one
kind of expression rather than the other (predicates as opposed to subjects) and no reason to associate the explanation of those logical properties with one kind of metaphysical entity rather than another
(properties as opposed to objects).

Ramsey developed a criticism of Russell that, in a way, reflects such
worries about the existence of negative properties and facts. Ramsey
offered a diagnosis of why Russell and others thought that the predicate of a sentence such as "Socrates is wise" is best represented by the
functional expression "x is wise" and that the predicate symbolizes the
form of the proposition. Ramsey suggests that if we consider some
property-specifying expression such as "wise," we can form two sets
of propositions: one set which includes any sentence with the word
"wise" in it, and another narrower set wherein someone or other has
been said to be wise. The narrower set includes such propositions as
"Socrates is wise," "Aristotle is wise," and "Plato is wise," for these are
all values of "x is wise." The wider set of propositions will also include
sentences that do not attribute wisdom to anyone; it will include such
sentences as "Neither Socrates nor Plato is wise." By contrast, we
cannot analogously form both a wider and narrower set of propositions
involving some subject expression such as "Socrates." There is the set
of propositions which include the word "Socrates," but within that set
of propositions, there is no narrower set of propositions which could
be said to be values of "Socrates is q." For any sentence in which
"Socrates" occurs, that sentence can be said to attribute a property to
Socrates. "Socrates is kind" and "Socrates is bald" attribute properties
to Socrates, but so does "Socrates is neither kind nor bald."[30]

Any sentence involving the word "Socrates" can be said to be about
Socrates and attribute a property to Socrates. That is true even of sen-

29   We can't have a logic that admits both without generating fallacies, but we've been
given no reason to prefer the logic that admits such properties over the one that admits
such objects.
30   Ramsey, "Universals," *Mind*, 34 (136) (1925), pp. 401–17. Reprinted in *The Foundations of Mathematics*, ed. R. B. Braithwaite (Paterson, NJ: Littlefield, Adams, 1960), p. 124.

tences which say that Socrates does not have some property, for it is a property of him that he does not have that property. So far there is no conflicting analogy. Any sentence involving "wise" may be said to be about wisdom and attribute a property to it. This is true even of sentences such as "Neither Socrates nor Plato is wise." The sentence says of wisdom that it has the property of not belonging to Socrates or Plato.

The asymmetry is this. Even if some property has been said to be had by wisdom when we say that wisdom is not possessed by Socrates or Plato, the sentence expressing that cannot be said to provide a value for x in "x is wise." No one has been said to *be wise*. The existence of a negative property of wisdom does not justify us in thinking that wisdom is instantiated in someone. By contrast, the existence of a negative property of Socrates *does* justify us in thinking that Socrates instantiates some property. So, in the set of propositions in which Socrates occurs, we cannot distinguish a wide from a narrow set of propositions, the narrower set being the ones that provide values for "q" in "Socrates is q." There is the set of sentences in which Socrates is said to have some property, but there is no *narrower* set in which the property Socrates is said to have that he instantiates ____. We don't know how to fill in the blank there. We would need a distinction between kinds of properties. We can divide the properties of wisdom into those it has in virtue of being instantiated in someone – this gives us the values of "x is wise" – and any other properties it has. But we cannot similarly divide the properties of Socrates.

Ramsey suggests that this asymmetry is not genuine, and it may be made to disappear, if only we distinguish

> among the properties of Socrates a certain subset which we can call qualities, the idea being roughly that only a simple property is a quality. Then we could form in connection with "Socrates" two sets of propositions just as we can in connection with "wise." There will be the wide set of propositions in which "Socrates" occurs at all, which we say assert properties of Socrates, but also there would be the narrower set which asserts qualities of Socrates. Thus supposing justice and wisdom to be qualities, "Socrates is wise," "Socrates is just" would belong to the narrower set and be values of a function "Socrates is *q*." But "Socrates is neither wise nor just" would not assert a quality of Socrates . . .[31]

If such a distinction could be made, the truth of such a statement as "Socrates is neither wise nor just" would not entail that there exists a

31   Ibid., p. 125.

quality, being unwise and unjust, such that Socrates instantiates that quality. There would be no disanalogy between subjects and predicates. Just as the sentence "Neither Socrates nor Plato is wise" does not assert of someone that he or she is wise – it provides no value for x in "x is wise" – so "Socrates is neither wise nor just" does not assert of Socrates that he has some quality and so supplies no value for q in "Socrates is q." In the case of both "Socrates" and "wise," we can distinguish a narrower set of propositions of the form "Socrates is q" and "x is wise" from the wider set of propositions in which "Socrates" or "wise" occurs, but which are not of that form. Thus, we have no reason to think that the sentence "Socrates is wise" is of the form "x is wise" as opposed to "Socrates is q," no reason to think that the predicate of the sentence and not the subject has the function of carrying the form of the proposition or serving as the propositional indicator.

In addition, the fact that we can form negative and compound predicate expressions gives us no reason to think that such predicates are genuine terms in this sense: we have no reason to think some real quality corresponds to every such combination of words. Similarly, we have no reason to think some individual corresponds to the names that have been combined or negated, as in "Tom and William" or "Not Tom."

Ramsey concludes that the alleged differences between expressions naming properties and those naming individuals arise only because Russell, as a "mathematician," is interested in classes or sets of things, not in their qualities. If we had an interest in distinguishing the qualities of a thing from its properties, then we would see that there is no principled reason to treat the predicate as the expression which has the form of the proposition and no reason to think that predicates, but not subjects, are genuinely compound, negative, and disjunctive.[32]

In conclusion, there is at least some question as to whether the particular–universal distinction does give us a principled reason either to take negation as attaching to the property-specifying expression or to think that the grammatical predicate (the relation-specifying and property-specifying expressions) forms a semantic unit of its own. The very metaphysical facts about the particular–universal distinction which

---

32 Ibid., p. 132. Ramsey's criticism of Russell is best represented in this way: *if* one is going to assume that the metaphysics of properties determines the form of the proposition, one should not be so quick to conclude that the form of the proposition in "Socrates is wise" is "x is wise." For on one construal of the metaphysics of properties, where we distinguish the simple qualities of a thing from its properties, the form of the proposition might equally well be said to be "Socrates is q."

Strawson uses to argue that negation attaches to the property-specifying expression would actually seem to show that if negation does "attach" to some expression in the sentence, it should and does attach to the relation-specifying expression. What is denied when we negate the whole sentence or the predicate of it is that the object *instantiates* the property. Furthermore, we have found no compelling reason to think that the relation-specifying and property-specifying expression may be merged into one semantic unit. Denying that an object instantiates a property is not obviously the same thing as affirming that the object has another, negative property. Thinking that it does has the result of compromising the reality of properties. Finally, even if we were to accept Strawson's explanation of the facts about negation, we have no reason for thinking that that property-specifying expression is the expression in the sentence which somehow relates the other expressions so that they together form a unity – no reason to think that that expression effects propositional combination: for Strawson fails to establish the necessary affinity between negation and propositional combination. Strawson fails to provide a single explanation based in the particular–universal distinction of the logical asymmetries between subjects and predicates and the semantic one (i.e., the referring–predicating distinction that explains the unity of the sentence).

6

Can a Unified Theory of Predication Be Given?

There are different distinctions between subjects and predicates or at least several different properties in virtue of which something is called a subject or predicate expression. We have so far distinguished these notions:

- *Grammatical subject and predicate*: the subject expression is the main noun-phrase; the grammatical predicate is the main verb-phrase.
- *Pragmatic subject and predicate*: the subject identifies what the statement is about; the predicate says something about that object.
- *Semantic subject and predicate*: the subject is the referring expression; the predicate is the attributing expression.
- *Logical subject and predicate*: the subject expression is that to which quantifiers are applied and the predicate is that to which negation, conjunction, and disjunction apply.
- *Metaphysical subject and predicate*: the subject introduces a particular (or something of a lower type relative to the predicate); the predicate introduces a universal (or universal of a higher type than that introduced by the subject).

In this chapter I will examine the relation between these properties. I first focus on whether the properties line up: is there some single thing that has the property of being the grammatical, pragmatic, semantic, and logical predicate, and does it name something of a certain metaphysical kind? If the properties do, or can be made to, line up in this way, is there some single explanation of why the predicate has these various properties? In pursuit of an answer to this question, I next discuss the kind of predicate required by logical theory. I set out Michael Dummett's argument that the predicates required by logical theory presuppose the unity of atomic subject–predicate sentences. If the unity of atomic sentences in turn requires that those sentences have a certain kind of predicate, then the predicates of logical theory presuppose the existence of a distinct kind of predicate required for sentential unity. Put it in terms of the distinctions set out above, there is no single thing that both has the property of being the logical predicate and the semantic predicate. If Dummett's presupposition argument is right, then we should not expect that what makes something a logical predicate (e.g., its introducing a universal) is the same thing that makes it unify basic subject–predicate sentences. This gives us reason for attempting to explain sentential unity in some way other than in terms of the metaphysical kinds introduced by the expressions.

1   The Relation between Various Kinds of Predicates

The pragmatic view would initially seem to challenge the view that various distinctions between subjects and predicates all line up. If identifying what the statement is *about* is associated with being the *referring* expression and having the property of *saying something of* that object is identified with being the *predicating* expression, then referring and predicating would not seem to be associated with grammatical categories or metaphysical kinds. For the same sentence "Socrates is wise" may be used to say of the particular Socrates that he has the property wisdom or may instead be used to say of the property wisdom that it is instantiated in Socrates. The referring expression might on one occasion be the grammatical subject "Socrates," which names a particular, but on another occasion, it may be the grammatical predicate "wise" that names the universal wisdom. And if the grammatical subject "Socrates" can function as predicating expression (as when someone asks "Who is wise?" and one says *"Socrates* is wise"), then the expression functioning to make the predication "Socrates" introduces a particular. This is at odds with Strawson's metaphysical thesis that an expression's introducing a universal (or a universal of higher type) is what makes it the predicating expression.

Strawson may reject this line of argument by rejecting the identification from which it began, saying that the semantic distinction between referring and predicating cannot be identified with "the being about and saying something of" distinction which is pragmatic. Or he may think that even if those are identified, what is fundamental to the semantic distinction between subject and predicate is the distinctive logical properties of subjects and predicates and the metaphysical kinds introduced by the respective expressions.

One problem with the latter line of thinking is that these logical features appear, on the surface, to be pragmatic as well. As Strawson himself points out, one can quantify over both parts of the sentence: there exists a substance, glass, which has the property of being elastic, or, alternatively, there exists a property, that of being elastic, that is instantiated in glass. Which part of the sentence one chooses to quantify over seems to depend on one's interests. Apparently, one can negate both parts of the sentence. Any part of the sentence that might be stressed in different contexts might be negated. Who sold his camera? "Not *Tom*." Or what did Tom sell? "Not *his camera*." Or "What did Tom do with his camera?" "Not *sell it*." All of these are denials of the statement "Tom sold his camera" and have equivalent truth conditions to "Tom did not sell his camera." The negation goes first with the grammatical subject, second with a part of the predicate (the direct object), and then with another part of the predicate (the verb "sell"). Again, this would be seem to be at odds with the metaphysical doctrine. For the metaphysical doctrine held that negation has to go with the expression in the sentence that introduces the highest level concept, but as we've just seen, it does not have to attach to that expression. This challenges Strawson's view that the kind of thing introduced by the expression explains the logical properties of the expression.

While this characterizes a line of argument against Strawson's metaphysical thesis, it is not a convincing one. The proponent of the metaphysical thesis can defend the view by arguing that *when* the grammatical subject functions as pragmatic predicate (and when negation goes with the grammatical subject), the grammatical subject then introduces a concept. Consider *"Socrates* is wise" uttered in answer to "Who is wise?" There, it would appear that although the grammatical subject introduces a particular, it functions as "pragmatic" predicate, saying something about wisdom. Strawson does not discuss this case, but he does discuss Ramsey's pair: "Socrates is wise" and "Wisdom is a characteristic of Socrates":

> If we take this at its face value, we are able, adhering to the grammatical test, to purchase immunity from saying that Socrates is predicated of wisdom, and to say instead that what is predicated of wisdom is the compound of universal and particular, *viz*. being a characteristic of Socrates.

> What we find here is, as it were, an anxiety to preserve the grammatical
> predicate-place of the categorially predicable, even at the cost of faking
> universals to keep up appearances.[1]

Strawson thinks, reasonably, we do not ever say that a particular
(Socrates) is predicated of a universal (wisdom). Instead, we create a
higher-level universal, 'being a characteristic of Socrates,' and we
predicate that of the lower-level universal, wisdom. This would enable
Strawson to offer the following defense against the pragmatic challenge. If we were to express more explicitly what we are saying in
saying "*Socrates* is wise," it would be that wisdom is a characteristic
of Socrates. This shows that when the stress falls on "Socrates" in
"Socrates is wise," "Socrates" does not simply introduce the particular
Socrates, but rather introduces the concept or property of 'being a characteristic of Socrates.' Thus, the asymmetry thesis is preserved. 'Being
a characteristic of Socrates' has its compatibility and incompatibility
ranges vis-à-vis wisdom. (Just as Fido's being a dog rules out his being
a cat, so wisdom's being a characteristic of Socrates rules out its not
being a characteristic of Socrates.) So when the grammatical subject
functions as pragmatic predicate, it will not introduce a particular but
a universal that competes with other universals for possession of what
is introduced by the grammatical predicate.

The proponent of the metaphysical thesis can take the same approach to the alleged counterexamples involving negation. Consider
these three perspicuous expressions of "Tom did not sell his camera":
"Whoever sold his camera, it was not Tom"; "Whatever Tom sold, it
was not his camera"; and "Whatever Tom did with his camera, he did
not sell it." "Not" never appears with the grammatical subject of the
sentence, and there is no reason to take the expression it modifies to be
one that introduces a particular, rather than an expression introducing
a concept – the concept, respectively, of not being identical with Tom,
not being the camera, or not being the selling of it.

The pragmatic distinction between subject and predicate lines up
with the metaphysical thesis: the expression which identifies what the
sentence is about will introduce something of lower type (a particular
or lower-level concept) relative to what is introduced by the expression
which says something of that item. When in the sentence uttered that
appears not to be the case, as in "*Socrates* is wise," there will be a more

---

1   Strawson, *Individuals: An Essay in Descriptive Metaphysics* (London: Methuen, 1959),
p. 175.

perspicuous way of expressing what is expressed when one stresses one or the other word, "Wisdom is a characteristic of Socrates." In that perspicuous expression, the metaphysical thesis holds good. There is, then, a canonical sentence where no violation of the asymmetry thesis occurs. To the question "Why is the sentence that does not violate the asymmetry thesis the preferred one?" Strawson may reply that it gives a single, unified account of subject and predicate across sentences of all types. It is preferred on theoretical grounds.

If it is true that the pragmatic, semantic, logical, and metaphysical features of subjects and predicates line up, what is the relation between these different features? It seems impossible that the logical or metaphysical features could explain the pragmatic facts or vice versa. Regarding the latter, that concepts compete for possession of particulars (or other lower-level concepts) is a fact about particulars and concepts that is completely independent of our interests or of whether an expression carries new or old information. Strawson may concede that different expressions in different contexts may be subject and predicate, but argue that the property owing to which an expression is subject or predicate is not explained by what the speaker is doing with the words, but by the metaphysical type the expressions introduce. Differences in context and stress serve only to *indicate* what the underlying logical form of the sentence is; they do not *determine* what it is.

Still, it is worth noting that, on this view, the words that comprise the sentence do not wear the logical form of the sentence on their sleeves. In "Socrates is wise," "Socrates" may introduce the particular Socrates, or the universal 'being a characteristic of Socrates,' depending upon whether it is the subject of the attribution of wisdom or the predicate predicating a property to wisdom. If pragmatic facts can explain why, in the one case, wisdom is predicated of Socrates or, in the other, why being a characteristic of Socrates is predicated of wisdom, then they may be able to explain why the expressions introduce what they do in the different contexts. If we distinguish the question "What makes one or another expression function as a subject or predicate on a particular occasion?" from the question "How can an expression be a subject or a predicate?" there may be an explanatory role for both the pragmatic and metaphysical theory. The pragmatic facts might supply an answer to the first question and the metaphysical facts an answer to the second.

Suppose, for example, that all kinds of propositional combinations – predicating, attributing, characterizing, instancing, describing, and so on – require that the expressions in the sentence introduce things of different types, one type of a higher level than the other. Then the reason the predicate has to be the expression that represents the higher-level property is, roughly, because in what is attributed, predicated, instanced, described, it is the higher-level property that is ascribed to the lower-level object or property. (Wisdom is what is predicated of or attributed to Socrates; wisdom is what is instanced in Socrates; and being wise is how Socrates is described or characterized as being.) This would vindicate Strawson's view that something cannot be a predicate unless it introduces a higher-level universal relative to what is introduced by the subject.

The pragmatic camp could, nevertheless, argue that metaphysical facts do not explain why one or another expression functions as a predicating expression. That an expression introduces a property that competes with other properties for possession of the object does not explain why an expression functions to effect propositional combination – to represent the property it introduces as instantiated in the object introduced by the subject expression. Indeed, in "*Socrates* is wise," it is only *if* an expression functions to predicate something of the referent of the other expression that it is plausible to take that expression, "Socrates," as introducing something of a higher type. So it is because an expression is effecting propositional combination that it is plausible to take that expression to introduce something of higher type, not vice versa. Cook Wilson and Ramsey would think that the pragmatic context – what the speaker is doing in uttering the words, what new information he is trying to convey, what in the context is presumed known or unknown – determines the function of the expressions, and so therefore why one expression functions to predicate a property of the referent of the other expression. (Of course, the pragmatic account must show how such contextual factors do explain that, if they do.)

It is not clear that Strawson himself would endorse this way of carving up what the pragmatic and metaphysical facts explain. He explicitly discusses the sorts of cases we've been considering, where pragmatic factors affect either the function of the expression or the placement of the negation, but thinks such cases pose no threat to his asymmetry thesis, because the pragmatic facts operate on a "different level of theory" or analysis than that of his asymmetry thesis. The asymmetry thesis concerns the common proposition propounded regardless of which expression is stressed or negated. The proposition expressed is the same whether one says, "*Tom* sold his camera," or "Tom *sold* his camera." The same is true of sentences involving negation: "It was not Tom who sold his camera" and "It was not his camera Tom sold" express the same proposition. Strawson says:

> The upholder of the asymmetry thesis will reply that the facts adduced in this objection are quite beside the point. The sense, invoked in the objection, in which negation may be taken now with one part, now with another part, of a proposition belongs to a different level of theory altogether from that to which the asymmetry thesis belongs. The thesis is not at all concerned with differences in the force with which a proposition or its negation may be propounded, but with the common propounded thing, the proposition or its negation. The point is that negation can never be taken together with the subject of the negated proposition as yielding a new expression of the same kind, or having the same role, as the subject of the original proposition; whereas negation can always be taken together with the predicate of the negated proposition as yielding a new expression of the same kind, or having the same role as, the predicate of the original proposition.[2]

Strawson's claim that negation can never be taken with the grammatical subject to yield a new expression of the same kind may be true. However, it is not clear that the grammatical predicate "not brave" forms a new expression of the same kind as "brave," so it is not clear there is any such asymmetry between subjects and predicates. Suppose the issue is *who* sold his camera. Consider these two assertions: "It was *Tom* who sold his camera"; "It was *not* Tom who sold his camera." The first says that the particular who sold his camera was Tom. The second rules out Tom as the particular who sold his camera. Compare these two assertions, when the issue is what property Tom has: "Tom is brave"; "Tom is not brave." The first says that the property Tom has is being brave; the second rules out brave as being the property Tom has. "Not Tom" does not name another particular. It serves only to rule out Tom as the particular who sold his camera. But, arguably, "not brave" does not introduce another property either. It simply serves to rule out brave as being the property Tom has. So in neither the case of the subject nor the predicate is a new expression of the same kind formed by attaching negation to the expression.[3]

---

2 Strawson, "The Asymmetry of Subject and Predicates," p. 98.
3 Of course, Strawson may argue that "*non*brave" names a negative property and is the same kind of expression as "brave." This would return us to this issue (already discussed) of whether negative properties are real properties.

Let us focus on Strawson's other point that pragmatic factors affect the wrong level of theory. He says that the asymmetry thesis is concerned "with the common propounded thing" – the proposition. In the proposition, the negation has to go with the predicate. We should now be concerned with the level of theory at which Strawson's theory is operating. We started out characterizing differences in the parts of the *sentence* in virtue of which those expressions functioned as subject or predicate expression. That functional difference was supposed to explain how the sentence expresses a proposition. Strawson ends up considering, not the sentence and its parts, but the proposition itself, the parts and form of "the common propounded thing." But it is by no means obvious that what is expressed by a sentence is an entity of any kind, still less that it is an entity with parts which have to be unified or to which negation may attach. Strawson himself, in *Individuals*, says that the literal implication of talk of two nonlinguistic terms, the constituents of the proposition, which must be brought together in producing the unified thing, the proposition, is "logically grotesque." He says, "But we need not necessarily be troubled by those implications; for, even in seeming to play on them, a philosopher may say nothing which could not be re-expressed without dependence on them."[4] From these comments, I take it that he does not mean to postulate propositions as entities.

His talk of the proposition and its form may be intended to distinguish the deep structure of the sentence, its logical form, from its surface structure. Strawson's point might be that the pragmatic factors affect the surface structure of sentences (on some conception thereof), but the asymmetry thesis is meant to be a characterization of the deep structure – a structure common to various sentences that express the same proposition. In the deep structure, subjects and predicates have different logical properties: negation, conjunction, and disjunction are properties of predicates, not of subjects.

The notion of a semantic subject and predicate in the deep structure is justified just in so far as it is required to give an adequate account of the semantics of the sentence. Strawson can say that it is justified because it is required for logical theory. The substantive question then becomes "What *is* the notion of predication needed in logical theory and how is it related to the notion of predication required for the unity of the sentence?" In this final section, though I depart from Strawson's work, I follow up on the question it raises. I examine whether a par-

4   Strawson, *Individuals*, pp. 140–1.

ticular conception of predication is required in the deep structure, so to speak, to properly account for sentences involving quantifiers and logical operators and to explain patterns of inference? And I examine the relation of the logical predicate to the kind of predicate required for sentential unity, investigating whether a single theory can be given to explain both these conceptions of predication. In what follows, I rely heavily on Michael Dummett's characterization of the kind of predicate Frege postulated in revolutionizing logical theory.

2 A Conception of Predication Required for Logical Theory and its Relation to the Unity of the Sentence

I have postponed for some time discussing the conception of predication required in quantification theory. Yet Frege's and Russell's conceptions of predication emerged from their work in the theory of quantification. One might think that, historically, it was the attraction of that particular conception of the predicate for quantification theory that made for a preferred way of analyzing the atomic subject–predicate sentence.[5] The assumption was that a single notion of predication was at work in the phenomena to be explained.

In his *Frege: Philosophy of Language*, Michael Dummett argues that Frege's account of quantification requires that there exist two different classes of sentences, atomic and complex, with correspondingly different kinds of predicates. Complex sentences include sentences with quantifier or modal expressions and sentences with logical operators. (The sentences "Mary loves John" and "Everybody loves somebody" while apparently of the same form are in fact of different form, the first being a simple sentence, the second a complex one.) According to Dummett, the analysis of certain complex sentences, those with more than one quantifier, does give us reason to postulate predicates that are specially incomplete. Such predicates, however, are not to be identified with particular words of the sentence nor are they of certain grammatical categories. So he thinks that Frege made a mistake when he,

---

5 One may have his doubts about whether this is true of Russell's theory. His analysis of sentences involving quantifiers involved the notion of a propositional function, where the propositional function provides a sentence frame containing a free variable, as in "x is wise." But, so far as the theory of quantification goes, we have no reason for thinking that the predicate rather than the subject is the propositional function, for we can quantify over subjects, as in "Socrates is something," and then Russell's analysis would be, "The propositional function 'Socrates is F' is sometimes true."

first, identified the "incomplete" predicate necessary for the analysis of complex sentence with a part of the sentence, the concept-specifying expression, and then second, held that such an incomplete expression was necessary for the sentence to express a proposition or thought. Contrary to what Frege said, Dummett thinks that no part of the atomic sentence is specially incomplete in the sense that the predicates of complex sentences are genuinely incomplete. In the simple sentence "Brutus killed Caesar," the relational expression "killed" may be

> regarded as a simple unitary expression, as much a linguistic entity capable of standing on its own as are the two proper names. Like them, it cannot form a sentence standing on its own (unless the rest of the sentence is understood from the context); but, like them, it constitutes a word that is physically capable of being detached from the sentence.[6]

Dummett concludes that no single notion of predication is to be found which is both required for logical theory and for the unity of atomic sentences.

Complex sentences are distinguished from simple sentences in the way they are constructed. According to Dummett, one insight that contributed to Frege's discovery of quantifier notation was that a sentence involving multiple quantifiers had to be "constructed in stages, corresponding to the different signs of generality occurring in it."[7] Any adequate account of sentences containing more than one quantifier, such as "Everybody loves somebody," must treat the sentence as having been formed in stages, first one part forming a unit of its own; then the other modifying that unit. The idea of different constructional histories is familiar to us in such expressions as "$(2 \times 4) + 3$" as distinct from "$2 \times (4 + 3)$." The operation in the parenthesis is performed first, that product treated as a unit that is then combined with the rest of the expression, resulting in different values corresponding to the different methods of construction. Forming the sentence in these separate stages is to be contrasted to forming it by combining the words simultaneously, in one act, as it were, as in the above sentence "Brutus killed Caesar." This differentiates the atomic from the complex sentence. An adequate analysis of complex sentences cannot treat the expressions as combined in one act, but an adequate analysis of atomic ones can.

6 M. Dummett, *Frege: Philosophy of Language*, 2nd edn. (Cambridge, MA: Harvard University Press, 1981), p. 28.
7 Ibid., p. 10.

The step-by-step analysis of sentences with multiple quantifiers has several theoretical virtues, among the most important of which is that it provides a systematic and non ad hoc way of disambiguating any such sentence, showing which quantifier falls within the scope of the other. We understand "Everybody loves someone" as meaning that for each person there is someone or other that he or she loves, not as meaning that there is some single person that everyone loves. The two paths of step-by-step construction may distinguish the two possible meanings. The history of the construction begins from a simple sentence containing names, for example "John loves Mary." One can form a sentence expressing that, for each person, there is someone or other that he or she loves, by first abstracting out the name "Mary" from "John loves Mary," forming the predicate 'John loves ξ,' then combining this predicate with "somebody" to yield "John loves somebody." Now abstract out the proper name "John," and this yields the new predicate 'ξ loves somebody,' which can be combined with "everybody" to yield "Everybody loves somebody."[8] The order of construction then in "Everybody (loves somebody)" is

1. John loves Mary. (Replace "Mary" with "somebody" and we get –)
2. There is an x such that John loves x. (Replace "John" with "everybody, and we get –)
3. For all y, there is an x, such that x loves y.

If (2) is constructed first and treated as a single unit, then the "everybody" will have to modify that *whole* construction. Thus, 3 is generated, but by this method it impossible to generate 3*, namely "There is an x, such that for all y, y loves x."

Contrast this with the constructional history that does yield that reading; that is, that there is some single person whom everyone loves. The order of construction in "(Everybody loves) somebody" is

1. John loves Mary. (Replace "John" with "everybody," and we get –)
2*. For all y, y loves Mary. (Replace "Mary" with "somebody," and we get –)
3*. There exists an x, such that for all y, y loves x.

Again, if 2* is constructed first and treated as a unit, then "somebody" will have to modify that whole, so generating 3*, but making it impossible to generate 3.

8　Ibid., p. 11.

The method of step-by-step construction can be used to account for phenomena other than quantification, leading to a uniform account of complex sentences. Particularly, "the combination of sentences by means of sentential operators has also to be regarded as part of the step-by-step construction."[9] For example, in "Some people are charming and sincere," "and" is joining expressions, but not by combining the two sentences "Some people are charming" and "Some people are sincere."[10] The sentence, instead, results from the application of "somebody" to the predicate 'ξ is charming and sincere,' which is formed by abstraction from some sentence such as "Peter is charming and sincere." And that sentence is itself formed from the two sentences "Peter is charming" and "Peter is sincere."[11]

Dummett thinks the formation of complex sentences is based on three kinds of operations: "the application of sentential operators to sentences to form new sentences; the omission from a sentence of one or more occurrences of a proper name to form a one-place predicate; and the application of a quantifier to a one-place predicate to form a sentence."[12] Besides the notion of step-by-step construction, the accounts of quantification and combination by sentential operators require a one-place predicate formed by the omission of a proper name. Dummett calls this a *complex* predicate and essential to it is that it is formed from an *already existing* sentence by *abstracting out* the proper name: "Here it is of great importance that the predicate itself is not thought of as having been built up out of its component parts."[13] It is instead a remnant of some previously formed sentence. By contrast, the predicate of an atomic sentence is built up from its parts – the constituent words – and is not formed from an already existing sentence.

Complex and simple predicates explain quite different phenomena. Complex predicates are postulated to explain sentences with multiple quantifiers, sentences involving logical operators and patterns of inference. Regarding inference, consider reasoning from "Brutus killed Caesar" and "Anyone who killed Caesar is an honorable man" to the conclusion "Brutus is an honorable man." Accounting for the legitimacy of the inference may involve recognizing the complex predicate 'ξ killed Caesar' as common to the premises and conclusion. The

---

9   Ibid., p. 15.
10   Ibid.
11   Dummet also argues that the notion of step-by-step construction allows the truth-conditions of sentences involving multiple quantifiers to be reduced in stages to the truth-conditions of atomic sentences. See p. 11.
12   Ibid., p. 16.
13   Ibid., p. 15.

complex predicate is required "only in order to state the general principle to which we are appealing when we recognize an inference."[14]
But "[t]he representation of the sentence as consisting of 'Brutus' and
'ξ killed Caesar' is quite irrelevant to any explanation of the way in
which the sense of the atomic sentence is determined from that of
its constituents."[15]

This is shown by the fact that different ways of analyzing the same
sentence may result in different predicates, depending upon the inference one wants explained. Suppose that Brutus's wife admired Caesar
and would hate anyone who killed Caesar. Then, for that purpose, the
predicate in "If Brutus killed Caesar, Brutus's wife hated Brutus"
would be analyzed as 'If ξ killed Caesar, then Brutus's wife hated ξ.'
But suppose, instead, that Brutus's wife had no special interest in
Caesar, but had an aversion to violence and especially to murder. The
inference depends on the fact that if anyone killed anyone, Brutus's
wife hated that person. Then the predicate in the above sentence might
be represented as 'If ξ killed ψ, then Brutus's wife hates ξ.' Even in
the same sentence there are alternative logical analyses of the predicate
that we might appeal to in explaining an inference.[16] Given that one
and the same sentence contains different such predicates, it is implausible that the predicates are necessary for explaining the unity of the
sentence. Dummett says, "the possibility of giving such an 'analysis' of
the sentence has no bearing on the process by which we form the sentence, or on that by which we come to grasp its sense."[17]

One might insist that the unity of the sentence depends just upon
the occurrence of *one or another* of the predicates. Dummett will say that
this fails to appreciate what a complex predicate is. In the representation of a complex predicate, the Greek letter – the ξ in "ξ killed ξ" –
is not merely a place-holder for a name. Rather, it indicates something
about how the referent of the names must be related to the relation
"killed" itself. So in the sentences "Brutus killed Brutus," "Cassius
killed Cassius," and "Brutus killed Cassius," the complex predicate in

14   Ibid., p. 28.
15   Ibid., p. 29.
16   Recall Frege's example in the *Begriffschrift* of the sentence "Cato killed Cato": on one
way of analyzing it 'killing Cato' is the function on another 'being killed by Cato' is
the function and on yet another 'killing oneself' is the function (*Begriffschrift*, §9, p. 66).
Which analysis is given makes no difference to the content we come to grasp, but only
with the way we come to grasp it. Frege goes on to argue that the distinction between
function and argument makes a difference to content only when the argument becomes
indeterminate (e.g., as when quantification is involved).
17   Ibid., p. 29.

the first two is 'ξ killed ξ,' but, in the third, it is 'ξ killed ψ.' The Greek letters in 'ξ killed ξ' indicate, by convention, that the names which might be substituted for the letters must name the same person, whereas the Greek letters in 'ξ killed ξ' indicate that the names need not do so.[18] Obviously there are other ways to indicate this besides the use of Greek letters, for example free variables, ordered pairs, and so on. The method of symbolization is not important. The point is simply that we need some way *in the symbolism* to indicate the difference between two notions of the "form" of the sentence: a simple notion that might be purely syntactic and a richer notion that is semantically determined. The simpler notion is that sentences which contain relational expressions introducing one-term relations must have one slot for a name; sentences introducing two-term relations must have two slots, and sentences with three-term relational expressions must have three slots, and so on. We might represent the form of those as 'aR,' 'aRb,' 'aRbc.' According to this conception of the form of the sentence, we've been given no indication of or restrictions on how the relata named by the names must be related to each other and to the relation R. When, however, one represents the form of the sentence relevant for constructing complex sentences and preserving inferences, the letters in the gap of the relation do indicate something about how the terms of the relation must be related to each other and to the relation in question, as in 'ξ killed ξ' versus 'ξ killed ψ.' The first tells us that the terms of the relation must be the same and is a suicide, the second that they may be different, and so may be a murder.

Dummett argues that this notion of a complex predicate cannot figure in any account of how the parts of the sentence combine to express a proposition, for such a predicate is not a part of the sentence but, rather, a feature the sentence has given that it has the meaning it does. The existence of the complex predicate presupposes the unity of the atomic sentence:

> The complex predicate 'ξ killed ξ' cannot be regarded as literally part of the sentences in which it occurs; it is not a word or string of words, not even a discontinuous string. There is no *part* in common to the sentences "Brutus killed Brutus" and "Cassius killed Cassius" which is not also a part of the sentence "Brutus killed Cassius," yet the predicate 'ξ killed ξ' is said to occur in the first two and not the third. Such a complex predicate is, rather, to be regarded as a *feature* in common to the two sentences, the feature, namely that in both the simple relational expression

18   Dummett, *Frege*, p. 31.

"... killed ..." occurs with the same name in both of its argument-places. ... It is precisely in this sense that an expression is said by Frege to be "incomplete"; it does not consist merely of some sequence of words or symbols, but *in the occurrence within sentences of such a sequence standing in a certain uniform relation to terms occurring in those sentences*. It is for this reason that it cannot literally be removed from a sentence in which it occurs and displayed on its own; we can only indicate the common feature of various sentences which we have in mind by the use, together with words or symbols belonging to the language, of the Greek letters, which represent argument-places. And it is, in turn, just because the incomplete predicate is thus not really an expression – a bit of language – in its own right, that we are compelled to regard it as formed from a sentence rather than as built up of its components.[19]

The complex predicate is not a word or collection of words, nor can it be identified with a grammatical category. That "Brutus killed Brutus" contains the predicate 'ξ killed ξ' cannot be explained by the three words considered *in isolation*; nor is it explained by the fact that the word "killed" names a two-place relation. Nor is it explained by the fact that the relata of the two-place relation-specifying word "killed" are the names "Brutus" and "Brutus," for we would still have to know that "Brutus" names the same object in each occurrence. Suppose "killed" specifies the two-place relation killing and the two occurrences of "Brutus" name the same person, is that sufficient for explaining why the predicate of that sentence is 'ξ killed ξ'? No, for that collection of symbols might still be just a list. It is only if that collection of symbols "Brutus killed Brutus" represents it as being the case that the man Brutus killed himself, that we can say it has the predicate 'ξ killed ξ.' The predicate is a feature present in the sentence given that the sentence means what it does. It is only if the parts of the sentence are unified to express a proposition that this feature of the sentence emerges. Thus, such a notion of predication can play no part in explaining how the parts of the sentence combine so that they together express the proposition they do.[20]

This discussion has taken us some distance from Strawson. Strawson suggests that, because of the kind of logical properties that accrue to predicates, the proposition must have a certain kind of subject and predicate. I interpreted this to mean that in the deep structure of the sentence a certain kind of predicate is required by logical theory.

19   Ibid., p. 31 (my emphasis).
20   See Dummett, p. 31.

Dummett argues that a certain notion of predication is indeed required by logical theory, but precisely because of the kind of predicate this is, such predicates play no role in the account of the unity of basic sentences. The logical predicate is a semantic feature common to many sentences, given that they have the meaning they do.[21] As such, the unity of the atomic sentence is *presupposed* in the idea of such a predicate. There appears, then, to be no single phenomenon of "predication" found in the notion of the logical predicate and in that part of the atomic sentence that predicates something of the object of reference. Dummett himself does not discuss whether the unity of the sentence is explained by some distinctive feature of the grammatical predicate, but he argues that the predicate is just another word in the sentence, no more complete or incomplete than another. He may reject the idea that any part of the sentence effects propositional combination. But if the unity of the sentence is to be explained by the distinctive function of the predicate, then what we should take from Dummett's argument is that such a predicate must exist and perform its function in order for there to be such a thing as a feature predicate. Thus, there is no single thing that has the property of being both the logical predicate and the predicate that effects propositional combination.

I draw two conclusions from this discussion. The first is that what is needed, fundamentally, to explain the unity of the sentence is an account of the unity of basic or atomic subject–predicate sentences. The unity of complex sentences – ones involving quantifiers and logical operators – can be explained, in some way, in terms of operations we perform on atomic sentences or on "feature" predicates that are abstractions from these already unified subject–predicate sentences.

Second, the facts about logical predicates give us no reason to think that the unity of atomic subject–predicate sentences is explained by the parts introducing things of certain metaphysical kinds – particulars and universals. If a certain kind of predicate must exist to effect, in part, the unity of atomic subject–predicate sentences and this predicate is distinct from and antecedent to that of the logical predicate, then, even if it is true that properties of logical predicates are explained by their

21   These predicates are in their nature general: such a predicate is the common property in what is expressed by various sentences. This might provide a different way of understanding Strawson's idea that it is the connection of a predicate with a property or concept, a thing of that metaphysical kind, that explains why we can form negative, disjunctive, and compound predicates. We can form such predicates, because they identify what is expressed by the sentences that have this feature in common, and it is what is expressed that is negated, compounded, or made disjunctive.

relation to universals, it won't follow that the properties of the atomic predicate in virtue of which it predicates a property to an object is explained by that expression's introducing a universal.

The recognition of this might free us from the association of the unity of atomic sentences with the distinction between the metaphysical kinds introduced by its parts. For that association comes about because philosophers have so often believed, first, that the predicate's designating a universal can explain its logical properties, and, second, that we should seek a unified account of predication. If the metaphysical kind can explain the logical properties of predicates, and if there is a single thing that has both the properties of the semantic predicate and the logical predicate, then the metaphysical kind designated by an expression might explain why that expression functions to make a predication to the object of reference. But if there is no single thing that has both these properties (for the existence of logical predicate presupposes the existence of a predicate that contributes to propositional combination), then we should not expect the relation of the logical predicate to a universal to explain the unity of the sentence.

What seems clear to me is that we do not gain an adequate account of sentential unity from consideration of the metaphysical nature of the things introduced by the parts of the sentence, despite the efforts of Frege, Russell, and Strawson to provide one. Strawson's analysis of concepts may provide a lucid explanation of the logical properties of predicates. But, in my opinion, he fails to establish the required connection between those logical properties and an expression's functioning to *predicate a property of* the object of reference. In the end, he does not show those logical properties are necessarily connected with the notion of predication required to account for the unity of the sentence. Nor does he show how the fact that an expression designates a concept or universal can explain its effecting propositional combination.

While I cannot say that no such account can be given, it seems to me that enough has been said to justify trying a different tack. The unity of the sentence has been made mysterious because, historically, it was enmeshed in the nature of the distinction between particular and universal or concept, and, sometimes, more problematic still, in the unity wherein the universal inheres in the particular or the object saturates the concept. Cook Wilson said:

> The futility of representing the problem of the relation of universal and particular as one of predication, or as the problem of predication, is revealed at once if we demand, as we reasonably may, that the technical

term "predication" be replaced by what it means. If predication means simple assertion, it would be absurd to describe the metaphysical difficulty of the inherence of the universal in the particular as a problem of assertion.[22]

As Cook Wilson here reminds us, the question about the unity of the sentence is just about assertion or representation. We might make better progress on that question by investigating whether the pragmatic distinction Cook Wilson himself sets out could explain how the parts combine to express a proposition, and to attempt to provide an account of basic subject–predicate sentences.

22   Cook Wilson, *Statement and Inference with Other Philosophical Papers*, vol. 1, p. 146.

Part III

A Pragmatic Account of the Unity of the Sentence

7

The Causal Asymmetry between Subject and Predicate and the Unity of the Sentence

1 Introduction

It is natural for us to think of a sentence as a static thing. Maybe we tend to think too much of written sentences and not of the active speaking of sentences. But our written language itself represents the sounds that people speak, and speech is what is fundamental in language. Speaking is an event, a kind of action.

When we say something, we perform an act that is made up of other acts, as one utters this and then another word. Whether the successive smaller acts combine to make the single larger act of saying something is not determined just by what the constituent acts may be or even by the order in which they occur. It depends on the context in which the successive acts occur, but the context matters, I think, mainly because it tells us *why* the words occur as they do. Even when the right words are uttered one after another in the right temporal order, the words might then together express a proposition or they might not. Their successive utterance might just coincidentally represent the words of a sentence, and their utterances together fail to constitute a single act of saying something. Consider the utterance "The cat is on the mat. Is its bed occupied?" This has the words "the mat is its bed" in it, but they do not make up something the speaker says. He does not say that the mat is its bed. It is not enough that they happen to fit together, in such a way that one *might*, in uttering them, be making that statement. They must be *fitted* together, somehow, by the speaker, or by what the speaker is doing in uttering them, or by the surrounding context. Just as the pieces of a jigsaw puzzle which are shaped so they will fit together must still be put in the right places to be fitted together, so words that will fit together to make a sentence must still be fitted together before a statement is made. It is hard to see what this additional factor that makes the words a sentence might be, except something the utterer *has done in* uttering the words in that order.

The "unification" of the utterance of several words into single assertions is an instance of something common to complex acts of all kinds. The sentence is a whole greater than the sum of its parts, because the sentence has representational properties its parts do not have. The simple sentence represents something as being the case, but no one of its parts does so. This phenomenon is not essentially linguistic. There are all kinds of acts comprising other acts which are nonetheless wholes having properties that none of their parts has. The batter's striking out is an act made up of three distinct acts, three swings, no one of which alone has the property the whole act has, of being an out. The swings of the bat constitute the act of striking out, because the batter does what he does in a particular context – he is "at bat," his swing fails to contact the ball, and the thrown balls he swings at are "pitches."

The idea has not been adequately tried that the unity of the sentence lies in the speaker's performing a certain act in a certain context. The rough idea is this: a sentence is what is said (or asked, commanded, exclaimed, etc.). Saying is an act comprising other constituent acts. What explains the unity of the act of saying explains the unity of the sentence. What explains the unity of the act is the way (the explanations of) the constituent acts are interrelated in the context in which they occur.

The attempt to give "pragmatic" explanations of semantic phenomena has long been a commonplace of the philosophy of language. It is a familiar idea since Wittgenstein's *Investigations* that the meaning of an expression is associated with the speaker's use of it in a particular context. And an expression's referring to an object has been identified with the speaker's using it to make reference to that object. The statement made is thought to depend on what, in particular, one has referred to, and what one has meant by the words one has uttered. What one says, to the extent that it depends on what one has referred to and what one has meant, depends at bottom on the intentions of the speaker in uttering those words. Paul Grice analyzed the meaning of a sentence in terms of what utterers of the sentence generally mean or would mean by it, and the fundamental concept "utterer's meaning" was identified with what the speaker intends his audience to come to believe by means of the recognition that he intends it to be believed.[1] Analyses of the "pragmatic" kind just mentioned suggest that the features of the context which explain the semantic properties of the utterance are principally ones that enter into the causal explanation of the act, as the intention to make a certain utterance is what causes the utterance to be made and, if the intention is of the right kind, what confers meaning upon that utterance.

Consider again a speaker who, as he uttered the pair of sentences "The cat is on the mat. Is its bed occupied?" uttered the string of words "the mat is its bed." This speaker presumably did not intend by "its mat is its bed" to impart any belief or to do any other single thing by the utterance of those words, and that would explain (along the lines of Grice) why he would not have meant anything by those words, and so why they did not mean that its mat is its bed. While this string of words have the syntactic potential, they do not have the *actual* unity of a statement, because – so it seems – there is no relevantly unitary explanation of their actually occurring in the context given. The explanation of the utterance "the mat" is bound up with the explanation of "The cat is on," while the explanation of "is its bed" is bound up with that of "occupied." There is no such connection between the explanation of "the mat" and the explanation of "is its bed." This suggests that the words combine to express a proposition when there is a single thing that would explain the utterance of the words or, at least, when the explanations of the constituent parts of the sentence are essentially interlocking or interdependent. We might look for the basic source of the unity of the sentence in the unity of such underlying explanations.

The simple underlying explanation may be just that the speaker uttered something which is grammatically a sentence, and in uttering that, intended to refer to something and intended to say something about that thing. In many cases, this seems to be all that is required in order for the utterance to express a proposition. But however true it may be – that one succeeds in saying something so long as one's intention to say something explains one's utterance – without an analysis of *intending to say*, this does not advance our understanding of the concept of saying: for intending to say something contains the concept under analysis, saying.

We might try, instead, a Gricean intention as the underlying explanation of the utterance of the sentence. What explains the fact that, in

---

1 Cf. H. P. Grice, "Meaning," *Philosophical Review*, 66 (1957), pp. 377–88.

the utterance of the sentence, the parts combine together to express a proposition is that the speaker intends to produce a certain belief in the audience, and that intention explains the speaker's making the utterance he does. This may suffice to define utterance meaning and maybe more abstract attributions of meaning as well. But it relies on the notion of the propositional content of the *belief* that the utterer intends the audience to come to have. It is a key feature of Grice's proposal that what the utterance means is *exactly* what the audience is intended to believe. While it is true that a single sentence may express a single belief, an explanation of the unity of a sentence in those terms is useless, for what constitutes a single belief is, in turn, nothing but what can be expressed by a single *sentence*. The two concepts take in each other's laundry. There is, in addition, a strong case for supposing that beliefs and other propositional attitudes themselves are representations with a componential structure (that they are complexes of simpler parts) and that the question about the unity of the propositional attitudes is so similar to the question about the unity of the statement that it is hopeless to attempt to account for the one in terms of the other.

So, to pursue the idea suggested by the pragmatic approach to the analysis of meaning, we will want to look into the inner structure of an utterance, not at the pragmatic properties of the complete utterance, but at the distinctive pragmatic properties of their parts. We have, already, in Cook Wilson and Ramsey, a tradition that associates the functional difference between subject and predicate with pragmatic facts, such facts determining whether an expression functions to identify what the statement is about or to say something about that object. The sentence represents something as being the case because the one part identifies what the statement is about and the other says something of that object.

This platitude opens the way to the account I will develop at length. But immediately, a question arises about the depth of an analysis in terms of the function of the parts. Certainly, if the function can be characterized only in terms of what an expression functions to *say* about something, or in terms of an expression indicating what object it is about which something is being *said*, the analysis will seem to be circular. For we want to know how the parts hang together in such a way that some single thing is said, and it is not very helpful to know that they hang together by one of them functioning to say something about the object that the other indicates is that about which something is being said.

My own investigation, to follow, locates the source of the unity of the proposition in relations of causal dependencies which I think underlie and define the functional concepts of subject and predicate, and my effort is devoted to spelling out the nature of the dependency relations themselves. My discussion will eventually concern a pattern of dependency between (roughly speaking) the respective causal explanations of the occurrence of the subject and predicate expression in the utterance of a string of words that expresses a proposition. The causal pattern I am concerned with is quite specific, but it is rich enough, I think, to allow substantial answers to a number of questions about how an utterance that has such an explanation constitutes a representation of a single state of affairs. I do not assert that every utterance of a sentence in which the speaker is allowed to be "saying" something, or "making a predication," or representing something as being the case is a case that exhibits the specific causal pattern with which I will be so much concerned. On the contrary, I think that in many cases, where something is said, nothing more is present in the causal explanation of the act than that the speaker intended to say something or intended his audience to come to have a certain belief. But since such cases involve, in one way or another, the semantic concept under analysis, such cases do not reveal, in any interesting way, how the parts of sentence combine to say something.

I will focus on cases of what I take to be a fundamental kind. But my aim is not to provide an account of how any and every sentence has unity. (The reader will easily be able to think of cases that do not work like the cases I describe.) Providing such an account would likely be as complicated as language itself. There are many kinds of sentences besides simple subject–predicate sentences, for example sentences that involve quantifiers and logical operators. If Dummett's interpretation of Frege is right, accounting for the unity of such sentences will involve understanding operations on more basic subject–predicate sentences. And once certain basic sentences have meaning, speakers can combine and recombine them and their parts in many different ways. Even the account of how very simple subject–predicate sentences have unity may differ, since the unity of some may be less basic than that of others, in the sense described above, that an account of their unity may be highly intentional and parasitic on the unity of other utterances of such sentences. So I do not suggest that every sentence does possess its unity in the same way. My project is simply to understand how *some* very basic subject–predicate sentences have unity and to do so, relying as little as possible on the semantic concepts under analysis.

I begin from the pragmatic distinction noted by Ramsey and explicated by Cook Wilson: which expression identifies what the statement
is about and which says something of that object depends, in Ramsey's
words, on "the point of view from which we approach the fact" or on
our "centre of interest."[2] If we are interested in what properties Socrates
has, "Socrates is wise" will say of Socrates that he is wise. If we are
interested in the question in whom is wisdom instantiated, that same
sentence may say of wisdom that it is instantiated in Socrates. Frege
thinks that what is regarded as the subject or predicate has to do with
how one comes to grasp the thought or proposition, where the same
thought may be grasped in different ways. The distinction may, as
Cook Wilson suggests, be a matter of which expression the speaker
intends to carry new or old information given the beliefs of the speaker
and audience. What is known or not known by a given speaker, what
is at issue and what is taken for granted in the particular context, determines the function of the expressions.

None of these philosophers tries to use this pragmatic distinction to
provide an account of sentential unity. Frege and Cook Wilson want to
emphasize that the distinction is of no importance to logic. Frege says,
"A distinction between *subject* and *predicate* finds *no place* in my representation of a judgment."[3] He justifies this by arguing that which
expression is subject and which is predicate has no influence on "the
possible consequences" of the judgment, because it does not in any way
affect the "conceptual content" of a judgment.[4] Cook Wilson says that
the subject – predicate distinction, properly defined, "is a matter of no
great moment, for the distinction is of no importance in logic proper,
and indeed of no use whatever for the solution to the usual problems
in logic."[5]

But even though the distinction does not correspond to one in the
"conceptual content" of what is expressed by a sentence, it does not
follow that the distinction does not contribute to the explanation of *how*
the sentence *comes to have* a conceptual content. It is true that the sentence "Theaetetus flies" expresses one and the same proposition and
that it functions the same in any argument, whether it is taken to say
of Theaetetus that he flies or say of flying that Theaetetus does it. At
the same time, it may be essential to its expressing that proposition that

2   Ramsey, "Universals," p. 116.
3   G. Frege, *Begriffschrift*, §3, p. 53.
4   Ibid., p. 54.
5   J. Cook Wilson, *Statement and Inference with Other Philosophical Papers*, vol. 1, p. 124.

there be one constituent that plays one of these roles and another that plays the other. Further, it may be that neither role can be played, by whatever expression might play it, unless the other expression plays the other role. This in fact is what seems to be the case: certainly no expression can function to say something about something unless there is an expression that functions to indicate what it is being said about, and no expression can function to indicate what it is about which something is being said unless some expression functions to say something about it.[6] The two expressions are complementary and the functioning of one dependent upon the functioning of the other. It is this fact that suggests that an understanding of the unity of the sentence might emerge from a deeper understanding of the way these two functions depend upon one another. Throughout, I will focus on those features of the causal explanations of the constituent acts – the utterance of subject and of predicate – that might explain the functional role of those parts. Unless otherwise specified, I will use the words "subject" and "predicate" to mean *pragmatic* subject and pragmatic predicate (in distinction from "syntactic" and "metaphysical") – the subject identifying what the statement is about, the predicate saying something of that object.

2   The Connection and Asymmetry between the Respective Explanations of the Subject and Predicate

Cook Wilson argues that whether an expression, for example "elastic" in "Glass is elastic," is used to make reference to the topic of elasticity or to say something about glass depends upon facts about the utterance of the sentence, the act of uttering it. It depends upon one's reasons for, or the causes of, one's uttering the expression "elastic." He then defines the distinction between subject and predicate as follows:

> The subject of the statement may be defined as what we were thinking about as we thought, or conceived it, before we arrived at the statement, or before we had the statement communicated to us, while the predicate is the new fact which we state about it or have communicated to us. Or, to put it otherwise, the subject is what we were thinking of, as we thought

6   The two expressions need not occur in the same sentence (as when someone says "gray" in response to the question "What color is the cat?") or may be implicit in the context.

it or conceived it, before forming the judgement, opinion, or belief which the statement expresses, or to which, at least it corresponds, while the predicate is the new fact, or what we suppose to be the new fact which we do not know about it; in other words the new thing which we state about it.[7]

This difference between subject and predicate is suggested by what the speaker is doing in uttering the words of the sentence, by the fact that he or she is making an assertion. Specifically,

> assertion is either for the information of others, or merely the verbal expression of knowledge or opinion we have arrived at for ourselves. Clearly the purpose of assertion is, in the one case, not to inform others of what they already know of a given subject, but to tell them something which will be new to them . . .[8]

The pragmatic facts that distinguish subject from predicate are characterized by the psychological states of the speaker and audience – their beliefs and interests, what they already know or don't know, what will be new or old information for them. But what is fundamental to the examples is the difference in which expression *purports to carry information*. Using Strawson's example of the sentence "Raleigh smokes," if one wants to know something about smoking, "Raleigh" will purport to carry information about that subject: "smokes" will not purport to carry information about Raleigh. By contrast, if one wants to know what Raleigh does, then "smokes" will, in that context, purport to carry such information about Raleigh, and "Raleigh" will not purport to carry information about smoking.

Once Cook Wilson defines the subject–predicate distinction and differentiates it from other distinctions, he does not develop it further. This was unfortunate, for there was already present in his characterization a good suggestion as to the source of the unity of the sentence. From the point of view of the speaker, the function of the pragmatic predicate is to provide information about the referent of the pragmatic subject. If the speaker intends the utterance of the predicate to provide information about the referent, that constrains what will explain or

---

7   Ibid., p. 118.
8   Ibid., p. 119. Cook Wilson refines his characterization of the distinction in the pages that follow. See pp. 120–4. But his general conclusion is that the question of what is subject or predicate "admits of no answer, if we have no help either from the context, or from stress or from special grammatical form" (p. 126).

cause the occurrence of the predicate. What explains the occurrence of that predicate should be determined by, dependent upon, what the *referent* is: in particular, what explains the utterance of the predicate should do so *because of* its relation to the referent. If, for example, the speaker intends to provide information about the cat, then what causes the occurrence of the predicate might be the property of the cat he wishes his audience to know it has. If the referent, in turn, explains his uttering the referring expression, then the separate utterances of subject and predicate are in that case not isolated or unconnected events. Rather, there is an interconnection between the explanations of the two utterances, the "tokenings" of the two expressions, the cause of the tokening of the predicate dependent upon the cause of the tokening of the subject. Thus, from the function of the pragmatic predicate, we can begin to find unity in the act of utterance – in the connection between the respective explanations of the tokenings of the two expressions – for the explanation of the predicate depends on that of the subject. This connection between the causes of the two utterances may explain why the expressions themselves manage to perform their different functions and why the whole utterance of which they are parts expresses a proposition.

The idea that the relation or interconnection between the causes of constituent events unifies the whole has application to other phenomena. It has an application to the question of what makes the several movements that constitute any ordinary complex action, like walking up the stairs, or throwing a stone, a single action. And it has a closer application to the phenomenon of natural representations. (Natural representations provide useful models because they exhibit what is essential to representation without the distractions of psychology or convention.) For instance, consider a rock formation from which some piece of geological history can be reconstructed, perhaps a stratified formation with a layer of coal above a layer of limestone. The coal is the remains of an ancient forest and may be said to "represent" a forest. The limestone is the deposit of an ancient sea and it represents a sea. But the whole formation does not just represent or "list" two things, the forest and the sea. Rather, the fact that the coal stratum sits above the limestone – that spatial relation – represents it as being the case that the sea came before the forest. The spatial relation between the constituents of the representation represents a temporal relation as obtaining between the forest and sea. What explains the unity of the representation is that the temporal relation between the causes, the forest and the sea, determines the spatial relation between the strata.

So there is, first, a relation or interconnection between the separate causal explanations of the constituent events, a temporal relation between the forest and the sea. Second, that temporal relation between the causes governs the spatial relation that obtains between the constituent deposits themselves. There is a causal law governing the production of the representation whereby what comes later in time gets deposited on top of what comes earlier. The fact that the coal and limestone stand in the spatial relation they do then carries the information that the sea was present before the forest. Following this analogy, we want to look for some relation between causes of the constituent words which will explain why the fact that the words stand in the relation they do – in the subject–predicate relation – represents the things designated by those words as related in some specific way.

Whether an utterance expresses a proposition is similarly determined by whether there is the right sort of interconnection between the explanations of the constituents of that utterance. Consider a case in which what explains the utterance of the predicate does not depend upon what explains the utterance of the subject. Here is such a case: you've been struggling to finish a crossword puzzle, the remaining item being a four-letter word and the clue being "the color of Forrest's coat." Just then, the animal control officer knocks at your door. You go to the door asking yourself who this Forrest might be. You are asked the color of your cat. You start to answer, "The cat is . . ." but at just that moment the solution to the puzzle dawns on you – it is the Confederate General Bedford Forrest: "Gray," you blurt out, distracted from the inquiry about the cat. It seems clear that, in such a case, you have not, in uttering that string of words, "The cat is gray," predicated the property of being gray to the cat (though you will mistakenly be taken to have done so). While you have uttered parts of speech, "The cat" and "is gray," of which one might make a sentence, you did not here utter the sentence "The cat is gray" and certainly you did not say that the cat was gray. The reason that you did not is that the explanations of the two utterances are not connected in the right way. In particular, something's being gray did not cause the tokening of "gray," because it was appropriately related to the object that caused the subject expression, the cat. Of course there is a "single" explanation of the occurrence of the words in that sequence, which I gave in telling the story – in the minimal sense that any "coincidence" has a single explanation. But it is not an explanation in which the causal factors mentioned are related to one another in a relevant way. It is not an explanation of the relevant kind.

The relevant kind is not easy to specify. There are other sorts of cases where we do regard two utterances as part of the same speech act, even though they come in a salient way from different sources. There is the wife who, in company, completes the sentences of her slow-talking husband. Telling their friends a story, he says, "The policeman got out of his car, came over and started to write me a ticket. Then he—" Before he can finish, the wife blurts out, "dropped dead on the side of the road." The subject and predicate of the sentence – the words "Then he dropped dead on the side of the road" – were uttered by different people. Yet, she has "finished her husband's sentence," so there was a sentence composed by the utterances of two people. The separate utterances together do make a statement, do represent something as being the case. Here the explanations of the occurrence of the subject and predicate expressions are connected in the right way. Roughly, what explains her saying "F" *is* connected in the relevant way to what explains his saying "x." The connection is not, so to speak, just at the level of the words uttered, but at the level of the referents of those words. For the utterances are connected in such a way that there is, putatively, a piece of information presented by the sequence of utterances, about what he was referring to when he said what he said before she butted in. Assuming that that object, or something about it, explains his uttering the words whereby he referred to it, the explanation of his utterance is connected to the explanation of her utterance.

So far, these cases are merely suggestive. What is needed is something much more concrete, namely an understanding of exactly what explains the functional difference – the pragmatic asymmetry – that Cook Wilson points out between the referring and predicating expression, and of whether that difference can explain the unity of the sentence. (Of course the difference concerns what the speaker is doing, in uttering the one or the other expression, but I wish to see whether there are not other and more revealing concomitants of this difference.) The difference in function may be brought out by seeing what factor changes from one context to another, when the function of the expression changes, so isolating those factors that explain why one or the other expression serves the function it does.[9] Cook Wilson does not himself develop such an explanation, but the method for doing so is implicit in his examples. As he points out, various expressions in the

9   Some of the material that follows is from my paper "The Unity of the Sentence and the Connection of Causes," *Philosophy and Phenomenological Research*, 58 (4) (1998), pp. 827–45.

very same sentence may perform these different roles, functioning either as a referring or as an attributing expression, depending upon what's being used to provide information about what. So all we need to do is see what changes from one context to the next in virtue of which the function of the expressions changes. This should serve to isolate the phenomenon of predication so we can see it for what it essentially is, separate from the syntactic and other semantic features of the expressions. For so long as we are considering the utterance of one and the same sentence, nothing changes in the syntax, and we may stipulate that nothing changes in the semantic value of the constituents. While in one utterance of the sentence, "smokes" does the predicating and "Raleigh" the referring, in another the roles are reversed: but in either case "Raleigh" is the grammatical subject and it designates Raleigh, while "smokes" remains the grammatical predicate and designates the property of smoking, and the truth conditions of the statement, whether it's about smoking or about Raleigh, are exactly the same. Since all semantic features stay the same except which expression functions as referring or attributing expression, the factor that determines what element does the attributing should stand out in relief.

I will here consider a limited number of fairly straightforward examples, my aim being to isolate those cases where the contrast is most sharp so the exact difference may be clearly discerned. This will uncover and characterize what it is that changes from context to context when the function of the expression changes. I will argue that what expression functions as pragmatic predicate is correlated with a certain causal fact or datum. But I postpone until later any explanation of how this causal fact might be made to account for the functional role of the predicate and the consequent unity of the sentence.

Consider, then, a single sentence, uttered in two different situations, in which the pragmatic subject and predicate switch around. To bring out the difference, we may, as Cook Wilson does, suppose that one or another question has been asked of the speaker. In the first situation, a child has lost both of her pets, a cat and a dog. She is asking around the neighborhood to see if anyone has seen them; a neighbor tells her he has just seen a cat and asks her, "What color is your cat?" She replies, "The cat *is gray*." The expression "The cat" functions here as the pragmatic subject, marking the cat as the referent of the sentence, while "gray" functions as pragmatic predicate, attributing the color gray to the cat. In the second situation, there is a rabid animal at large that has bitten someone in the neighborhood, but all the victim knows is that the animal that bit him was gray. Animal control officials are now going around the neighborhood asking what pets in the area are gray, and they ask the child, "Do you know of any gray pets in the neighborhood?" Pointing at her cat, she says, "*The cat* is gray." Here "gray" functions as the subject, marking the color gray or, more fully, gray pets as the topic, while "The cat" functions as the predicate, supplying information about what pet is that color.

In each case, the question asked indicates what information is being sought, and identifies what that information is supposed to be information about. "What color is your cat?" identifies the color of the cat as the topic. The respondent is to provide information about that. In other words, *the cat's being the color that it is* is to be the reason she says what she does. (Notice the issue is the reason someone says what she does, not what conscious process of reasoning precedes the utterance.) The other question "Do you know of any gray pets?" identifies gray pets as the topic, and the answer is to provide information about what pet has that color. *A certain pet's being of the color gray* is to be the reason the child says what she does.

In both cases, the inquirer identifies what is to be the reason for her saying what she says in response. If reasons are causes, it identifies what is to be the cause of her saying that.[10] The questions serve to define the range of possible appropriate explanations or causes of the response. What constitutes the difference in the two cases is not necessarily that distinct actual states of affairs explain the utterance as the subject differs, for the cat's being gray and gray's being the color of the cat are not two distinct states of affairs. The difference is, rather, that different *ranges* of possible states of affairs *might* explain it (consistently with the directives of the operative question). Where the issue is the color of the cat, the color of the cat, whatever it may be, is to explain the utterance: the range of states of affairs that could explain the utterance consistently with the directives of the question is thus either the cat's being *white* or the cat's being *gray* or the cat's being *black*, and so on. The child is supposed to single out one of these possible states of affairs as the actual one. Where the issue is instead whether there are any gray pets around, what is to explain the utterance is some pet's being gray. The range of states of affairs that could explain the utterance consistently with the directives of the question differs accordingly: it is the *cat's* being gray or the *dog's* being gray or the *goat's* being gray, and so on.

10 In speaking of its cause or explanation – as if there were a single one – I shall always mean the salient cause or explanation as distinguished from background causal conditions.

Of course, things may not go as they are supposed to go. The child may not respond to the question at all or she may, as children often do, say something irrelevant to the question asked. And what ultimately matters to what *her* utterance means is not what the questioner asks but what the child is doing in saying what she says. But suppose that, in each case, she intends to answer the relevant question. Now how might the difference between the ranges of states of affairs that could cause the utterance in the two cases explain why one or the other expression does the predicating?

Consider first, the case where the issue is the color of the cat. If the color of the cat, whatever it might be, is to explain the occurrence of the utterance, then the color that does figure in the explanation of the utterance will do so *because of its relation* to the cat: in the simplest cases, because that color *is* the color of the cat. Suppose the child says that the cat is gray because the cat is gray, so it is the color gray that explains the token utterance "gray." Here the color gray, rather than some other color, is the cause of the utterance of the predicate because of its relation to the cat – in this case, because it is the color of the cat.[11] It would not in this case cause the utterance by virtue of being the color of the *sky*, for instance. But in this case (where the question is the color of the cat), the cat's being the cause of "The cat" does not depend on its having the color that causes the utterance of the predicate. For if we ask, "Why was the cat the object that explains the utterance of 'The cat' in the utterance 'The cat is gray'?" the answer is *not* that the cat is gray. The reason that the cat, rather than the dog or goat, explains the utterance of "The cat" (or of the grammatical subject) has nothing to do with the fact that the cat is gray. The speaker and hearer are talking about the cat because it is lost, not because it is gray. So the cat's capacity to cause this reference to itself does not depend on its being gray or any other particular color. Had the cat been white (and the speaker knew it), then other things being the same, "The cat" would still occur in the utterance – though followed by "is white." In other situations, the cat may be the topic for reasons other than the fact that it is lost. But so

11   To say that the property gray is the cause of the utterance is, of course, imprecise, since strictly states of affairs or events are causes, not properties. My talk of an object or property causing an utterance will always be short for "the object or property 'figuring in the explanation' of the utterance." But the latter language is too cumbersome to use and obscures the presentation of the idea. When the nature of the interconnection between the causes of subject and predicate is later technically specified, it will be a relation between constituents of the states of affairs that give rise to the respective utterances of subject and predicate.

long as what is at issue is the color of the cat, then, whatever it may be that explains the cat's being the cause of the tokening of "The cat," it will not be the fact that the cat has the color it does.

This asymmetry might instead be described at the level of psychological states. One might prefer to think that the relevant cause of the utterance of the predicate "gray" is not the color of the cat, but the child's belief about the color of the cat. Suppose that the child believes the cat is gray. If we ask, "Why does the belief that causes the utterance involve the concept gray rather than the concept black or white or tabby?" the answer is because the child believes that gray is the color *of the cat* (or she believes it is the color of the object she believes to be referred to by "The cat"). The utterance "gray" wouldn't have been caused by a belief involving the concept gray, if the child had not thought that it is the cat that is gray: her thinking that the pig is gray would not have caused the utterance. But the reason it is a belief about the cat (rather than the dog or horse or pig) that causes the occurrence of the subject "The cat" is not because the child believes that the cat (but not the dog, horse, or pig) is gray. It is because she believes the issue before her concerns the color of the cat.

Thus, there is an *asymmetry* between the respective explanations of the tokening of the subject and the tokening of the predicate that may be described either in terms of the psychological states of the agent or, as I prefer to do, in terms of the more distant states of affairs in the world outside the agent's psychology.[12] In this case, whatever color it may be that figures in the explanation of the utterance of "gray," it does so because, and only because, it is the color of the cat. The capacity of some color to be the cause of the utterance "gray," in this context, depends upon that color's relation to the cat – here on its being the color of the cat. But the converse is not the case. The capacity of the cat (or anything else) to explain the utterance of "The cat" does not depend similarly upon the cat's being the color it is. If the cat were another color, then the cat would have the same potential to cause "The cat" in

12 I prefer this because the characterization is simpler to state and grasp on the level of the external states of affairs causally relevant to the utterance. Talking about beliefs or intentions often complicates and obscures the structural facts I am trying to call attention to. I am also worried that many readers will be unimpressed with an account of semantic properties of sentences that seems to fundamentally ride piggy-back on the semantic properties of psychological states. But, the reader who, for whatever reason, thinks that *only* the psychological states matter will see that the asymmetry is there also on the psychological level and, throughout, may substitute the relevant psychological description.

the utterance (though the predicate would then differ accordingly, other things being equal). That causal potential depends instead on the circumstances that make the cat the topic of conversation. Notice, what is at issue is why *one thing rather than another is the thing* that causes the expression (whatever the expression turns out to be). This may strike some as a curious kind of "causal explanation," and I will discuss this later, once the asymmetry is more fully developed.

What causes the predicate expression depends on the specific character of the object that causes the subject expression. But the subject expression does not depend, for its occurrence, on the specific property (here, the color) that causes the predicate. Thus, there is a causal factor that fixes one element of the representation relative to the other, the latter element being determined by the former. The former fixed element then begins to take on the aspect of a subject, and the latter element that of a predicate: for, in the causal context, there is a potential variability in a predicating element vis-á-vis a certain stability of the subject element. This variability may be thought of as the *epistemic* possibility (from the inquirer's point of view) of the object's having any of a range of colors. It is, for instance, associated with the subject's possibly being white or black or orange, with a prior ignorance on the part of the audience of which color it actually is. While what color the cat is is undetermined, what object the statement is about is not undetermined. The cat is the topic, the role of the predicate is to supply information about the cat's color. And it is the color of the cat that is to determine the predication made. The separate explanations of the subject and of the predicate are connected: the explanation of the predicate is dependent upon that of the subject expression. But the explanation of the subject is not similarly dependent on that of the predicate. The relation is one of *asymmetric dependence* of the cause of the predicate on that of the subject.

The exact nature of the dependency may be further developed by examining cases that deviate from the straightforward one with which I have introduced the idea. Suppose a perceptual mistake occurs, for example the lighting is poor, and, in fact, the cat is white. Here, the cat's being white causes it to look to her as if the cat is gray, and again she says, "The cat is gray." Even so, the reason that that color, white, is the cause of the utterance, rather than some other color, is that that color belongs to that cat. (Had it belonged to the dog, it would not *ceteris paribus* have been the cause.) But the cat, rather than some other animal, is not the cause of "The cat," because it is the color white. Suppose, instead, that the child is lying. She believes the cat is white and consequently says, "The cat is gray." Again, the reason that the color white, rather than some other color, is the cause of the tokening of "gray" is that white is the color of the cat.

The causal facts I am discussing leave open the possibility that the statement being made is false, which is, of course, essential. The tokening of the predicate depends upon the causal power of a certain property. But that property need not actually *belong to* the object that causes the tokening of the subject expression to exercise that power. It just needs to be appropriately related to it. So, even in these basic cases, it is not a necessary condition of the predicate's making a predication, that it be caused by some property of the object of reference.[13] The property that causes the predicate might belong to some other thing that the speaker mistakes for the referent, and the attribution may be not merely false, but "misdirected" and the property misattributed. Seeing a gray squirrel and mistaking it for the cat, I say "The cat *is gray*." This statement may attribute the color gray to the cat, despite the fact that the property causally responsible for the predicate belonged to the squirrel, not the cat. What that property is attributed to need not be the thing that actually has the property that is causally operative, for it will be attributed to the referent of the subject term. This is because what determines the referent of the subject term is independent of what determines the occurrence of the predicate term. By contrast the predicate term does depend, for its occurrence, on there being a certain relation between something's causing its occurrence in the sentence and whatever it may be that explains the occurrence of the subject term. Here, the squirrel's being gray is the cause of my saying "gray" only because that property of the squirrel is related as it is to the cause of "The cat" – namely, by its being mistaken for the color of the cat. So the asymmetry may be present even when we are not perceiving the object of reference. The dependency just requires that *whatever it is* that explains the occurrence of the predicate, it will do so *because* of its relation to what explains the occurrence of the subject. Thus the dependency is one in which the one causal event happens because of the other causal event, and so the asymmetric dependency may extend beyond perceptual reports.[14]

13 Nor, incidentally, will the predicate's being caused by a property of the object of reference be sufficient for its making a predication, for there must be a kind of guarantee in place. That nature of that guarantee is explicated below.

14 It can, for example, allow for utterances based on inference. Suppose that knowing that Bob has a horse, I infer that his horse is white, because I know that Bob idolizes the Lone Ranger and I figure he is going to buy a horse that is the same color as the Lone

While the state of affairs that causes the occurrence of the subject and the state of affairs that causes the predicate both depend for their being causes on their relation to something else, significantly, the cause of the predicate expression depends for its being a cause on its relation to the *cause of the subject expression*. By contrast, the cause of the subject expression does *not* depend for its being its cause on its relation to the cause of the predicate. In the simplest cases, the property that figures in the explanation of the occurrence of predicate does so only because it belongs to the object that figures in the explanation of the subject. But the converse is not true: the object that figures in the explanation of the subject does not do so because it possesses the property that figures in the explanation of the predicate. Further, it is not just that this *particular* property depends on its relation to that particular object for its figuring in explanation of the predicate. Rather, *whatever* property it is that figures in the state of affairs that explains the utterance of the predicate "gray," whether that is the property of being gray or white or calico or whatnot, that property depends for its role in causing "gray" on its relation to the object that causes the utterance of "The cat."

Moreover, that property depends for its causal role on its relation to *whatever* object it might be that causes the utterance of "The cat," whether that be the cat, the dog, or the goat. This more general claim – that whatever property figures in the explanation of the predicate does so because of its relation to whatever object figures in the explanation of the subject – can be substantiated by considering cases of mistaken reference. Suppose that the child, confusing cats and dogs, uses the words "The cat" to refer to her dog. When she is asked the color of her cat, she thinks of her gray dog and says, "The cat is gray." The reason the color gray, rather than some other color, was the color that figured in the explanation of "gray" is because that was the color of the object that caused the utterance of "The cat," namely the dog. But the dog, rather than some other animal, did not figure in the explanation of "The cat" *because it was gray*. What determines that that property figures in the explanation of the occurrence of the predicate is not just

Ranger's horse. The Lone Ranger's horse "Silver" was white. So I believe that Bob's horse is white. Asked about Bob's horse, I say "Bob's horse is white." The interest in Bob's horse explains my saying "Bob's horse," and Silver's being white explains my saying "is white." Still, the latter causal fact depends upon the former. Silver's being white explains my saying "white" in this context only because of the relation of Silver to Bob's horse. That relation is this: if I had not thought Bob would have a horse the same color as the Lone Ranger's, then Silver's being white would not have been the cause of that utterance of the predicate "white."

its relation to a particular object, but also *the fact that that object explains or causes the occurrence of the subject term*. If that object (the dog) had not figured in the explanation of the subject term, that property (gray) would not figure in the explanation of the predicate term.

I will call this dependency of the cause of the predicate on the cause of the subject "nexus-dependency." There is a relation, a nexus, between the cause of the subject and that of the predicate. (The character of this dependency will be more closely specified later.) While the kind of dependency will remain the same across cases, the particular relation that the constituents stand in (by virtue of which the one depends in the required way on the other) may differ. As we have seen, it may be because the property is exemplified in the object that it is the cause; or, instead, because the property is mistaken for or inferred to be a property of that object, that that property is the cause of the predicate.

We have found that when the grammatical predicate is the pragmatic predicate, it has a nexus-dependent cause. Is this a coincidence or is it fundamentally connected to the function of the expression? The strategy was to study what changed from one context to another in virtue of which the function of the expression changed. So we need to see whether, when the grammatical *subject* functions as pragmatic predicate – as the information-carrying expression – it too has a nexus-dependent cause. If it does, that would establish a *correlation* between an expression's functioning to make an attribution and its having a nexus-dependent cause. We must consider a case in which, in the utterance of "The cat is gray," "The cat" functions as pragmatic predicate and "gray" as pragmatic subject.

Such was the case when the child uttered the sentence "*The cat* is gray" in response to the question "Do you have any gray pets?" Here "gray" is the pragmatic subject and "The cat" the pragmatic predicate. Now, if the proposal is correct, "The cat" will have a nexus-dependent cause and "gray" will not. Suppose that the statement made by the utterance is true. Knowing her cat's color, the child says in answer to the question, "*The cat* is gray." Her cat's being gray explains her saying, "The cat," and that the property of being gray was the property asked about explains her saying, "gray." In this case, the cat figures in the explanation of the utterance of "The cat" rather than some other animal only because it has whatever property figures in explanation of the utterance "gray," namely (in this case) the property of being gray. But the color gray, rather than some other color, does *not* figure in the explanation of "gray," because it is the color of the cat. The color gray figures in the explanation of "gray," because that is the color the authorities asked about. The pragmatic predicate "the cat" does, as predicted, have a nexus-dependent cause, and the pragmatic subject "gray" does not. And this remains true even if the statement is false or a lie. Suppose, for example, the sentence is false because the child's cat is not gray: confusing cats and dogs, her dog's being gray causes her to utter the words "The cat" in her utterance of "The cat is gray." Still, the dog is the object that figures in the explanation of the utterance of "The cat" rather than some other animal, only because it has the property that figures in the explanation of the utterance "gray." But again, the reason the color gray figures in the explanation of the utterance of "gray" rather than some other color is not because the dog is that color.[15]

To be clear about the kind of causal explanation that the nexus-dependency supplies, it is useful to see how it is analogous to and different from some other kinds of causal explanation. When it is said that whatever color causes the predicate is its cause only because it belongs to whatever object causes the occurrence of the subject expression, that is not an explanation of how a particular state of affairs gives rise to the particular predicate uttered: how the cat's being white results in the occurrence of the word "gray" rather than some other word. It instead identifies a principle that determines why one cause rather than another is selected; it is a kind of "historical" explanation.[16] The claim is that *but for* the causal connection between the cat and the utterance of the subject expression, there would be no causal connection between *this* color and the utterance of the predicate term. This color among colors was selected as the cause of the predicate, because it belonged to the cat and because the cat was the cause of the subject term. There is one causal event wherein the cat's being white caused the occurrence of the predicate, because there was another causal event wherein the cat's being lost caused the occurrence of the subject.

This sort of historical causal explanation is somewhat unusual. Ordinarily, the answer to "Why is X, rather than Y, the cause of Z?"

15 And, as in the other case, there will be a more general formulation of this: whatever object causes the occurrence of the predicate "the cat," it is the cause of that rather than some other object only because it belongs to whatever property it is that causes the utterance of "gray," but not vice versa.

16 Compare a selectional explanation in biology that is also historical. This giraffe has a long neck because that trait was selected for. That is to say, this giraffe has a long neck, because those of its ancestors who had long necks fared better and reproduced more than those of its ancestors who had short necks. This is a historical explanation of how there came to be a certain effect, a trait. The nexus-dependency is instead a historical explanation of how something came to be a cause.

would cite some relevant feature that X has and Y does not have (e.g., X is present in the environment but Y is not, or X's properties are causally linked to the properties of the effect Z, but Y's are not). However, in the case of the nexus-dependency, we say X, rather than Y, is the thing that is the cause of Z, because *something else*, A, rather than B, was the cause of some other event C. There being a causal event wherein it was X that caused Z depends on there being a distinct causal event wherein it was A that caused C. (The color white, rather than gray, orange, or black, was the cause of "gray" because the cat, rather than the horse, goat, or squirrel was the cause of "The cat.") This kind of explanation is not unprecedented. Consider the following analogy. Suppose that researchers develop drugs for human beings only from those drugs that first work in animals. Suppose, contrary to fact, that mad cow disease is cured by the drug Proto R. Mad cow is in fact closely related to a human disease called Creutzfeldt-Jakob. Of all of the drugs agents that they were working on that might have cured mad cow, Proto R worked first. Because Proto R worked in cows, a variant of that, R2, was developed to cure Creutzfeldt-Jakob disease. Now if someone were to ask, "Why is it R2, rather than some other substance, that is the thing *used* to cure the Creutzfeldt-Jakob bacterium?" the answer would be, because Proto R cured mad cow disease. Granted, there may be other substances that might have been used to cure Creutzfeldt-Jakob, other drugs that have the power to do so. The properties of these other substances might have had the same effect. Still, the reason it is R2 and not those other substances that was used to cure Creutzfeldt-Jakob is that Proto R cured mad cow. The causal explanation being offered gives a historical explanation of why X, rather than other things, came to be the thing actually linked to a certain effect Z. It came to be so linked because of another causal linkage that exists between a different cause A and its effect C.

In the case of the sentence, the causal linkage between a state of affairs (that causes the predicate) and the utterance of the predicate is determined by the causal linkage between another state of affairs (the state of affairs that causes the utterance of the subject) and the utterance of the subject. Both linkages are determined by such pragmatic factors as the question asked or the intentions of the speaker. Those psychological or pragmatic facts select for certain causes of the utterance rather than others, and they determine what states of affairs in the world outside the agent's psychology will govern the production of the utterance. They establish a connection between the separate explanations of the utterance of subject and predicate, for in the speech situation, the subject expression's being caused by the particular thing that causes it determines what state of affairs causes the predicate. It is because that object causes the subject expression that that property causes the occurrence of the predicate. Or, where verb-phrase supplies the pragmatic subject, it is because that property is the property that causes the subject that that object is the object that causes the pragmatic predicate.

3   The Contribution of the Nexus-Dependency to an Explanation of Sentential Unity

The causal relation that exists between a state of affairs and the utterance of the predicate depends upon the causal relation that exists between a state of affairs and the utterance of the subject. Now the question is "Can the dependency that has been described between these causal explanations connect the separate utterances of the subject and predicate expression in such a way as to explain their constituting a whole, a sentence that represents something as being the case?"

An expression's having a nexus-dependent cause is correlated with its being the pragmatic predicate of a sentence. But the correlation may be purely accidental or it may be the result of some other phenomenon, that phenomenon being the one that genuinely explains the predication. So we need to understand whether the fact that the predicate expression has a nexus-dependent cause plays some role in determining the representational content of the utterance.

I will argue that, in the examples considered, the nexus-dependency can explain such aspects of the unity of the sentence as these: why the utterance represents not just a property and an object, but a property *of an* object, not just a cat and a color but the color of a cat; why it represents a property *of the object being referred to*, rather than some other object; why the predicate functions as an information-carrying expression rather than the subject; and how the asymmetry of function in the expressions explains the sentence's representing something as being the case.

Before proceeding to these matters, the nexus-dependence relation must be specified more closely. Whether a property is nexus-dependent upon an object or an object upon a property has been seen to change from context to context. So the metaphysical kind, object or property, denoted by an expression does not determine whether its cause is the nexus-dependent one. Rather, in a simple sentence consisting of two expressions "AB," the nexus-dependency might be a relation between any two constituents of the different states of affairs that cause or explain the utterance of the two expressions – a relation wherein a constituent of the state of affairs that causes the one expression depends for its figuring in the explanation of the occurrence of that expression on its relation to a constituent of the state of affairs that causes the other expression. Suppose that, in the utterance of sentence "AB," there is a state of affairs that causes "A" and a state of affairs that causes "B." The state of affairs that causes "A" has a constituent α and the state of affairs that causes "B" a constituent β.

β is nexus-dependent on α if and only if, the state of affairs that caused "B," was a state of affairs composed of β, rather than some other constituent δ, only because

(i) β stands in some relation R to α and δ does not, and

(ii) α was a constituent of the state of affairs that caused "A."

Let us consider why the examples suggest conditions i and ii. (Here I will use examples in which the statement made is false. While that makes things a bit more difficult to follow, it also makes it clear that nothing I am arguing rides on the statement's being true. From here on out, I will primarily focus on the case where the property is nexus-dependent upon the object. But in cases where the role of pragmatic subject and predicate are reversed, that relation will also be reversed, the object instead being nexus-dependent upon the property.) In the first example, where the cat's being lost explained the child's saying "The cat" and, suppose, the cat's being white explained the utterance of "is gray," the reason the color white, rather than some other color, figured in the explanation of the utterance of "gray," was because of the relation (i) between that color and the cat – in this case, because that color belonged to the cat. Thus, the reason it was a state of affairs composed in part of the property of being white, rather than some other color, which caused "gray," is because white was a property of the cat. But it was not just because white belonged to the cat that that color, rather than some other one, caused the tokening of "gray," but also because the cat caused the tokening of the subject term. That is how condition ii comes in. The color white is the color that causes the occurrence of "gray" because of its relation to some object. But what object? Whatever object it is that causes the occurrence of the subject term "The cat." If that object is the cat, then it is because the cat caused the occurrence of the subject term that this property, white, caused the occurrence of the predicate term. But, if the actual situation were such that the cat did not cause the subject term, then the cat's color, white, would not have caused the predicate term (unless, of course, white were relevantly related to the object that *did* cause the subject). Thus, white will figure in the explanation of the predicate only if it is relevantly related to *whatever* object it is that figures in the explanation of the subject term.

We can now begin to see how this causal dependency might explain several aspects of the unity of the sentence. I will proceed by posing specific questions and saying how the nexus-dependency provides an answer. When all of these questions are answered, I hope to have supplied an account of how, in these cases, the words are combined in such a way as to represent something as being the case or so as to predicate a property of the referent. Let us begin from this question:

1. What is the connection between the utterance of the predicate expression and the utterance of the subject expression in virtue of which the predicate expression predicates a property of *the object named* by the *subject* expression?

No predication is made to the object picked out by the subject expression when it is considered in isolation, for example when I greet my cat at the door and say "Frostie." So why is it that when that expression is combined with "is gray," a predication is then made to *that* object, that cat. Of course, when the expressions are combined in the right way "Frostie" will then refer to an object, and the predication will be made to the referent. But this is so as it were by definition of "referent": a thing "referred to" is just a thing of which some predication is made. Since the concept of reference is tied up analytically with the concept of predication and saying (asking, etc.), we must look for an account that goes deeper. We need some explanation of how the subject and predicate expressions are connected in such a way that the predication made is made to the object named by the subject expression.

When the nexus-dependency is present, it is no coincidence that the property that figures in the explanation of the predicate depends on some object *and* that precisely *that object* is the cause of the subject expression. Rather, the nexus-dependency *guarantees* that the property that figures in the explanation of the predicate term will do so because of its relation to the object that figures in the explanation of the subject term: it is because that object figures in the explanation of the subject expression and because the property is related to that object, that that property figures in the explanation of the predicate.[17] Thus there is a *lawful* connection between the state of affairs that explains the occurrence of the subject term and the state of affairs that explains the occurrence of the predicate term. Notice that in the examples considered, the object in question, that is, the thing upon which the cause of the predicate is nexus-dependent, has been the referent.[18] If we assume that the object that figures in the state of affairs that causes the occurrence of the subject term is the referent, then the nexus-dependency guarantees that the property that explains the occurrence of the predicate is related to and determined by the referent.

The fact that this guarantee exists may explain why the utterance of the sentence predicates a property to the referent in particular, rather than to some other object. Given the nexus-dependency, the referent's being what it is, in part, determines what state of affairs causes the tokening of the predicate. It is because, for example, white is instantiated in whatever object causes the subject expression that white figures in the explanation of the predicate. Since the object that causes the subject expression is the cat, that fact determines that it is the *cat's being white* – that state of affairs – that is the cause of the predicate. The predicate expression is caused by some property of an object (the cat's being

17 In cases of "vacuous" referring expressions, there may be no object related to the utterance of the subject expression. But here we may follow standard views. A vacuous referring term, e.g. "The present king of France," may either refer to someone inaccurately or refer to no one at all. If it refers to someone inaccurately, the present prime minister perhaps, then the utterance of that sentence will succeed in making a predication because there is some object – the present prime minister – on which the cause of the predicate depends for being the cause of the predicate. When the expression refers inaccurately and succeeds in making a predication, the predicate does have a nexus-dependent cause. If, on the other hand, the term "The present king of France" is genuinely vacuous, then the view predicts what in fact seems true – that no predication is made. No predication is made, for there is no thing that relevantly causes the utterance of "The present King of France" upon which the cause of the predicate depends for its being its cause.

18 I am not attempting to give an account of reference. By assumption, in the examples in question, the cat was the referent. We then found that the cause of the predicate is nexus-dependent on that very object, the referent. Though I won't pursue the idea, the nexus-dependency may bear on which object is the referent: the referent might plausibly be that object some property of which is the cause of the predicate only because that object is the cause of the subject. This would suppose that the intentions of the speaker, not the standard meaning of the referring expression, determine the referent.

white) in effect because the subject expression is caused by that *same* object (the cat). The predicate expression then predicates a property to that object rather than to others for this reason: it is some property of that object, not others, that causes the tokening of the predicate, and that property causes it because that object, not others, is the referent (or, at least, because it is the cause of the subject expression).

Other cases will be more complicated. Returning to an earlier example, if the fact is instead that the property of being gray causes "gray" because it is the color of the squirrel and the squirrel is mistaken for the cat (the cat being the relevant cause of the subject), it is the relation of the color of the squirrel to the referent, the cat, that is, the being-mistaken-for-the-cat-relation, that determines it is a state of affairs wherein the squirrel is gray that will cause the predicate. Still, the predicate predicates a property to the referent, the cat, because some property is the cause of the predicate in virtue of its relation to the referent and because the referent, rather than some other object, is the cause of the subject expression "The cat."

This should explain why, *if* the sentence predicates a property of an object, it would make the predication to the referent in particular. But it does not yet explain why a predication is made to any object. Nor does it explain why the subject and predicate are combined to represent some single unitary thing formed in some way from both the contribution of the subject and predicate. The sentence "The cat is gray," for example, may be said to represent the cat just in case it represents *something about* the cat.[19] And what it represents about the cat is determined by the contribution of the predicate. Given the particular predicate uttered, the sentence represents the situation or state of affairs with regard to the color of the cat. It represents not separately a cat and a color gray, but the color of the cat. This raises the question:

2. Why do the words in the sentence combine to represent a unitary thing – a state of affairs or situation with regard to some property of an object?

Here I will focus my explanation on the most straightforward examples, as my aim is only to illustrate how the nexus-dependency might explain this aspect of the unity of the representation.

19 Analogously, the sentence may be said to represent the property of being gray just in case it represents something about that property. What is represented by the whole sentence – its object – is something more than what is designated or referred to by either of its parts.

In the straightforward cases in which the child is characterizing the color of her cat, whatever property figures in the explanation of the predicate does so only because it belongs to whatever object it is that figures in the explanation of the subject. So whether the speaker's statement is true or not, even if she is lying or misperceiving the color of the cat, still the color that causes the utterance of the predicate is its cause because it belongs to the object that causes the subject, "The cat." (Remember that when she misperceived the color of the cat or wanted to lie about it, it was the cat's being white that caused the utterance of "gray." Even so, white was the color that was the cause of the utterance because it belonged to the cat.) If the object that causes the subject expression were different, then, other things remaining the same, the property that caused the predicate would change to be a property of *that very object*. Imagine, for example, it is a dog, not a cat, that causes the occurrence of the subject expression. Then it will be the color of the dog, not the cat, that causes the occurrence of the predicate. Thus, there is a lawful connection between the cause of the subject expression and the cause of the predicate expression. Necessarily, whatever property it may be that causes the utterance of the predicate term, it is the cause of it because it is a property of whatever object causes the utterance of the subject term. In these cases, that nomic connection guarantees that the predicate expression will be caused by a property of the referent (the object that causes the occurrence of the subject expression), caused by that property *because it is a property of the referent* (of the object that causes the occurrence of the subject expression).

In this sort of case, the nexus-dependency also guarantees that the predicate expression in a certain way "tracks" the causally operative property of the referent. Importantly, it does not guarantee that it represents that property of the object correctly, so the utterance may be false. Suppose that the color that causes the predicate does so only because it belongs to the object that causes the occurrence of the predicate. This means that if the color of that object (the cat) had been different, then other things being equal, the color that caused the occurrence of the predicate and the predicate expression itself would have been different. Suppose the cat's being white caused the child to say, "The cat is gray," because the lighting was poor. (So the utterance is false.) Now, imagine that the cat were orange, instead of white. Then it would have been the cat's being orange, not white, that caused her to utter the predicate, and presumably, other things being equal, a different predicate expression would have been uttered. Changes in the color of the cat would result in changes in the color that caused the occurrence of the predicate and in the predicate expression uttered. The predicate expression, then, tracks (or co-varies with) the color that causes it, and the color that causes it co-varies with the color of whatever object is causing the occurrence of the subject expression. The predicate expression tracks a property *belonging to* the object of reference.[20] If the predicate tracks a property of the object of reference, the utterance of the sentence could then *represent* that property of that object.

To see that this is so, we must consider what exactly we mean when we say that a representation represents a situation, state of affairs, or property of an object? The property of the object that is represented cannot be the very property predicated, because the predication may be false, and what is represented should be specifiable in advance of our knowing whether it is represented correctly or incorrectly. As Dennis Stampe puts the point:

> In discussing the representational view of sentences, the question always arises, What might a sentence represent, when what it says is false? (And it is pointed out that it could not be a fact that it represents, as if it *could* "represent a fact" if it said something true.) It must surely represent the *same* thing, whether it is true or false, i.e. whether it represents the thing rightly or *mis*represents it.[21]

If we are to allow for the possibility of misrepresentation, what is represented can only be a property that the object has whether the predication is true or false. What is represented cannot be identified with the specific property that the thing is represented as having. For the same reason, it cannot be identified with the state of affairs the sentence represents as being the case. The *object* of the representation cannot be identified with its *content*. If the statement is that the cat is gray, what is represented cannot be the *grayness* of the cat, or the state of affairs wherein the cat is gray, for the cat might not be gray. But, as Stampe suggests, what is represented may be the generic or "determinable" property. It may be the *color* of the cat, of which gray is a determinate instance. Or it may be the state of affairs *with regard* to the color of the cat.[22] For whether it is true or false, the color of the cat is what is rep-

20 In the more deviant cases involving mistaken reference, things will be less simple, and the relation between nexus-dependent constituents will not be instantiation.
21 D. Stampe, "Show and Tell," in *Forms of Representation*, ed. B. Freed, A. Marras, and P. Maynard (New York: American Elsevier Publishing, 1975), pp. 221–45. See p. 223.
22 Ibid., pp. 223–4.

resented by the statement that it is gray. Interpreted in this way, what is represented may be a unitary object formed from the contribution of both the subject and predicate, yet the same thing is represented whether the representation is true or false.

This way of specifying the object represented also allows a fuller conception of the function of the predicate. So far, I've said that the predicate is the expression that "purports to carry information" about what is represented. Suppose that what is represented is some determinable property of the referent. The predicate expression would then purport to carry information about that determinable property. Its distinctive function is to make that determinable *determinate* – that is to say, to represent that determinable property in a determinate way, or as being some particular property of that general kind. It represents the cat's color as gray, or his size as huge, or his weight as ten pounds. That is the way the utterance of the sentence succeeds in representing some determinate thing as being the case.

If the nomic connection established by the nexus-dependency could answer the questions

3. How does the utterance represent some determinable property – the color of the cat, or temperature of the air, or the size of the shoe? and,
4. Why does the predicate function to make determinate that determinable?

then it would provide an account of the unity of those sentences in which the dependency is found. For then we would have an account of the unitary object of the representation – for example, the color (generic) of the cat – as well as of the representation's content – that the cat's color is gray. I take it that explaining how the sentence "The cat is gray" represents the color of the cat and represents his color as being gray would suffice for explaining how the property of being gray is predicated of the cat.[23]

In the earlier cases considered, one utterance of "The cat is gray" represented the color of the cat and "gray" functioned to make the

23 Whether it does suffice will depend upon precisely what one means by "predicating a property of an object." If only sentences (not beliefs or other representations with representational content) and only certain kinds of sentences are held to "predicate" properties to objects, then the account won't suffice. But if what one means is simply that the representation has truth-evaluable content, then it may suffice.

color determinate, and in the other utterance of that same sentence, the utterance represented the identity of the gray pet and "The cat" functioned to make that matter determinate. The two distinct utterances of the sentence express the same proposition. That shows that neither the sentence in the abstract nor the proposition expressed by it determines, with full specificity, what is represented by the utterance or which expression functions as predicating expression. Nor can that be determined just by looking at the actual states of affairs that cause the utterance: for, by an accident of the situation, the causally effective state of affairs may be the same, as it is when the color of the pet is gray and the gray pet is the cat.

What may explain what is represented by the utterance and which expression functions to make that object determinate is the particular *procedural history*, as it might be called, of the utterance. The difference between the two utterances "The cat is gray" in virtue of which one tracks the color of the cat and the other tracks the identity of the gray pet may be conceived as arising from a difference in the two distinct routes, programs, or procedures that would issue in the same utterance, expressing one and the same proposition in either case: two routes to the same destination. The programs begin from one or another distinct array of relevant possibilities, in the one case, a set of possible colors (gray, white, orange . . .) in the other case, a set of possible pets (the cat, the dog, the ferret . . .). The set of possibilities collects determinate instances of the determinable, which is the thing being represented, the color of the animal, in the one case, and the identity of the gray animal in the other. The predicate, then, is the term expressing the one determinate instance selected, as it might be "gray" in the one case, "The cat" in the other. It is the route by means of which the proposition comes to be expressed that determines what is the object of representation and so which expression will function as the information-carrying expression. What makes one or the other term function as a predicate is not its syntax, but the procedural history of its utterance – its having a certain selectional history or profile.

The nexus-dependency between subject and predicate accounts for the fact that the utterance has one or another procedural history. This may be illustrated as follows. When the child is asked the color of the cat, it is presupposed that the cat is going to occupy a place in the color range or in that region of logical space. If the child responds to the question, her utterance will single out the relevant place in the range, locating a place in space within the color range that the cat occupies. If the nexus-dependency is present, whatever color is the cause of the utterance is its cause because it is (or is thought to be or is mistaken for, etc.) the color of the cat. But the object that causes the occurrence of "The cat" is not its cause because it has the color gray. This asymmetric dependency makes certain counterfactuals true. We can, for example, say that in this case, if white had not been the color of the cat (or was thought to be or was mistaken for it), that color would not have been the cause of the predicate – some other color would have been. Change the color of the cat, and, other things being equal, one changes the color that is the cause of the predicate, and changes the color predicate uttered. This makes the procedural history of the utterance one such that the relevant possible causes of the utterance are the possible *colors* of the cat and the relevant possible utterances of the predicate are color *predicates*.[24] If the possible causes of this utterance are the cat's being black, the cat's being white, the cat's being orange, and so on, then the utterance will locate the cat in the color range of logical space.

The color of the cat – whatever it is – is to cause the utterance of the predicate because it is the color of the cat. The fact that some color or another, whatever color the cat happens to be, is to be the cause of the predicate because it is the color of the cat, corresponds to the fact that the utterance will locate the cat in some region *or other* of the color range. It determines the relevant determinable, the object of representation, as the color of the cat as opposed to the size of the cat or its shape and as opposed to the identity of the gray pet. The possible causes of the utterance of the predicate (the different colors) correspond with the possible regions of logical space in the color range that utterance might determine. It is indeterminate what region in the color range that cat will be represented as occupying. The expression that then makes that determinate by identifying a particular color, for example "gray," will then be the *predicate* – the information-carrying expression – because it is the expression that narrows the relevant possibilities, making determinate the relevant region of logical space. "Gray" rather than "The cat" functions as the information-carrying

24   It should be clear that I am not making the implausible psychological claim that the speaker runs through in her mind the various colors and predicates before she utters what she does, nor am I describing the psychological process of reasoning. Rather, I am describing her reasons for making the utterance. Those reasons make the above counterfactuals true. And those counterfactuals determine what are the possible causes and utterances.

expression because it makes determinate that determinable, purporting to carry information about the color of the cat, and representing it as gray. In that way, the proposition that the cat is gray comes to be expressed, or, following Frege, "grasped," by following a certain route to it, because of the particular causal or explanatory history of the utterance.

When one utters the sentence "The cat is gray" in answer to the question "Which of your pets is gray?" one follows a different route to the proposition expressed. In this case, it is presupposed that some pet or other is gray, and here, unlike the other case, already a particular color in the range of color space has been located. (Before, we had the cat occupying some color place or other in the range color, here we have some animal or other occupying the color place gray.) The question is not what color in the range but which of a class of objects belongs in the color place gray. It is a matter of placing the right object out of an array of possible objects (pets) in the preselected property space gray. The counterfactual causal dependency established by the nexus between subject and predicate again selects the relevant set of possible causes of the utterance. If whatever pet causes the occurrence of the grammatical subject is its cause because it has (or is thought or inferred to have) the property of being gray, then changes in which pet is gray will result in changes in the object that causes the occurrence of the pragmatic predicate and in the pragmatic predicate uttered: if the dog is gray, then the dog would be the cause of the utterance, or if the goat is gray, it would be the goat, and so on. Thus, the selectional history of this utterance is defined by a different set of possible causes. The various possible causes of this utterance are *the cat's* being gray, *the dog's* being gray, *the goat's* being gray (not the cat's being *gray*, the cat's being *orange*, the cat's being *black*). This utterance, unlike the other one, is supposed to specify a gray pet. The utterance is a representation of the identity of the gray pet: *identity* is the relevant determinable, because the object that causes the occurrence of the pragmatic predicate (and grammatical subject) is its cause, only because it is the color gray (or is thought to be, mistaken for) and because that color is the cause of "gray." Again the causal possibilities mirror the parts of logical space to which the property gray might be assigned. The particular expression uttered, "The cat," will be the information-carrying expression because it makes determinate what pet is located in the color place gray.

This difference in procedural history may be illustrated as follows:

	Case 1	**Case 2**
The utterance represents:	the color of the cat or	the identity of the gray pet
Actual utterance:	"The cat is gray"	"The cat is gray"
Possible utterances:	"The cat is white"	"The dog is gray"
	"The cat is calico"	"The squirrel is gray"
	"The cat is black"	"The goat is gray"
	"The cat is tortoise-shell"	"The rat is gray"
Possible causes:	The cat's being gray	The cat's being gray
	The cat's being white	The dog's being gray
	The cat's being calico	The squirrel's being gray
	The cat's being black	The goat's being gray
	The cat's being tortoise-shell	The rat's being gray
Possible propositions expressed:	that the cat is gray	that the cat is gray
	that the cat is white	that the dog is gray
	that the cat is calico	that the squirrel is gray
	that the cat is black	that the goat is gray
	that the cat is tortoise-shell	that the rat is gray

We might characterize the distinctive function of the predicate by employing Strawson's idea – that the predicate is the expression which introduces a term that carves out a particular region of logical space – and interpreting it dynamically. The predicate expression is the expression that functions to narrow down the relevant possibilities, making determinate the location of an object in logical space, or, in different terms, making determinate some determinable.[25] In each case, the cat is located in the color space gray by the utterance. But the utterance locates the cat in that color space in two different ways, by narrowing down one or another of two different sets of relevant possibilities.

The one utterance tracks the color of the cat, in the sense that causal counterfactual dependencies between the subject and predicate map possible colors of the cat onto possible utterances and propositions expressed. In the case where the causal counterfactual dependencies run in the opposite direction, the utterance tracks the identity of the

25 This provides a way of understanding Strawson's claim that the predicate always designates something of a "higher type" than what is designated by the subject. The predicate is that expression which makes determinate some magnitude or other determinable. Determinate magnitudes and determinables will always "compete for possession" of the referent with other determinations in their range and so be of "higher type."

gray pet, because the counterfactuals instead map possible gray pets onto possible utterances and propositions expressed.

The representation represents what it does, one or another determinable, because of the route by means of which the proposition comes to be expressed. The idea of a procedural history used here offers an interpretation of the traditional idea that a representation represents what it does because it has a form in common with what it represents. It is a standard view that a sentence is distinguished from a list, because in the sentence, unlike the list, there is a correlation, not just between words and the things designated by the words, but between the relation that the words stand in to each other and some relation between the things designated. The correlation requires not that the relation between the elements of the representation is entirely the same as that between elements of what it represents, but just that there is some kind of structural similarity. The two-dimensional map of Earth may represent the three-dimensional sphere, even though the relation of points on the map are not everywhere the same as that of corresponding points on the sphere, because there is nevertheless a mapping that in some way preserves the structure of the array on the sphere. There is a sameness of form.

The representation is said to represent what it does because it has a form in common with it. Form is a similarity relation across instances. But it has proved difficult to discover what the relevant terms of this similarity relation might be in the case of representations and what they represent. A true sentence might be said be similar in form with the fact it represents, but the problem is that a false sentence does not represent a fact. Russell thought there could be no *single* thing, no unitary object, corresponding to the false proposition, no such thing as 'that Charles I died in his bed.' Apart from the consideration that such entities offended Russell's sense of reality, he hoped to arrive at a genuine understanding of the unity of the proposition. This is certainly not provided by postulating such prefabricated unities as the "objective" that Charles I died in his bed, and saying that the representation has a form in common with that entity. Russell's implicit rule was to restrict the account to actually existing things, Charles, dying, his bed. But then the question was how to provide a notion of form common to the representation and what it represents.

Wittgenstein's conception of possible states of affairs allows for an interpretation of common form that may bend but does not break Russell's rule. It does not break the rule, because possible states of affairs are ways that actually existing things could combine to form states of affairs. No complex nonexistent entity is postulated; for the form of the possible state of affairs is not a property of some complex (which may not exist), but a matter of the possible ways that the constituents of actual states of affairs, constituents that do exist, can combine in states of affairs. For Wittgenstein, form is a strongly modal notion. The isomorphism between the representation and what it represents is understood in terms of possibilities, specifically possibilities of combination – the possible ways the objects named could combine and the possible ways the names that make up the sentence could combine. Those possibilities must be the same. This identity of form is achieved because the possible ways the object can combine in states of affairs govern the ways the words naming those objects can combine in sentences: the names can combine in a sentence only if the objects named can combine in a state of affairs. The form of the name and of the object it names is identified with the possible ways it can combine. In that way, the form of a proposition and of a state of affairs are reduced to the form of its parts, actually existing entities.

The examples we have considered suggest a different notion of form, though still a modal one and still one in which the possible combinations of objects govern the possible combinations of names.

5. What is the form common to the representation and what it represents in virtue of the former represents the latter?

The instances relevant for defining that form are not the logically possible combinations of objects, on the one hand, and of names on the other, but the *causally* possible ones given what the speaker is doing in making the utterance. The table offered above displays the difference between the possible causes, utterances, and propositions expressed in the distinct utterances of "The cat is gray," and suggests a corresponding notion of "same form." As we've seen, the nexus-dependency between subject and predicate makes certain causal counterfactuals true. Those counterfactuals describe ways that objects and properties can combine to form states of affairs that are potential causes of the utterance. The way that objects and properties can combine to form states of affairs that would be possible causes, given the nexus-dependency, governs the way that the words can combine to form possible utterances. The possible causes are mapped onto the possible utterances, where the mapping is governed, not as in Wittgenstein, by what is logically possible, but instead by what is causally possible *consistently with the speech situation.*

Form is a similarity relation across instances, and in this conception the relevant instances are the possible causes, the possible utterances, and the possible propositions expressed. In the first case, what is common to the possible causes is that the cat is some color or other, the possible sentences that the words "The cat" occur together with some color word or other, and the possible propositions that the cat is said to have some color or other. The isomorphism between the causes, utterances, and propositions consists in the fact that differences in the color of cat result in different color predicates being uttered and different colors being predicated in the propositions expressed. In the second case, what is common to the possible causes is that some animal or other is gray, the possible utterances that the words "is gray" occur together with some animal-specifying word, and the possible propositions that some animal or another is said to be gray. It is the relation of the particular utterance made to its possible causes and the possible utterances it might have been that determine the object of representation – in one case, the color of the cat, in the other, what pet is gray.[26]

Such a conception of the form of the representation provides an account of the object of representation, where what is represented is a unitary entity (formed in a way from the contribution of subject and predicate) meeting Russell's criteria. It allows for both true and false statements (for the same thing is represented – for example the color of the cat – whether the sentence is true or false) and it posits no unreal entities (propositions or 'that such and such is the case'). This conception of the form of the representation can also provide a fairly fine-grained specification of the object of representation. Remember, on Wittgenstein's conception of form, the sentence represents what it has a form in common with, and it has a form in common with "reality." The sentence represents reality. Since the form common to the sentence and reality is the form of states of affairs, he could say it represents a state of affairs, some state of affairs. But his account of what was represented in terms of form was no more determinate than that. Form gave him no way of differentiating what was represented by "The cat is gray" and "The cat is huge."

26 Notice that while the utterance is causally related to some determinable, such as the color of the cat, I have not supposed that it is caused by such a thing. Arguably, determinables, such as the color of the cat, the size of the shoe, the weight of the horse do not cause determinate events. In any case, on the present view, it is because of the relation of the utterance to determinate states of affairs that it represents the determinable it does.

Whereas, on the notion of form I am proposing, the sentence "The cat is gray" represents the state of affairs with regard to the color of the cat, not his size, because given its form – its causal history – it tracks the cat's color, not his size. Whereas, presumably, "The cat is huge" would track his size not his color. Even where the sentence carries information about several things, this notion of form can explain why one rather than another of those things is the object of representation. Suppose that a particular utterance of "The cat is gray" carries information about the color of the cat and about the identity of the gray pet. What does the utterance represent, the color of the cat or the identity of the gray pet? The utterance represents that with which it shares a form, and the form is a similarity relation across possible causes and possible utterances. So in the case where the color that causes the utterance "gray" is its cause, only because it is the color of the cat, the utterance will represent the color of the cat. That is because, in that case, changes in the color of the cat would result in changes in the color that caused the predicate and, presumably, in the predicate uttered. The possible causes of the utterance are then the possible colors of the cat, and the possible utterances are color predicates. The predicate expression would change with the color of the cat. That is the case both when the sentence is true and when it is false.[27] So the utterance can have a form in common with the color of the cat even if carries no information about it (as the utterance is standardly interpreted.) The utterance, then, tracks the color because there is an isomorphism between the color of cat and the utterance of the predicate.

By contrast, in this case, there is no such relation between the identity of the gray pet and the occurrence of the subject term: this utterance does not track the identity of the gray pet. We cannot say of this case that if the cat had been a different color, the cat would not have been the cause of the subject term. Change what animal is gray and that does *not* change the identity of the object that causes the subject term or the subject term uttered. That is because the cat is not the cause of the subject term *because* it is the color gray. (So the alternative possible causes of this utterance are not the cat's or the dog's or the goat's being gray.) Thus, the grammatical subject term would *not* change to *vary* with which animal is gray. The isomorphism that exists, given the

---

27   Remember, even when the cat's being white caused the utterance of "The cat is gray," white was the cause of it rather than some other color, because white was the color of the cat. So, if the cat's color were different, the color that caused the utterance of the predicate would change to be the color of the cat (other things being equal).

actual causal dependency, is one between the color the cat and the grammatical predicate term, not between what animal is gray and the occurrence of the grammatical subject term. So while the utterance "The cat is gray" may carry information about the color of the cat and about which pet is gray, it represents the color of the cat, because the properties of that utterance – here the utterance of the predicate – is correlated with the color of the cat. Given the way it was produced, this utterance tracks the color of the cat but not which pet is gray.[28]

Wittgenstein thought that it is the fact that the words are combined or related in the way that they are that explains their representing the things they name as related. I am suggesting that the relevant fact about the way they are combined (or related) is that the utterances are combined in a causal context wherein the cause of the predicate is asymmetrically dependent on the cause of the subject. This may go some way towards explaining what Wittgenstein's theory had a problem explaining. In my earlier discussion of his view, I argued his notion of form and structure did not suffice to explain why words which are such that they could go together to express a proposition actually *do* go together to express a proposition. When names are just arbitrarily combined into collections that are syntactically sentences, as when the turtle accidentally inscribes a sentence in the sand or the wind blows

28   To say that this notion of form can give a concrete specification of the object of representation is not to say that, for any representation, it is clear what its object is. There are cases where it is not clear what is represented, e.g. the case where the color of the squirrel causes the utterance of "gray" in "The cat is gray," but only because the squirrel is mistaken for the cat. If that object, the cat, had not caused the occurrence of the subject expression, that property, gray, would not have caused the occurrence of the predicate expression (unless, of course, gray did turn out to be the color of the object wrongly taken to be the cause of the subject term). So if the object that caused the occurrence of the subject expression had been different, the property that caused the occurrence of the predicate would also have been different. The property that causes the predicate changes, not so as to be a property of the referent, but to be a property of the object mistaken for the object of reference, the squirrel. What does the whole utterance represent – the color of the squirrel or the color of the cat?

One might plausibly say that since the property which causes the predicate co-varies with a property of the squirrel but only because that property of the squirrel is mistaken for the color of the cat, the utterance represents the color of the cat. Alternatively, using those same two facts, one might say that it represents the color of the squirrel. Unbeknownst to the speaker, her utterance represents the color of the squirrel, because it is the color of the squirrel that actually co-varies with the utterance of the predicate given that she has mistaken that squirrel for the cat. The nexus-dependency explains why we have conflicting intuitions, why we might interpret it one way or another, and why on either way of interpreting it, the utterance has a certain kind of unity and does not merely separately represent a property and an object.

together words torn from the newspaper, their combination does not represent a state of affairs. Yet the latter case is apparently a collection of symbols that are structured and have what Wittgenstein would regard as a form common to reality. So what is it about the way they are combined that makes some collections genuine representations and others not?

The fact that the utterance of the words has been combined in a causal context where the cause of the one utterance is nexus-dependent upon the cause of the other may explain their combining together to comprise a genuine representation. Cook Wilson's and Ramsey's "subjective distinction" between subject and predicate can be understood in terms of objective features present in the speech situation, and then an account of predication emerges. The psychological and contextual factors including the interests and intentions of the speaker, what is in doubt and what is not, make the cause of the predicate asymmetrically dependent upon that of the subject. That asymmetric dependency is a matter of there being certain counterfactual causal dependencies between the external state of affairs that causes the predicate and that which causes the subject. Those counterfactual causal dependencies determine the possible causes, possible utterances, and possible propositions expressed. The fact that there are causal counterfactual dependencies explain, why the words constitute a representation. And the fact that the dependencies run in one direction or the other explains why the representation represents the one thing or the other – the color of the cat or the identity of the gray pet. It explains why one expression or the other – "gray" or "The cat" – will function to make the determinable subject matter determinate, purporting to supply information either about the color of the cat or the pet which is gray. That there is an object of representation and what it is is determined by the causal history of the utterance, by how it would come to carry certain information, by the interrelation of the actual causes of the utterance. That is what is contained in the metaphor of the "route" by means of which the proposition comes to be expressed. And it is such causal counterfactual dependencies that give us a determinate conception of the form and hence the object of the representation.[29]

29 There will be other cases where the counterfactual dependencies established by the nexus-dependencies explain the utterance's representing a property of an object in ways other than by making the utterance track that property of the object. Suppose, e.g., I believe only fat cats are gray, and I know that Sally's cat is fat, and so when asked the color of her cat, I say, drawing an inference, "The cat is gray." Now there is a nexus-dependency (being fat is a cause of "gray" only because it belongs to the object that

What remains constant, regardless of the route, is that there is a functional difference between the parts of the sentence wherein one of the expressions functions as the information-carrying expression, and that is the expression that has a nexus-dependent cause.

This explanation needs further development. Supposing that there is such a structural isomorphism between the sentence and some property of an object, one might yet ask why *that* structural isomorphism is one *constitutive* of representation. (Granted it is not the arbitrary combining of words into what happens to be a sentence, but why does the sentence's tracking a property of the object of reference entail that it represents it?) Answering that question would require a particular theory of representation – of what makes one thing a representation of another. In the present chapter, I have tried to explain how the nexus-dependency might account for the unity of the sentence independently of any particular theory of representation or meaning, precisely because the facts explored here might fit into various such theories. In the next chapter, I will show how the structural isomorphism in question could explain why something is a representation on a particular theory of representation, namely on a causal or information-based theory. The account will remain incomplete until that explanation is provided.

Still, in the causal facts, we have reason to identify the object of representation in one way or another – the color of the cat or the identity of the gray pet. The facts explain why a representation might represent a certain determinable. When the utterance of "gray" is nexus-dependent upon that of the "The cat," there is reason to suppose that "The cat is gray" represents the color of the cat. And given the causal history of the utterance of the sentence, the predicate is variable in this sense: it would change with changes in the property of the object represented. Changes in the color of the cat would have resulted in a different color predicate having been uttered (other things being equal). This does not yet suffice for explaining why the expression functions to make determinate that determinable, but it may suffice, I think, if a last question can be answered:

causes the occurrence of "the cat" and because I believe being fat is correlated with being "gray"), and that will make certain counterfactuals true in virtue of which the utterance represents the color of the cat. But this utterance does not track the color of the cat, because it is not true that if the cat had been a different weight – thin, e.g. – that its being thin would have been the cause of the predicate and a different color predicate would have been uttered. (Since I do not happen to believe that all thin cats have one color, the cat's being thin won't cause me to utter a color predicate at all.)

6. If the predicate predicates a property, why is the property predicated
   the one *designated* by the expression rather than the one that causes
   the utterance of the expression?

This fact is not explained by the nexus-dependency. The explanation of
it will, however, fit into the kind of analysis being proposed. The
speaker utters the particular word he does because of what it means.
The cause of the predicate causes that word rather than some other
to be uttered, because of what tokens of that type mean. Using my
standard example, the color white is the cause of "gray," rather than
"white" or "black" or "orange," in the sentence "The cat is gray"
because tokens of the type "gray" designate the property of being gray.
Now I suggest that if (1) given the causal history of the utterance of the
sentence, the utterance represents the color of the cat, a determinable
property, and (2) the color predicate uttered would vary with changes
in the color of the cat, and (3) the predicate uttered designates a color,
and (4) the speaker uttered the predicate expression he did because it
designates the color it does, then in his utterance of "The cat is gray,"
"gray" functions to make determinate the determinable property
'color of the cat.' That is, it predicates the property of being gray to the
cat. All of this is consistent with the fact that the color of the cat is not
gray, and thus with the possibility of misrepresentation.

   This gives us a fairly complete explanation of various representational aspects of the unity of the sentence. The sentence represents not
separately some object and some property, but a property (generic) of
the object of reference, because the property that explains the occurrence of the predicate is its cause only because it belongs to (is
mistaken for or inferred to be a property of) the referent. That
nexus-dependency between the separate causal explanations of the
subject and predicate expression establishes a lawful connection – an
isomorphism – between that property of the object and the sentence
which can explain why the utterance represents that property (generic)
of the object. An expression functions to make determinate that
property of the object, because it would change with changes in that
property of the object and because the speaker uttered that expression because it designates the determinate property it does. When
these various features of the causal explanation are considered
together, it is plausible to think that the sentence represents an object
as being some determinate way or that it predicates a property of the
object of reference. The interrelation of the explanations of the utterance of subject and predicate bind them together to form a whole, with

representational properties that neither of them separately has. The whole utterance comes to have its characteristic representational properties because of the way that the causes of the separate utterances are connected in the act of utterance.

8

Limitations, Applications, and Externalist Theories of Meaning

I have proposed a pragmatic account of the unity of some very simple subject–predicate sentences. This chapter focuses on some ways of extending that account and relating it to sentences of more complex structure, locating it in the terrain of contemporary theories of meaning, and drawing out some of its implications. In particular, I will show how the notion of 'nexus-dependency' might be extended to explain some basic "ways of talking about the world" that J. L. Austin classified. I then locate the account in current externalist, causal, or information-based theories of meaning, arguing that it can answer certain questions that arise on such theories. And finally, in fairly speculative remarks, I will discuss a notion of what I call "event meaning" that may emerge from the account, which I argue is less psychologically based than is Grice's notion of speaker's meaning.

I have considered a very limited number of examples, all of them of basically only one type and have considered these examples only as they might occur in the making of an assertion. I explained that I would confine my attention to these on the assumption that they are basic. I am supposing both that complex sentences are built up from such simple sentences, and also that the principles I have employed might serve or be modified to serve in a fuller account of the unity of the sentence. I will do little to substantiate that idea but will make a few remarks to that end.

The general program envisioned here is predicated on the idea that the unity of the sentence is at bottom a property of the *utterances* of sentences, not of the sentence in the abstract, independent of the context of its use. So we should not look for the basic explanation of sentential unity in the grammatical, logical, or metaphysical properties of the expressions. Rather, if we were to generalize from the cases studied here, we should look for an explanation in terms, broadly, of the explanatory dependencies that come to obtain between the respective causes or explanations of the tokenings of the expressions as a result of what the speaker is doing in uttering the words. (The nexus-dependency is probably just one kind of interconnection that gets established when the parts of the sentence function asymmetrically, as subject and predicate.)

To extend the account would first require an account of other kinds of speech acts besides assertions: questions, commands, suppositions, and many other kinds of speech acts that a speaker might be performing in saying even "The cat is gray." The account I have offered of that sentence derives its unity from the unity of the act of uttering its parts, owing to the way the explanation of the utterance of one part depends on the explanation of the utterance of the other. But the detail of the explanation may distinguish between the speaker's *asserting that*, and her *asking whether* the cat is gray. In either case, what explains the occurrence of "gray" (the color gray, ideally) depends upon what explains "the cat" (the cat). But in the one case this is so because the speaker is describing the latter as instantiating the former and in the other case because the speaker is asking whether the latter instantiates the former. (He is describing it, perhaps, because he intends his audience to think that he thinks the cat is gray and he is asking whether it is gray because he wants his audience to indicate whether it is gray.) It seems as if other distinctions of illocutionary force may be treated in some similar way.

Second, I have considered only simple sentences, and among those I have not considered modifiers like adjectives and adverbs. The relation between a term and its modifiers is a kind of asymmetric dependency relationship not totally unlike the relation between subject and predicate. It seems plausible to think that if we can understand the unity of "the cat is gray" as I have suggested, we can understand the unity of "dark gray" along the same lines. (The phrase presumably means that the gray is dark.) But not every modifier–modified relation is like that.

Among "nonattributive" modifiers there are quantifying adjectives like "all" and "some" and "no." If Frege is right as he is interpreted by Dummett, an adequate account of the semantic properties of sentences such as "Everybody loves somebody" requires it to be constructed by an ordered application of certain operations to basic subject–predicate sentences. This would mean that the product of such operations does not have a structure that mirrors that of the subject–predicate sentences from which it derives. "Everybody loves somebody" is not built up from its parts in the same way as is the basic sentence "John loves Mary." Likewise in operations like negation, conjunction, disjunction, and conditionalization, these operations are applied to wholes derived from basic subject–predicate sentences. The unifying structure of the basic sentences need not survive when it occurs in complex sentences. (The kind of nexus-dependency between the subject and predicate that was present in the basic sentence "The cat is gray" need not hold in that same sentence as it occurs in "The cat is gray and the dog is brown" or in "It is not the case that the cat is gray.")

To go further we would need some way to understand the role of these "operations" in the utterance of a sentence in which these quantifier terms or connectives occur. It is always difficult to understand the relationship between the derivations and operations and constructions posited in an analytical account of the grammatical or the logical/semantic form of a sentence, on the one hand, and what a speaker is actually *doing* in uttering a sentence of that form. And my "pragmatic" account is formulated in terms of what the speaker is doing. If the analytic account is formulated in terms of rules in the application of which the sentence is generated, it is not to be supposed that the speaker applies those rules and generates them in speaking the sentence in the same way the analyst might apply them. Still, it may be satisfactory to speak provisionally of these rules as somehow governing the actual processes (whatever they are) that underlie the utterance of the sentence. In the simple cases I have treated, I have conceived these as causal processes in which the speaker's utterances of this or that word in a sentence are explained by the reasons she has for uttering them, and the interconnection of those reasons. And I have taken the basic question about unity to be why do these words occur together in the utterance, and the basic answer to be, because the reasons for the occurrence of the one are tied up with the reasons for the occurrence of the other.

In the standard uses of language, the reasons one utters a particular word *are* reasons for uttering it because the word means what it does, and therefore because the truth conditions associated with the word are what they are. So the way the rules according to which the abstract sentence is constructed govern the causal processes that underlie the analysis of the token sentence is by way of their determining truth conditions that govern the activity of the speaker. The causal explanations of the speaker's successive utterances of the several parts of the sentence are related together so as to comprise a single act because of the role of the speaker's knowledge of the rule, and the truth condition it determines, in the explanation of the parts of the act.

While this may be true of the utterance even of simple sentences, their *unity* should not be explained by appeal to truth-conditions, precisely because definitions of meaning in terms of truth-conditions presuppose the notion of a sentence. For the notion of a truth-condition is that of a condition which truth can be predicated, and it is only a relevantly unified expression to which truth or falsity can be predicated. For the same reason, it should not be thought that "truth-conditional" definitions of the meaning of predicates yield an account of the unity of the sentence. A truth-conditional account of what some predicate, for example "gray," means would appeal to the condition under which *sentences* of the form "x is gray" would be true. This is not in any way to reject "truth-conditional" semantics, but only to comment on its role in the total theory of language. But once one has an account of the unity of basic sentences that provides the stock upon which other operations are performed, then there is no apparent circularity in the appeal to the speaker's knowledge of the truth-conditions governing the utterances she makes.

Consider complex sentences in which simple sentences are joined together by the occurrence of the simplest operators "and" and "or." (These operators create *co-ordinate* structures, so it would be a mistake to look for any asymmetrical dependency between the conjoined or disjoined clauses of the kind we find between subject and predicate, or modifier and modified expression.) The utterance of a string of words of the form "p and q," if the string says a single thing, does so because it is a single act, and this is the case if there is a single explanation of the several utterances it is made up of. This single explanation involves the speaker's attention to the rule determining the truth condition for conjunction in the utterance of "p" and the utterance of "q" in the context "___ and ___." Her attention to that rule constrains her against the utterance of "p" if it is not true that p. (If the connective were "or" she would not be so constrained.) The explanation of the one utterance is related to the explanation of the second via the causal role of the speaker's knowledge of the meaning of "and."[1]

1 "Not" will sometimes work similarly, as an operation performed on some sentence "s is F" with the speaker's knowledge of the meaning of "not" governing its occurrence in the larger utterance of which the sentence "s is F" is a constituent. But sometimes it may work as it does in the basic cases. What property doesn't the cat have? "The cat is not gray." There the property that causes the occurrence of the predicate is to do so

These remarks are intended only to illustrate one direction that might be pursued in attempting to explain the unity of the sentence in terms of the unity of the act of utterance. To confirm or disconfirm the general thesis that the unity of the act explains that of the sentence would require an investigation into all the different kinds of sentences and the many varieties of speech acts. Having acknowledged the limits of my investigation, I want at this point to demonstrate how well the proposal developed above characterizes the sentences to which it applies directly, not just in general, but in particular structure-revealing ways, when it is applied to the subvarieties of acts in which such sentences are uttered.

1 Austin's "How to Talk: Some Simple Ways"

In this much admired but little discussed article, Austin "isolates" and "schematizes" what we have in mind when we distinguish such speech acts as describing, calling, stating, placing, instancing, and others.[2] He initially lists eight such models that we have "for talking about the world," but thinks that "This sort of investigation of the nature of speech-acts might go on more or less indefinitely."[3] Austin himself shows what is different in what the speaker is doing in virtue of which we regard the acts as distinct kinds of act. He is skeptical of general characterizations that cut across all speech acts or even across a single family of speech acts:

> Names for speech-acts are more numerous, more specialized, more ambiguous and more significant that is ordinarily allowed for: none of them can be safely used in philosophy in a general way (for example, "statement" or "description") without more investigation than they have, I think, yet received. . . .
>
> To some extent we probably do, even in ordinary language, make use of models of the speech-situation in using the terms that we do for speech-acts. At any rate, the construction of such models can help towards clarifying the varieties of speech-act which are possible. Any such model, even the simplest, seems bound to be fairly complicated –

because the cat doesn't have it. It would track properties the cat does not have, and so on.

2 J. L. Austin, "How to Talk: Some Simple Ways," in his *Philosophical Papers* (Oxford: Oxford University Press, 1961), pp. 181–200.

3 Ibid., p. 197.

too complicated for the standard subject–predicate or class-membership model. . . .

A feature, for example, in which different speech acts even of the same family may differ very much is that commonly discussed in an entirely general way under the name of "truth": even, say, with speech-acts which are assertions, we often prefer for one a different term of approbation from that which we prefer for another, and usually for good and understandable reasons.[4]

It is significant that Austin never calls the family of speech acts he discusses by any name. He does not, as I did, call it "saying." The only general characterization given of them is the one least descriptive – "ways of talking about the world."

What is interesting about Austin's cases, for my purposes, is that despite the differences between them, there is something common to them, and the models all seem to fit what might be described as a subject–predicate model. So where Austin draws attention to what is different about the speech acts, I want to draw attention to what is the same. In each case, the different things the speaker is doing establishes a nexus-dependency between the causes of the constituent utterances, and the expression that has a nexus-dependent cause is the one that functions to carry information about the referent of the other expression. Austin's cases illustrate that it is possible to arrive at the same place – for the truth-conditions of the utterances and the proposition expressed are the same – by means of doing quite different things. A single notion of predication may be found, I think, running through these cases. Of course, these four speech acts are all in the genus "assertion" (if we may use that term despite Austin's disapproval) and are of the most simplified kind, so they do not show to what extent that notion of predication is generalizable across different genuses or even in more complicated speech situations within that genus. But they do provide evidence that supports the general model: that, in doing what she is doing, the speaker establishes connections between the causes of the constituent utterances and so makes it a unity.

Austin classifies the four simplest species as "placing" (what he also calls "cap-fitting"), "casting" (or "bill-fitting"), "instancing," and "stating." He illustrates the difference between them with reference to a single sentence "1227 is a rhombus" uttered in different speech situations. Throughout, we are to imagine that there are various figures named by the numerals – 1227, 1228, 1229 – and various words naming

4   Ibid., pp. 197–8.

properties or types (Austin calls them "T-words") such as "rhombus," "square," "rectangle." Consider the sentence "1227 is a rhombus" as uttered in these different situations: (1) A child is making a drawing that includes a rhomboid figure. Wanting her picture to be precise, she asks "Where can I find a rhombus to trace?" When her friend hands her 1227 and says, "1227 is a rhombus," he *casts* 1227 as a rhombus, or presents something that fits the *bill* "rhombus." Compare that with situation (2): The child doesn't really know what shape corresponds to the word "rhombus" and is trying to figure that out as she is shown examples of various figures. She says, "Show me a thing that has the property of being a rhombus." When the teacher points to 1227 and says, "1227 is a rhombus," he is citing an *instance* of a rhombus. This differs from (3) *placing* the object: suppose the child has the figure 1227 before her and is clear what kind of shape the figure is but is not clear what to call it. She asks, "What is this called?" When she is told that "1227 is a rhombus," the child can then *place* the object in the category "rhombus." Contrast that with (4) *stating*: here, the child sees the figure 1227, but because it is too far away, she can't make out what shape it is. (If she could, she would know what to call it.) She asks, "What shape is that figure?" and the speaker states, "1227 is a rhombus."

Austin uses two notions to distinguish between the four cases: "direction of fit" and "onus of match." Direction of fit has to do with whether a word naming a type (a "T-word") is being fitted to an object or an object is being fitted to a T-word. Notice that in both casting ("Where can I find a rhombus to trace?") and instancing ("Show me a thing that has the property of being a rhombus"), when one says "1227 is rhombus?" the T-word is given and one is fitting an object to the T-word. Conversely, when placing ("What is 1227 called?") and stating ("What shape is that figure?"), when one replies "1227 is *rhombus*," the direction of fit runs in the opposite direction: for there the object is given and the T-word is fitted to the object.

The direction of fit determines which expression will function to carry information about the referent of the other expression: the term being fitted to the other one is the information-carrying expression. The cases differ in that in placing and stating "rhombus" is the information-bearing expression, whereas in casting and instancing it is "1227." But in each case, there is one expression that functions as an information-bearing expression. I will argue that the expression that is an information-bearing expression has a nexus-dependent cause.

The notion of "direction of fit" cannot by itself distinguish the four species, for the speech act of placing has the same direction of fit as stating, and casting has the same direction of fit as instancing. Austin introduces another notion, which he calls the "onus of match," to distinguish placing from stating and casting from instancing. Onus of match has to do with what in the context is presumed to be in doubt or at issue. According to Austin, we fit the object to the T-word or the T-word to the object "on the ground that the *type* of item and the *sense* of the name match. But in matching X and Y, there is a distinction between matching X *to* Y and matching Y *to* X, which may be called a distinction in point of onus of match."[5] In the one case, the type of the object is taken for granted, and "the question might be whether the sense of the T-word is such as really to match it": this is placing and instancing.[6] While one is perfectly clear what the object is like, one is in doubt about what word correctly characterizes it. In the other case, stating and casting, "the sense of the T-word is taken for granted, and the question might be whether the type of item is really such as to match it."[7] One knows perfectly well what the word means, but is in doubt about what the object is really like. I will argue what is in doubt or at issue in each case, what the "onus of match" is, explains the presence of the nexus-dependency.

First, consider the difference in onus of match between casting and instancing, where in both cases one says "*1227 is a rhombus*" being given the name "rhombus" and fitting the object 1227 to that name. The difference in onus of match is brought out in understanding the different things that might be at issue when someone makes that statement. In the casting example, the child knows what the property of being a rhombus is, what the type is, but was casting around for an object that is a rhombus because she needs one to trace. The issue is what object is of such a type that it matches the sense of "rhombus." The interest is in linking the sense of the name "rhombus" to the object via the type of thing the object (1227) is. Thus, the object that causes the occurrence of the object-specifying expression is to be its cause because it has the property of being a rhombus. But the property that causes the T-word to be uttered is not to do so because it belongs to the object 1227. (That is to say that if 1227 were rectangular, being rectangular would not be the cause of the T-word, but if 1229, instead of 1227 were rhomboid, 1229 could be the cause of the object-specifying word.) Thus, the expression "1227," which is the expression being fitted to the other, has a nexus-dependent cause. The nexus-dependency is

5   Ibid., p. 188.
6   Ibid., p. 190.
7   Ibid.

established by the interest in linking an object to the name ("rhombus") via the sense of that name. Given that interest, whatever object causes the occurrence of the object-specifying word is to do so because it has the property of being a rhombus.

Compare that with instancing where the child is not sure what the word "rhombus" means. Someone tries to inform her of what rhombuses are (of what the word "rhombus" means) by showing her an instance of a rhombus, an object that has that shape. Here the onus of match changes. When 1227 is cited as an instance of a rhombus, the question is whether the sense of "rhombus" is such as to match this object's, 1227's, type.[8] The interest is in fitting an object to the T-word because the object is of the type it is. Thus, whatever object causes the occurrence of the object-specifying word is to do so because it has the property of being a rhombus. But the property that causes "rhombus" is not to do so because 1227 has it. Again, the information-bearing expression has a nexus-dependent cause, and the nexus-dependency is established by the onus of match.

Consider now Austin's cases of placing and stating. There, in both cases, when one says "1227 is a *rhombus*," one fits the T-word to the object in answer to the question "What is this called?" In placing, one is not in doubt about what the object is like but about what property it has in virtue of being like it is, or what name correctly applies to it in virtue of the object's being like it is. The interest is in linking some T-word to the object via the sense of that T-word. The question is "What is the right category to put this in given that it is the way it is?" This makes the expression "rhombus" have a nexus-dependent cause, for the type (property) that causes the occurrence of the T-word is to do so because it is the type that 1227 is (because that property belongs to 1227). By contrast, the object that causes "1227" is not the object that causes it (rather than some other one) because it has the property of being a rhombus or because it is of the type it is.

Contrast that with stating. In stating, we are again fitting a T-word to an object. But here what is in doubt is not the sense of the T-word or what property or category is what, but rather what this object is like. For example, one may be seeing it but be unable to make out its shape. So the question is "What is the shape of this object?" In this context, the property that is the cause of T-word is supposed to be the cause of it because the object in question has that property. But the object that causes "1227" is not its cause, because it has the property that causes "rhombus." Thus, "rhombus," the information-bearing expression,

8 Ibid.

has a nexus-dependent cause. This is explained by the onus of match.

What constituent is fitted to the other may differ, and our interest in fitting the one to the other may differ, even when we use the same sentence, and this, in part, determines what speech act we are performing, whether stating, instancing, placing, or casting. Still, in doing these different acts, using the same sentence, we say the same thing. We arrive at the same proposition by different routes. This is because there is something common to these varieties of saying. There are constant features of the acts. The fact that whatever element is fitted to the other has the property of being the information-carrying expression is constant. When one places or states, one fits the name of a type to the object, and it is the name of the type, "rhombus," that functions as information-carrying expression. By contrast, when one casts or instances, one fits the item to the name of the type, and it is the name of the item "1227" that functions to carry information.

Another constant in these four speech acts is that the element which purports to carry information about the referent of the other has a nexus-dependent cause: what explains the tokening of that element depends asymmetrically on what explains the occurrence of the fixed element. In each case, what the speaker is doing, what is at issue or in doubt, establishes those dependencies. In casting and instancing, it is because she is fitting the object to the name, via either the sense of the name or the object type, that the property which causes the predicate does so because it belongs to the object that causes the subject. In placing and stating, it is because the speaker is fitting the name of the type to the object, by way either of the sense of name or object type, that the object which causes the subject does so because it instantiates the property which causes the predicate. What the speaker is doing may be explained by the sorts of subjective factors Cook Wilson, Ramsey, and Austin cite. But, in the end, what gets established in one way or the other, by fitting the T-word to the object or the object to the T-word, is a constant source of the unity of the sentence, lying beneath the interests and psychology of the speaker. For, whether one is stating, classing, placing, or instancing, one fits one or another of the elements to the other. The element fitted to the other is the information-carrying expression and it has a nexus-dependent cause. The unity of the subject–predicate sentence is explained by the interconnection and interdependence of the cause of the predicate on that of the subject.

Pragmatic or contextual facts about the utterance, including psychological states of the speaker and audience – their interests, purposes, what they know or don't know – select for certain causes and establish explanatory dependencies. Those causal interdependencies, once established, explain certain representational properties of the utterance. The particular psychological factors that are operative may be said to be irrelevant in just this sense: that anything else that served to establish the same causal connections would serve as well. It would not matter to the utterance's meaning what it does if the relevant causal asymmetry got established by convention or by nature instead of by intention. Still, it would be owing to those causal interdependencies that the parts of the representation are related so as to represent something as being the case.

There are, of course, other psychological states than these that enter into the production of utterance, and perhaps they are essential to the utterance. The states of affairs in the world that give rise to the utterance do so *via* a causal chain that extends from the external objects the statement is about, through the beliefs of the utterer about those objects, to the intentions to utter, and finally to the utterance itself. Those mental states are the more proximal cause of the utterance. For instance, the color of the cat (or squirrel) may cause an utterance *via* the speaker's perceptions of and/or beliefs about the color of the animal. We have seen that the nexus-dependency characterizes the level of belief as well. The belief that causes the utterance of the predicate will be asymmetrically dependent upon the belief that causes the utterance of the subject. In one sort of example, the belief that causes the utterance of the predicate "gray" involves the concept gray (or white) because the speaker believes that that is the color of the cat and because it is a belief about the cat which causes her to say "The cat." Change the belief that causes her to say "The cat," make that belief be about a different object, and the color concept which figures in the belief that causes the predicate would change to be one which she believes belongs to that other object.

So the nexus-dependency of "the cause" of the predicate on "the cause" of the subject characterizes at least two levels of causal analysis. It is present at the external level of objects and properties that give rise to the utterance and on the internal level of the mental states caused by those states of affairs. For certain reasons one might favor an "internalist" account of the unity of the sentence framed in terms of the interconnection of such beliefs. For one thing this would obviate problems about nonexistent referents and vacuous predicates, and it would also greatly simplify the account of how an utterance may be meaningful although it says something false.

The trouble, of course, is that this would seem to explain the unity of the statement in terms of the other states, beliefs in particular, which are themselves propositional and which themselves have unity. An account in terms of beliefs drives the basic question back, and merely transforms the terms of it. On many accounts of belief, beliefs themselves are composite entities with a constituent structure that mirrors the sentence: we can distinguish what the belief is about and what is believed about that thing.[9] It is plausible to think that there is something in the belief itself – some constituent of it – that corresponds to and determines what it is about, on the one hand, and what is believed about it on the other. That is, it is reasonable to think that beliefs themselves are composed of correlates of predicates and subjects, or perhaps that, in believing something, one is applying a *concept* or applying a predicate. It is also reasonable to think that this constituent of the belief, this application of a concept, depends on a second mental constituent that represents the thing to which it is applied. This mental constituent – the thinking of or the intuition of the object in question – is the correlate of the subject of the statement. On any such view, beliefs are not merely lists of concepts, but represent something as being the case, some single thing. Essentially the same questions that arise about the unity of the sentence arise also about the unity of the belief: How are its parts combined into something propositional, into the single thing that is believed?

An additional reason for avoiding an internalist account is methodological. It seems clear that if an account of the semantic properties of *sentences* is to shed any light on the semantic properties of *belief*, the semantic properties of the sentence cannot be explained in terms of psychological states that have those very same properties: for the explanation of the semantic properties of the psychological states needs to appeal to something outside of the psychological states under analysis. This is why I have framed the description of the asymmetry on the external level of states of affairs, and I will go on to explain how the nexus-dependency may fit into an externalist theory of meaning. The aim is to provide a more basic account of the unity of the sentence; "more basic" in two senses: first, that it provides an account of the unity of the sentence that, in its general features, might be applied to the unity of psychological states which are "propositional," and, second,

---

9 Beliefs are not *composed* of concepts (or of concepts or of intuitions) as sentences are composed of phrases or words. But beliefs can be said to "involve" concepts, i.e., involve the *application* of them.

that it relies less heavily on the sorts of semantic concepts internalist accounts tend to use rather than to analyze.

That being said, I want to say something in defense of the merits of such an internalist account. It may not be fundamental in the ways being sought above, but it would be wrong to accuse it of deriving the semantic properties of the utterance from the very same semantic properties as they characterize the belief the utterance expresses. Consider the view that a string of words expresses a single thing because their utterances have been caused by an intention to produce a belief that has that same single thing as its content. Such an internalist account provides no explanation of how the parts of *anything*, sentence or belief, have been unified to have a single thing as its meaning or content. By contrast, on the account I have proposed, the representational properties of the sentence would not be derived from the belief that has that same content. The unity would not be derived from the relation of the utterance to a *single* belief, and the belief that has the same content as the sentence would not necessarily figure in any way in the explanation of the utterance of the sentence. Rather, in utilizing the nexus-dependency between the beliefs that give rise to the constituent utterances, the separate utterance of the subject and predicate would comprise a single unitary act, because of an interconnection between the mental constituents of the separate beliefs that give rise to the utterances, the belief that causes the subject crucially determining the belief that gives rises to the predicate.

2   The Role of the Nexus-Dependency in Causal/Information Theorectic Accounts of Meaning

Causal and information-based theories of representation

There are semantic theories that try to cut through the psychological intermediaries, or proximal causes, of the meaningful utterances to the external "objective" states of affairs that are correlative to their meaning, and to attribute their meaning to some nomic or causal relations between such states of affairs and the meaningful item. And, though they are not widely recognized as doing so, the causal/information based accounts of meaning given by Dennis Stampe, Fred Dretske, and Jerry Fodor can be seen as extending Grice's program of reducing semantic to pragmatic properties. On all of these views, the fundamental semantic properties of expressions are properties inherited from facts about what the standard utterer of those expressions is doing, specifically what objective state of affairs (what objects and what properties) standardly cause and constitute the utterer's reason for uttering tokens of expressions of the type.[10]

Stampe's and Dretske's accounts begin in the idea that something is called a representation by virtue of its capacity to present some other object to us, not, of course, in the flesh, but at second hand – present it in such a way as to show us or tell us something about that object. This "presentation" is an epistemic phenomenon. The defining epistemic potential of representation is recognized quite explicitly by Leibniz:

> That is said to express a thing in which there are relations [*habitudines*] which correspond to the relations of the thing expressed.... What is common to all these expressions is that we can pass from a consideration of the relations in the expression to a knowledge of the corresponding properties of the thing expressed.[11]

Properties of the representation "correspond" systematically to the properties of the object, so that the form, if not the flesh, of the object is present in the representation. Because of that correspondence or "isomorphism," we can come to know some property of the object from some distinct property of the representation. What is represented is just what one would come to know something about from the representation. The height of the mercury column, for example, is isomorphic with the temperature of the air: an increase or decrease in the temperature correlates, respectively, with a rise or fall of the height of the mercury. The thermometer represents the temperature of the air,

10 See D. Stampe's "Show and Tell," in *Forms of Representation*, ed. B. Freed, A. Marras, and P. Maynard (New York: American Elsevier Publishing, 1975), pp. 221–45; "Toward a Causal Theory of Linguistic Representation." Reprinted in *Contemporary Perspectives in the Philosophy of Language*, ed. P. A. French, T. E. Uehling, and H. K. Wettstein (Minneapolis: University of Minnesota Press, 1979), pp. 81–102; "Verification and a Causal Account of Meaning," *Synthese*, 69 (1986), pp. 107–37; "Content, Context and Explanation," in *Information, Semantics and Epistemology*, ed. E. Villanueva (Oxford: Basil Blackwell, 1990), pp. 134–52; F. Dretske's *Knowledge and the Flow of Information* (Cambridge, MA: MIT Press, 1981); "The Epistemology of Belief," *Synthese*, 55 (1983), pp. 3–19; "Misrepresentation," in *Belief*, ed. R. Bogdan (Oxford: Oxford University Press, 1986); *Explaining Behavior: Reasons in a World of Causes* (Cambridge, MA: MIT Press, 1988); J. Fodor's "Semantics, Wisconsin Style," *Synthese*, 59 (1984), pp. 231–50; *A Theory of Content* (Cambridge, MA: MIT Press, 1990).

11 G. W. Leibniz, "What Is an Idea," in *Philosophical Papers and Letters*, ed. L. E. Loemker (Dordrecht: Reidel, 1977), pp. 207–8.

because that is what one could come to know something about from the rise and fall of the mercury.

A *causal* or a *nomic* theory of representation is one that goes on to explain the epistemic potential of a representation – its potential to convey information about, to present its object to us – in terms of the causal or lawful relations that obtain between the properties of the object on the one hand and properties of the representation on the other. When there is an appropriate necessary connection between some property of the cause and some property of the representation, then that property of the representation will represent that property of the cause. In Dretske's example, if only someone's pushing the doorbell could cause the doorbell to ring, then the ringing of the doorbell carries the information that someone is at the door.

Whether a representation does carry information about its object in particular circumstances is a perfectly objective matter. A signal, event, or structure is such that it carries information about some state of affairs if there is the right sort of causal or nomic connection between the properties of signal and those of the state of affairs. The properties of the signal and those of the state of affairs must be connected in such a way, that we could read off the properties of the state of affairs from those of the signal, if we knew how to read the representation. As Dretske expresses the point:

> A message . . . carries information about X to the extent to which one could learn (come to know) something about X from the message. And, in particular, the message carries the information that X is a dingbat, say, if and only if one could learn (come to know) that X *was* a dingbat from the message.[12]

Even when information is defined in terms of knowledge, the conception of information remains objective. For whether something F contains information about G is not a matter of what we actually know or believe. Rather, it is a matter of the causal or nomic connections that exist between the properties of F and G, connections whose existence may have nothing to do with us, though they may be such as to afford us knowledge. (For they may be such as to eliminate the possibility that our belief is mistaken.)[13]

---

12   Dretske, "Epistemology of Belief," p. 71.
13   See Dretske's "Conclusive Reasons," *Australasian Journal of Philosophy*, 49 (1971), pp. 1–22.

Of course, something might be a representation without anyone actually coming to know anything from it. Indeed, in the case of many natural representations, we may not know how to read them or even that they exist. Stratified deposits, tree rings, and the like represent facts about the history of the earth, whether we know how to read them or not. So what seems to matter is that the properties of the representation and that of its object are connected in such a way that one *could* come to know something about that property of the object from the representation.

That weakening to "could come to know" is necessary not just because there are representations in which information is present that we do not know how to elicit from them, but also because something can be a genuine representation although it inaccurately represents its object. In that case, it does not actually contain the *information* that x is f (since x is *not* f); but nonetheless (since it is a *mis*representation), it is correctly interpreted as representing x as f. While a representation may be inaccurate and misinformative, still it qualifies as a representation only if it in a relevant way might show or tell us how things stand, thus, perhaps, only if there are conditions under which it *would* carry genuine information about its object, conditions under which we could, from the representation, come to know something about its object. This, at least, is a central claim of Stampe's causal and Dretske's information-based accounts of meaning.[14]

These accounts take the relation between the properties of the representation and those of the object that can yield knowledge to be a causal or a nomic one. This idea is suggested by the causal theory of perception. What object one is perceiving is not determined by what object one believes one is seeing or the object that most resembles the visual percept one has, but by the object whose properties causally explain the properties of the perception. This may be extended beyond

---

14 Neither Stampe or Dretske say that it is a representation of an object *in virtue* of the fact that one could come to know something about it, if it were accurate. The account or theory of why something is a representation and why it represents what it does is a matter of the causal–nomic relation between the representation and some state of affairs or object. Thus, it is in virtue of their being such causal–nomic connections that the representation is a representation. Those causal–nomic relations can, however, explain why representations have a certain property – that they present objects to us in such a way as to afford knowledge of the object, under certain conditions. Thus, the theory can explain the fact that representations are *called* representations (or that we regard something as a representation) because of their ability to afford knowledge of their objects.

perception.[15] The distorted photograph of the cat may be a representation of her properties and not of a chicken's, even if the properties of the photo make the cat look like the chicken – even when the photo resembles a chicken more than it does the cat. What the photo most *resembles* may not be what it *represents*. Further, what a representation represents and what people take it to represent may not be the same. I may mistake the photo of the cat for one of some particular chicken, but that does not make it a representation of that chicken. In mistaking the photo of the cat for one of the chicken, I may come to have true beliefs about the properties of the chicken. Because what looks to be a chicken looks to be white, I believe some particular chicken is white. As it happens, coincidentally, the chicken is white. That does not make it a representation of the color of the chicken. It is still a representation of the cat and of the color of the cat.

These points seem undeniable. The question is how they are to be understood. The causal account gives this explanation: given the conditions in which it was produced, the cat's color and not the chicken's cause the color of the figure in the photo, and given that connection between the cat's color and color of the figure, and holding that fact fixed, it is the color of the cat we could know from the photograph, if the representation had been produced in a certain right sort of way, so that it had *not* turned out to be distorted. If contrary to fact, this very photograph had been produced in the right sort of conditions – the camera was working, the light not too bright or dim, the negative not smudged, and so on – then this representation would have carried information about the color and shape and whatnot of the cat. We could have come to know something about her from it.[16]

Stampe suggests that if we generalize from this, what matters to what a representation represents is what properties of an object actu-

15   David Kaplan extends it to partially provide a conception of what beliefs are about, and he extends it to pictures, saying, "If one or several witnesses describe the criminal to a police artist who then constructs a picture, I shall say that it is a picture of the criminal, even when after such a genesis the resulting picture has quite ceased to resemble the criminal" ("Quantifying In," *Synthese*, 19 [1969], p. 196; see §9). Stampe argues that it is a causal relation between some property of an object and that of the linguistic representation which determines the object of the representation – what the utterance is about – even where that comes apart from the object referred to. See his "Show and Tell," pp. 231–41.

16   This, I am told, goes against some accounts of the individuation of photographs. Such accounts would seem to run counter to the intuition that it is perfectly acceptable to say that this particular photograph might have had different properties, if, say, the lens had stayed open longer, or if the sunlight had not been so bright.

ally cause (or stand in another causal relation to) the properties of the representation in such a way that the representation would carry information about it, if the representation had been produced in what he calls "fidelity conditions":

> The causal relation we have in mind is one that holds between a set of properties F(f1 . . . fn) of the thing (O) represented, and a set of properties Φ (φ1 . . . φn) of the representation R. The specification of sets F and Φ will consist of predicates that identify certain constituents, and certain relations among those constituents, of O and R respectively. The relevant causal relationships between O's being F and R's being Φ will be one that normally, if not necessarily, preserves an isomorphism between the structures thus defined.[17]

And "fidelity consists broadly speaking in the absence of distortion, in the proper and accurate working or utilization of the representation generating device."[18] It may involve reference to the function of the device, in which case the specific conditions will differ from one kind of representational device to another. In Stampe's account, something qualifies as a representation only if it has properties that are causally related to some property of some object in such a way that *if* fidelity conditions were to have governed its production, then it would tell us the facts with regard to that property of the object. Only that *counterfactual* conditional need be true, so the favored conditions need not prevail in actual fact when the representation is produced.[19] What is represented by the representation is determined by the truth of the counterfactual conditional, which remains true whether its antecedent is true or not. As a result, what is represented remains constant whether the conditions that prevail are favorable or not, whether the representation is true or false.[20]

---

17   Stampe, "Toward a Causal Theory of Linguistic Representation," §6.4, p. 84.

18   Stampe, "Show and Tell," p. 226.

19   Ibid., pp. 225, 228–30; and "Toward a Causal Theory of Linguistic Representation," p. 46.

20   One can see from this exposition of Stampe's account of the object of representation, that his account is designed from the outset to provide for the possibility of misrepresentation. It is evidently believed by some that Stampe's and Dretske's theories do not allow for misrepresentation. This is wrong. That belief may stem from Fodor's flawed characterizations of these theories. (See his "Semantics, Wisconsin Style" or *A Theory of Content*, ch. 2.) For example, in Stampe's case, Fodor runs together the distinction between the object of representation and the content of the representation, a distinction that enables Stampe to state a causal theory that precisely allows for the possibility of misrepresentation. See Stampe's defense of his view in "Verification and a Causal

This provides a theory of what makes one thing a representation of another. In the last chapter, we were left with the question of whether the structural isomorphism (between the utterance and some property of an object) established by the nexus-dependency is one constitutive of representation. I will argue that, on this theory of representation, the structural isomorphism is constitutive of representation, for when there is such a structural isomorphism, the utterance of the sentence is causally related to a property of an object in such a way that one could come to know something about that from the utterance had it been produced in fidelity conditions. The theory of representation supplies an answer to the question why (or whether) the isomorphism established by the nexus-dependency is constitutive of representation. But the account of the isomorphism also supplies something that is missing from these causal or information-based theories of meaning and representation.

The causal theory of representation and the unity of the sentence

A central task for a theory of representation is to explain what the nature of that correlation or isomorphism is that holds between the properties of the representation and the properties of the object in virtue of which the one represents the other. These theories hold that the correlation is a causal or nomic one. The representation is *causally* related to some property of an object in such a way that it would carry information about that property, if fidelity conditions had obtained. But how is this to be understood?

There are causal theories of reference that attempt to explain how the referring expression refers to what it does, and causal theories of content that attempt to explain how the thing represented is represented. But it is another thing to explain how the whole sentence is causally related to some property of an object, for example the color of the cat, in such a way that it would carry information about that property of the object, under certain favored conditions. This is a question about the compositional character of the sentence. The phenomenon in question is an essential aspect of the unity of the sentence. Causal theorists have not attempted to explain how the parts of the representation are combined in such a way that they represent some determinable property of an object, or a determinable property, specifically, of the very object referred to or represented.

Account of Meaning" and my "Asymmetric Dependencies, Ideal Conditions, and Meaning," *Philosophical Psychology*, 9 (2) (1996), pp. 235–59.

It might be said that these causal/information accounts do not have a problem with the unity of the sentence, because the causal–nomic relations may be construed as relations between sentences and states of affairs, and states of affairs *are* unitary constructions or combinations of the properties, relations, and objects that enter into them.[21] And it might be assumed that the unity of the sentence is simply a reflection of or derivative from the unity of that state of affairs, and nothing more needs to be said about it. But this is not right. Of course, one may *identify* the meaning of the sentence with the state of affairs that would cause it under fidelity conditions. But this is not to *explain* why the parts of the sentence hang together in such a way as to *be* correlated with some unitary state of affairs that might, in this way, be identified with its meaning.

It is no coincidence that there is a systematic relation between the parts of the sentence on the one hand, and the distinguishable elements of that state of affairs on the other. Everyone might agree that it is owing to the relation of the parts of the sentence to one another that the sentence has the unitary meaning it does. The meaning of a sentence is "compositional." And, presumably, it is because the parts of the sentence are semantically related to the elements of the state of affairs that "is" its meaning, that *that* state of affairs, rather than another one, *can* be identified as its meaning. So the unity of the sentence is not a mere reflection of the unity of the correlated state of affairs.

The right course for the causal theory of representation is to attempt to *explain* the unity of the sentence in terms of the relevant relations between the elements of the states of affairs that cause it and the occurrence of the expressions that constitute the sentence. But it is not easy to see how this is to be done. For if we abandon the superficial idea that the unity of the sentence merely derives from that of the state of affairs identified as its meaning, then we must look to the states of affairs that determine, according to the theory, what its meaning is. And the first problem is that there is not one of them: there are, at least, *two*.

The basic problem is that there are different representational properties that contribute to the sentence's having a meaning, and such causal theories explain those distinct representational properties by appeal to distinct states of affairs. For example, such causal theories

---

21   Robert Stalnaker, in his book *Inquiry* (Cambridge, MA: MIT Press, 1984), depends upon this assumption when he uses what he calls Stampe's notion of "indication" to develop a holistic theory of content. I think the assumption is wrong.

take the referent of the subject to be something actually involved in the causing of the representation (or of the utterance of the sentence); and they take the content of the representation (compare the contribution of the predicate) to be a property that need not actually belong to that object, and accordingly need not actually be a cause of the representation or any of its parts. (For the statement may be false.) And yet, the particular thing represented as having this property is the object being referred to, that is, the actual cause of the statement or the subject of it.

The subject, roughly, corresponds to an object in some *actual* state of affairs that causes the utterance, but the predicate to a property in a state of affairs that would cause it *ideally* (not actually). The object that actually causes the utterance is represented as having the property that *would* cause it *ideally*. So the first point is this. There is not some *one* state of affairs, from which the unity of the sentence can be said to be derived. For the actual state of affairs that does cause it may not be the state of affairs that would cause it ideally. The unity of the sentence, then, cannot be the unity of "the" state of affairs that causes it.

More fully, the point is this: there are several "representational properties" of the sentence that contribute to its having a meaning. Consider the sentence "The cat is gray." The referring expression *refers* to a certain object, the cat, and the predicate expression *designates* a certain property, that of being gray. The sentence as a whole *represents* some determinable property of that object – the color of the cat or the state of affairs with regard to the color of the cat. And what is represented, the color of the cat, is represented *as being something or other*, here it is represented as being gray: to identify what it is represented as being may be said to identify the "content" of the representation. The meaning of this utterance includes in some way all of these representational properties.

My claim is that there is no causal relation between an actual or possible state of affairs to which the utterance is related that will explain, in one swoop, all of these representational properties, and so the unity of the sentence cannot be derived from the unity of any such state of affairs. The reason that there is no single state of affairs that will explain these various semantic properties is this: at the heart of these causal/nomic theories is the idea that a sentence "refers" to what it does, for example the cat, and represents what it does, the color of the cat, because it is actually caused by the cat and its color (or stands in some relevant other actual causal relation). So to explain the "aboutness" of the representation – what is referred to by the referring expression and represented by the whole utterance – one must appeal to a causal/nomic relation between the utterance of the sentence and some actual state of affairs.

But one cannot, similarly, explain either what is designated by the predicate or the way the object is represented as being with reference to any determinate property in the state of affairs that actually caused its utterance. Where the lighting is bad, the cat's being white may have caused the utterer to say, "The cat is gray," but "The cat is gray" does not represent the color of the cat as white, nor does "gray" designate the color white. More generally, if the meaning of any sentence were specified with reference to the actual state of affairs that causes its utterance, no sentence could be false, since the very state of affairs it represents as being the case would have to obtain, if that state of affairs is the cause of its utterance. In these theories, the semantic value of the predicate expression is specified counterfactually, with reference to a *possible* state of affairs – what *would* cause it to be uttered *were* certain specified conditions to hold. The upshot of this is that there is no single state of affairs actual or possible to which the sentence is related that can *explain* the various representational properties of the utterance in virtue of which it has the meaning it does. As Frege, Russell, and Wittgenstein found, each in his way, giving an adequate account of the joint competing constraints of objectivity and possibility of misrepresentation entails there is no "whole" out there in the world – at least no actual or possible state of affairs – from which to simply derive the unity of the sentence.

Of course, as we have seen, there *is* one state of affairs that may be identified with the *meaning* of the sentence, or, better put, there is one state of affairs such that to identify it is to identify the meaning of the sentence. But again, we cannot understand the unity of the sentence to *derive* from the unity of this state of affairs. We cannot do so, because the state of affairs in question can be identified *as* the meaning of the sentence, only because the string of words that is the sentence hangs together in such a way as to represent that particular state of affairs as the way things are. To avoid such circles, we have to explain the principal representational properties of the utterance, constitutive of its "unity," in a way that does not presuppose that the sentence uttered has the meaning it does.

While there is no single state of affairs to which the utterance is related that can explain its representing what it does, there is an interconnection – a nomic connection established by the nexus-dependency – between the states of affairs that cause the utterance of the subject and predicate expression, which can explain why the whole utterance represents what it does. According to Stampe, it represents what it does, because there is a structural relation between a set of properties F(fi ... fn) of the object and Φ (φi ... φn) of representation, which is such that if fidelity conditions had governed the production of the representation, the representation's being Φ would have carried information about the F of the object. The nexus-dependency establishes just such a structural isomorphism. When the nexus-dependency is present, there is a relation between a set of properties F of the object and Φ of the representation: the terms of this relation are the possible causes of the utterance on the one side and the possible utterances made on the other. If the color that caused the utterance of "gray" was its cause only because it belonged to the cat and because the cat was the cause of "The cat," then the color of the cat co-varies with properties of the representation. Change the color of the cat and the color that causes the predicate and the predicate expression itself changes. The possible causes are the possible colors of the cat and the possible utterances are possible color predicates. There is a structural isomorphism between the color of the cat and the utterance of the predicate expression that makes the sentence "track" the color of the cat (though as I've argued, it need not track it correctly).

That structural isomorphism is the form common to the representation and its object in virtue of which the former represents the latter. According to the theory of representation under consideration, a representation represents what it would carry information about, had it been produced under fidelity conditions. While there being a nexus-dependency between the cause of the utterance of the subject and that of the predicate in no way entails that the representation carry genuine information about its object (the color of the cat), it does entail that the utterance *would have* carried information about that property of the object, the color of the cat, *if* it had been produced under fidelity conditions. Suppose that the utterance is color tracking but false: because of the poor lighting, the child misperceives the color of the cat, and the cat's being white causes her to say, "The cat is gray." Still, because the nexus-dependency holds (because the color that causes her to say "gray" is its cause only because it belonged to the object that causes the occurrence of "The cat"), the utterance tracks the color of the cat. If, other things being equal, the cat had been a different color, it would have been the cat's being that color which caused the utterance of the predicate and a different predicate would have been uttered. Now imagine that, contrary to fact, fidelity conditions *had* governed the production of the representation. Here fidelity conditions will insure that the speaker is not misperceiving the object, is not lying, is capable of uttering the words she intends, and so on. Had those conditions obtained, the child would have uttered the predicate "white," and her utterance would then have carried information about the color of the cat. Given the presence of the nexus-dependency, the utterance she actually made, "The cat is gray," is causally and structurally related to the color of the cat in such a way that, if fidelity conditions had obtained, the utterance would have carried information about the color of the cat, even though it does not now do so.

The existence of the nexus-dependency itself does not depend upon conditions being normal or ideal for its nomic connection to be established; that is, whether one is lying, mistaken, or speaking the truth, the property that causes the predicate is its cause only because of its relation to whatever object causes the predicate. But the nexus-dependency establishes a structural relation between the property of the object and the utterance of the sentence which is such that, if fidelity conditions had governed the production of the sentence, it would have carried information about that property of the object. Thus the nexus-dependency establishes a connection between a property of the object that causes it and a property of the representation which can explain why the utterance represents that property of the object. It may explain, therefore, this aspect of the unity of the representation. And the unity the representation has it has owing to the connection between the various explanations of the utterances of its parts – because of its relation to several states of affairs – not to some single one.

Natural and non-natural meaning: the possibility of misrepresentation

I suggested in the Introduction that while many representations are semantic composites, there is something distinctive about the way in which mental and linguistic representations are compositional. In the end, the analysis I propose of these may seem to involve the same kinds of causal processes that explain natural phenomena. Why then are the capacities of our representations different from and sometimes greater than those of representations found in nature?

One clear difference between natural or "found" representations and representational devices (gauges and the like) we have created, on the one hand, and our mental and linguistic representations, on the other, lies in the difference in the *range* of things they may represent. Thermometers represent the temperature of the air, altimeters the altitude of the plane, the tree rings the number of annual cycles, and perhaps a few other things in passing (the temperature of the mercury, etc.). What these things can represent is highly restricted. Sentences and thoughts, by contrast, can represent most anything, or perhaps absolutely anything. This difference is explained partly by the fact that our perceptual and mental faculties are sensitive to information about more kinds of properties than are thermometers and other such representational devices. They can also generate more kinds of representations.

But it is not just that we are sensitive to more kinds of information, for it is not just what we represent, but *the way* we represent it that is distinctive. We represent things as being ways that they are not. Our minds and language do not, like many natural representations, simply mirror what goes on in the natural world. So some of our representations have "nonfactive" content; that is, they represent something as being the case that may not be the case in fact. We can be wrong, and lie, and create representations of states of affairs that don't exist. In metaphor, we can represent the way things are by ways that literally they are not. It is this "nonfactive" aspect of our representations that many philosophers believe distinguish our representations from other "natural" representations, from ones that occur in nature without the involvement of purposes or conventions or mental processes.

It is not a matter of controversy that both the representations we make and the representations found in nature have what Grice called "natural meaning" or content. Natural meaning is factive. If the patient's spots mean measles "naturally," then the patient's having these spots entails that he does have the measles. Otherwise, it is not correct to say that the spots *mean* measles (as opposed to "suggest," etc.). Natural signs like tree rings, paw prints, stratified deposits have natural meaning – they contain actual information that may be taken from them, provided that one knows how to read them. The presence of that information constitutes a kind of *content*: there is information *contained* in them. (By information I mean genuine information: misinformation is not a kind of information.) Any information contained in them, given the way they were produced, is a part of their "natural meaning": so, the paw print may contain information about the size and weight of the animal, what kind of animal it was, how long ago it was there. It represents naturally all of those things and the information it contains about each of those properties identifies a part of a paw print's natural meaning.

Our linguistic and mental representations also have natural meaning: they contain information about our psychological and physiological states, about our neural states and states of the world outside of us, whether we know how to read this information from them or not. But such representations also have "nonfactive" meaning. The statement "The cat is on the mat" means the cat is on the mat even if the fact is that the cat is *not* on the mat and so even when it does not carry the information that the cat is on the mat.

This raises a question about how the representation can have the content it does, when the content is not necessarily identified with information it actually carries. And it raises a question about how a representation can genuinely *represent* something, for example, the color of the cat, even if it does not carry any *information* about that, as normally interpreted. Consider the latter question first. What a linguistic utterance represents is not determined by the information that the utterance carries. First, because an utterance may represent something, for example the color of the cat, even if, as normally interpreted, it carries no information about that. Second, representations don't represent *everything* they may carry information about. ("The cat is gray" may represent the color of the cat and not the identity of the gray pet, even when it carries information about the identity of the gray pet.)

I have suggested that what is represented is explained by the procedural history of the utterance. When the nexus-dependency is present, the utterance may track some property of an object, without tracking it correctly, but in such a way that it has the epistemic potential that is characteristic of representations. Echoing Stampe and Dretske, that epistemic potential is that the representation is such that it could show or tell us something or could carry information about that property of the object, if it had been produced in certain conditions. When the nexus-dependency is present, the representation is such that it would have carried information about the relevant property of the object, had certain fidelity conditions governed its production. The cat's being white may cause the speaker to say, "The cat is gray," because the lighting is poor. So long as the nexus-dependency is present, the structural isomorphism between the color of the cat and the utterance will be present – change the color of the cat and that changes the color which causes the predicate and the predicate uttered – and the utterance will track the color of cat, but not track it correctly. Because the utterance was not produced under fidelity conditions, it does not carry the information that the cat is gray, but it nevertheless represents the color of the cat, because it is causally related to the color of the cat, in such a way, that had fidelity conditions governed its production, it would have carried information about the color of the cat.

Consequently, the representation here represents something it carries no information about.

Furthermore, unlike the natural representation, the sentential representation does not represent everything that it does carry information about. The representation may represent the color of the cat and not the identity of the gray pet, even when it carries information about the identity of the gray pet, because there is no structural isomorphism of the relevant kind between the representation and the identity of the gray pet. (Of course, considering the utterance as a "natural" event, it may carry information that the cat is the gray pet, and if it does it will have that "natural" meaning.) An utterance "The cat is gray" may carry the information that the cat is gray and so the information that the child's pet, the cat, is a gray animal, but represent only the color of the cat: for there may be no structural isomorphism between the identity of the gray pet and the utterance which is such that the utterance tracks the identity of the gray pet. (Changes in the animal that is gray will not result in a change of the animal which caused the utterance of the subject or in the subject expression uttered.)[22] Consequently, there is a way of identifying what the utterance represents, non-naturally, in terms of the way the utterance is actually caused to occur that nonetheless allows for the possibility of falsity. Thus, the nexus-dependency may provide an explanation of one aspect of an utterance's having non-natural meaning – of how it can represent, non-naturally, what it does.

But, ordinarily, an utterance will have nonfactive meaning or content only if the representation represents its object *as being some way* and the object might not be that way. So we have to have some way of identifying the way the object is represented as being that is distinct from the

---

22   This same sort of explanation can be employed to differentiate co-extensive predicates. Cats with "tortoise shell" coloring are about 98% female. Suppose 100% of tortoise shells were female. In any instance that the utterance "The cat is a tortoise shell" carried the information that the cat was a tortoise shell, it would thereby carry the information that she was female. Yet the sentence "The cat is a tortoise shell" does not necessarily represent the gender of the cat, for it may not have a form in common with the gender of the cat. Suppose the utterance of "The cat is a tortoise shell" is color tracking, then there would be co-variation between the color of the cat and the properties of the utterance. Since it is changes in color that affect the predicate and since other cats of other colors are both male and female, this utterance is not *gender* tracking. If the gender of this cat were different (male), but her color the same (this involves imagining that tortoise shells are not exclusively female), then the property that caused the utterance of the predicate (its being a tortoise shell) would not change so as to vary with the gender of the cat and no alternative predicate term would be uttered.

way the object actually is. This is an issue not about the object of the
representation, or what it represents, but about its *content*, or how what
it represents is represented. Some philosophers believe that what distinguishes our mental and linguistic representations from so-called
"representations" found in nature is that only the former can represent
their objects as being some way that they are not. It is argued that in
characterizing some natural representation as a misrepresentation, we
impose an interpretation of our own on it. After all, it may be urged,
it is not as if the tree trunk were trying to tell us its age, or as if it were
the biological function of the tree rings to record its age. This is merely
information that we, not the trees, have an interest in.[23] The issue is
whether there is a nonarbitrary way of assigning content to natural representations that makes them "intrinsically" capable of misrepresentation. Part of what it means for the content specification to be intrinsic
is that the representation's having the content it does has to have something to do with the existence of the representation, so we are not just
imposing a content on it.[24] Some philosophers go further, arguing that
if a sign cannot in that sense misrepresent its object, it is not "really"
a representation at all. If the signs found in nature are not capable of
*mis*representing things, then only our linguistic and mental representations will turn out really to be representations, with their
representational capacities being essentially different from natural
phenomena that might wrongly be called "representations."[25]

Despite the fact that I think these sorts of arguments are largely
unconvincing, I think there are important differences between the way
in which natural representations and mental or linguistic representations are constructed and that those differences may explain the
intuition these philosophers have that only mental and linguistic
representations are really capable of misrepresentation. It is not clear it
follows, though, that the analysis of linguistic and mental representations is *essentially* different from those found in nature.

There is the following difference between natural and linguistic representations. While the parts of a natural representation do not occur

---

23   Daniel Dennett, e.g., asserts that it is in only in the context of users and their intentions "that we can single out some of the occasions of state Q as 'veridical' and others
as 'mistaken'" ("Evolution, Error, and Intentionality," in his *The Intentional Stance*
[Cambridge, MA: MIT Press, 1987], p. 291).
24   That may be part of what is behind Dretske's idea that to be a representation it has
to have the function of indicating what it does, for if its function is to indicate something,
than what it indicates does have to do with why the representation came to exist.
25   Dretske, *Explaining Behavior*, pp. 66–71.

as they do because of what they individually mean or represent, the parts of a linguistic representation – a sentence – typically do do so. Words *do* occur in sentences because of what they mean – because tokens of the type mean what they do. The speaker utters the words "gray" in "The cat is gray," because it is a token of a type that means gray. Or she utters "gray" because the property of being gray would cause "gray" to be uttered under fidelity conditions. The causal process that produces the utterance proceeds, as it were, in consultation with the standard meaning of the constituent parts of the utterance. A determination of the meaning of the parts is intrinsic to the process that gives rise to the construction. It is not so with natural representations. Constituents of natural representations are not caused to occur because tokens of that type have the meaning they have. In the stratified deposit, it is no part of the causal process which gives rise to this representation that its constituents are caused to occur because of what tokens of those types represent or indicate. The coal did not come to be in the stratified deposit *because* other tokens of the type (coal deposits) represent ancient forests. Or consider the single tree ring that, because of odd climatic conditions, was produced over a period of two years, rather than the usual one. This tree ring was not caused to occur because of what other tree rings standardly indicate. Given the way it was caused to occur, by the passage of two years, we have no reason to identify its meaning with what tree rings normally or standardly indicate, that is, one year of growth.

By contrast, in the case of the utterance of the sentence, there is a way of connecting what *would* cause the utterance of the predicate under fidelity conditions to what *does* cause it, and so a way of understanding the meaning of the utterance in terms of its actual causal history. Words are uttered because of what they "timelessly" mean. When the cat's being white caused the speaker to say, "The cat is gray," she chose to utter the word "gray," rather than some other word precisely because of what tokens of that type mean. The timeless meaning of the words enters into the *actual* causal explanation of the occurrence of "gray" in this tokening of "The cat is gray." Importantly, there are intentionally less rich ways of describing this than an appeal to the meaning of the word type. We could say that is only because being gray would cause the utterance of "gray" under fidelity conditions that, here, the cat's being white caused the utterance of "gray." Or following Fodor, but for the fact that something's being gray causes the utterance of "gray," something's being white wouldn't cause the utterance of "gray." Fodor argues that the white/"gray" law depends upon the gray/"gray" law, but not vice versa.[26] But however this fact is described, it gives us a principled reason to think that gray is the color that the cat is represented as being. (This is on the assumption that other things are true of the representation as well, for instance, that it is a representation of the color of the cat, and "gray" functions to identify its color.) But the cat is white. Well, then, *this* utterance in and of itself *mis*represents the color of the cat. This particular utterance is a misrepresentation, given its intrinsic representational properties, for the fact that tokens of the type mean what they do explains the existence of this token. Thus, even though the content of the representation is explained with reference to the internal process by means of which this representation is caused to occur, the representation can be a misrepresentation. (So it is certainly possible to provide an account of misrepresentation on a Stampe/Dretske type theory.)

This difference between the natural and the linguistic representation may or may not be an essential difference, justifying such doubts as whether tree rings really "represent" the age of the tree. However that may be, it is not a difference that should make us think that no uniform account of meaning or representation can be given across representations of all kinds. It is a difference in *what* enters into the causal chain by means of which it is produced. So it is not that the representational properties are not determined by the causal relations that reach from the world to the representation. That is the same in both. It is rather that certain things enter into the causal chain that explain the production of the linguistic representation, here, the speaker's beliefs about the meaning of tokens of that type, that do not enter into the causal chain that produces the natural representation. That makes it the case that there is a sense in which linguistic representations are *intrinsic mispresentors* and natural representations are not, for, in the case of the linguistic representation, there is way of specifying their content, given the way that they were actually produced, according to which they can be misrepresentations.

Something can have nonfactive content only if the representation represents its object *as being some way* and the object is not that way. If the meaning of the predicate may be identified with what the type standardly means, then we begin to have a way of understanding how the representation can intrinsically represent its object as being some way that the object is not. But that is only part of the story. In particular, we will have reason for identifying the content of the representation in this

26 Fodor, *Theory of Content*, p. 91.

way only when that explanation is seen together with other aspects of the explanation of the existence of the representation. For a representation has nonfactive content, only if it genuinely represents some property of an object (state of affairs, etc.) even though it may not in fact carry information about that property of the object. This, I have argued, can be explained by the nexus-dependency, which establishes a structural isomorphism between some property of an object and the utterance of the sentence which is constitutive of representation. If the utterance represents some determinable property of an object, and one of its constituents functions to make that determinable determinate, and the determinable property it represents the object as having is the one designated by the expression, then the utterance may be said to represent something as being the case, and in such a way, that what it represents as being the case may be false.

3   Event Meaning

Emerging from this discussion is a notion of meaning that I will call "event" meaning: event meaning is a kind of nonfactive meaning that the utterance has given its actual causal history, in the sense just discussed. In particular, the event meaning will include both *what* is represented by the occurrence of the event and *the way* that object is represented *as being*, and both that object and content will be determined with reference to the actual causal history of the event, but in such a way that misrepresentation is possible. What is represented will be determined by the nexus-dependency – by the causal counterfactual dependencies between subject and predicate that are true of the utterance given the way it was caused to occur. And the way the predicate represents its object is explained by the actual explanation of the predicate in the utterance of the whole sentence, including the fact that the particular predicate was uttered because of what tokens of that type mean. The notion of event meaning is a more basic notion of meaning than what Grice called "utterer's" meaning in at least two respects. First, it might be possible to explain the content of psychological states that have propositional or representational content in terms of event meaning. Second, the explanation of the representational content of an utterance is less dependent upon reference to psychological states with that same content or to psychological states that employ the semantic concepts under analysis.

Regarding extending the account to psychological states, I have suggested an explanation of the unity of linguistic utterances of subject–predicate form and have shown how the suggestion might fit into the general framework of causal or informational accounts of representation. But the causal/information theorectic accounts considered are intended to apply to psychological states. Fodor's account is a theory of mental content. Both Dretske and Stampe formulate a general theory of representation, intended to apply to representations of all kinds. The fundamental properties of the representation that make them have the content they do – that is, their causal/nomic relations to states of affairs and the functions they subserve – are properties that mental states can possess. So the question arises of whether the kind of explanation I proposed could extend to *mental* representations that are propositional.

If such representations have sentential or other componential structure, it would seem that the general lines of the account might carry through. The unity of the mental act or event would be explained by a certain unity in the cause of the event, in certain cases, perhaps, by causal or nomic relations that come to exist between the separate explanations of the tokenings of the parts of the mental event as a result of how the event is caused to occur. These causal or nomic dependencies between the cause of the constituent events might explain how the constituent events themselves together become related to some state of affairs in such a way that together they would carry information about it, under certain favorable conditions.

In some cases, even the details of the explanation of speech and of thought may run along the same lines. For example, just as "saying" is a kind of catchall for different speech acts that an utterer might be performing, so the word "thinking" is a genus with many species. There are many things a person may be doing, many mental acts she may be performing, in thinking of a certain thing. Many of these mental acts might be expressed by speech acts of the same name. For instance, classifications of the thought that "that figure is a rhombus" may parallel Austin's classifications of "our talk about the world." In having the thought "that figure is a rhombus," a person might be giving an *instance* of a rhombus, *casting* something as a rhombus, *placing* an object in that category, and so on. Suppose the thought comprises concepts or, as in Kant, an intuition (of the figure) and the concept of a rhombus. In the thought, the intuition and concept are combined in such a way that the object is represented as being a rhombus. The unity of the thought might be explained by the nexus-dependency between the causes (or explanations) of the separate tokenings of intuition and concept in the thought. That causal dependency is established by what the thinker is doing in having the thought, by what, in her mind, is in doubt, by her interests, or, maybe vaguely, just by what, in the present state of affairs, strikes her in a certain way.

Suppose, for example, that in thinking "That object is a rhombus," a person needs a rhomboid figure, and in looking around the room, she lands on a certain object and thinks to herself, "That figure is a rhombus." Given her interests – that she is looking for an object to *fit the bill* "rhombus" – the object that causes the occurrence of "that figure" is its cause rather than other objects, because it has the property that causes the occurrence of "rhombus," that is, because it has the property of being a rhombus. But the property of being a rhombus is not the cause of "rhombus," rather than some other property, because it belongs to that object. The object that causes the occurrence of "that figure" is nexus-dependent upon the property that causes the occurrence of "rhombus." In *placing*, the nexus-dependency runs the other way. The child has an object before her, but is not clear what property it has in virtue of being like it is. She is trying to figure out what shape it is given the way it is shaped. She thinks, "That figure is a rhombus." There the property that causes the occurrence of "rhombus" is its cause, rather than another property, because it belongs to that object. But that object, rather than other objects, is not the cause of "that figure" because it has the property of being a rhombus.

The causal dependency that runs in one way or another is established by what the thinker is doing in having the thought. The thinker may come to have the same thought by means of various routes. The causal histories that issue in the thought may be different. But the interdependency between the causes of the parts of the thought makes certain causal counterfactuals true in virtue of which the thought has a form in common with some property of an object or state of affairs: it tracks a certain property of an object, in such a way that the thought would have carried information about that property of the object, if it had been produced under fidelity conditions.

The descriptions I've given of what the thinker is doing have been dependent upon other of her psychological states. First there is the matter of what the speaker is doing in having the thought, and that depends on such psychological factors as what she is interested in, what is, in her mind, in doubt or what she wants to know. This parallels the case of speech. In the case of the utterance of a sentence, what the speaker intends to be doing depends on her interests or her beliefs about what the audience does or does not know. In both cases, such psychological factors select for certain objective states of affairs as causes of the constituent utterances, and, more importantly, establish explanatory dependencies between those causes.

Even though the beliefs and intentions of the speaker enter into the explanation of the utterance or mental event in several places, it is not clear that they *essentially* determine the representational properties of the utterance or mental event. Consider, first, the psychological factors that select for certain causes. They establish certain explanatory dependencies, so that the cause of the predicate term is asymmetrically dependent upon that of the subject term or vice versa. Certain psychological factors explain how a certain causal setup comes to exist: why the property that causes the occurrence of the predicate is asymmetrically dependent upon the object that causes the occurrence of the subject (or vice versa). Still it is that causal setup – that asymmetric dependency itself – that explains the representational properties of the utterance or event. It is the asymmetric dependency that explains what is represented by the utterance and which expression will function as the predicating expression. The mental or linguistic utterance would have the same representational properties it has if the asymmetric dependence were the same, but the psychological factors were different or even if something nonpsychological, but natural, had established the nexus-dependency.

In the case of speech, there will be other sorts of intentions that enter as well. There are Gricean intentions: one utters the words intending to produce a belief in one's audience by means of their recognition of one's intention. (These intentions and beliefs are constitutive of the "speaker's meaning" of the utterance.) Even so, the event meaning of the utterance may be distinguished from this notion of its speaker's meaning. The representational properties of the utterance may have a life of their own independent of the Gricean intentions and beliefs of the speaker, for the event may not have the representational properties the speaker intended and may have representational properties the speaker did not intend. So event meaning is not the same as speaker meaning.

This may be illustrated, first, in the case of reference. I assume that *reference* is essentially intentional: the referent of an expression is the object the speaker intends to pick out by his use of the expression. Stampe gives this example: imagine a case where someone is describing, from memory, a person he remembers as his great grandfather. But suppose that unbeknownst to him, it is his great grandmother he is remembering, and it is his memory of her that explains the description he is giving. So it was because her nose was crooked that he utters the predicate "crooked nose," and because her eyes were gray-blue that he says "gray-blue," and so on. Who is he describing – his great-grandfather or great-grandmother? We might very well say, "He thinks he is describing his great-grandfather, but, in fact, he is describing his great-grandmother." Stampe argues that, while the speaker may be referring to his great-grandfather, he may be describing his great-grandmother.[27] We might say, "Forget the conventional meaning of the words and the intentions of the speaker, and ask what *this* utterance *really* is a representation of: whose properties might *it* really tell us something about?" Unbeknownst to the speaker, his utterance is *about* his great-grandmother, and represents some property of hers, not of the referent. Now, the speaker may intend his audience to come to believe (etc., à la Grice) that the great-grandfather has a crooked nose. That belief identifies the "speaker's meaning" of the utterance, but it does not identify what I am calling its "event meaning." The event meaning of "He had a crooked nose" is that she had a crooked nose, for, given the way in which the utterance is causally related to her properties, it is a representation of her, not of him.

There are also cases in which the utterance may represent something as being the case, even though the speaker did not intend it to do so. A speaker may intend to be making a list of objects in his room and of properties instantiated in his room. But the way he goes about it is by picking objects in the room, saying the name of that object and then listing a property that that very object has.[28] So he says, "table, brown, chair, big, stove, hot," and so on. Suppose, in addition, that the asymmetric dependency is present. The reason that the property which causes the property-specifying word is its cause is because it belongs to whatever object causes the antecedent object-specifying word. Were another object to cause the object-specifying word, another property, a property of *that* object, would cause the property-specifying word. The speaker does not intend that his audience come to believe that the chair is brown or that the stove is hot by means of their recognizing his intention that they believe it, for he has no intention that they believe it, even

27 Stampe, "Show and Tell," p. 240.

28 This example was given to me by Alan Sidelle. Some might think it is a counterexample to my proposal, because the nexus-dependency is present, but the utterances don't represent anything as being the case. I think that they *do* represent something as being the case, despite the fact that they are not intended to and that they are not sentences.

if he has an audience and wants his audience to understand what he is doing. So his utterance does not have what Grice would call an "utterer's meaning."[29] Nevertheless, the words that come out of his mouth comprise a representation of the color of the table, the size of the chair, and the temperature of the stove, because those words are causally related to those properties in such a way that if fidelity conditions had governed their utterance, they would carry such information about them. The property-specifying words make determinate the relevant determinable, representing the color of the table as brown, the size of the chair as big, and so on. Thus, though these are nonstandard examples, they are utterances that express propositions.

Of course, the utterance the speaker made is not the utterance of a *sentence* unless it is of a certain grammatical kind, so the kind of unity such sequences of words exhibit should not be called "sentential unity." But the point I would make is that the unity of the sentence is *basically* just a kind of unity that might be common to many different kinds of events in virtue of which they have propositional content. Of course, once that kind of unity is associated with strings of words of certain grammatical forms – sentences – or we have conventions for regarding strings of certain grammatical forms (sentences) as having that unity and others (lists) not, then propositional combination will be associated with certain grammatical forms. It will be associated with that grammatical form, whether or not the particular event of that form, in fact, tracks some property of an object, whether or not it would carry information about it had it been produced in certain conditions. Knowing and utilizing these conventions a speaker may utter "x is F," intending his audience to come to believe that x is F, and that may suffice for his having "said" that x is F, even if he is saying what he is saying with no knowledge of x or any beliefs about whether it is or is not F, even if he is attributing F to x if only because F is the first property that popped into his head. That is because it is sufficient to say something that the speaker uttered a grammatical sentence intending to say something (or, better, intending that his audience come to have a belief by means of their recognition that he intends them to believe it). That suffices, perhaps, only if saying is associated with certain grammatical forms, some of which have or had genuine event meaning.

---

29   If he did have such intentions, then his utterance would take on the aspect of a sentence and his act that of saying.

The notion of event meaning does not explain what is said by the utterance with reference to the intention to say something. Nor does it explain the content of the utterance with reference to a belief with the same content. Furthermore, the speaker's beliefs and intentions about the representational properties of the utterance do not determine what representational properties the utterance actually has. That being said, it is unclear whether a notion of event meaning could be entirely divorced from an agent's psychological states. Perhaps, what mental states we have always depends upon what other mental states we have: what we believe depends upon what other things we believe, and how and why we come to have the particular thoughts we do depends upon what our interests are, what we know and don't know.

An attempt to divorce altogether the explanation of the utterance or mental event from the agent's psychological states would show what is controversial. Imagine the following scenario: there is a causal process in which, in certain circumstances, properties of objects cause noises to be emitted from a person's mouth regardless of his intentions or beliefs. So the person makes these noises even when he intends not to, and the beliefs he has regarding the properties of these objects are irrelevant to which noises are emitted. So far this seems entirely possible. But now suppose that the nexus-dependency is present, so that whatever property causes the utterance of the property-specifying word does so only because it is a property of whatever object causes the object-specifying word. Is it possible to provide an understanding of that "only because" without the agent's having certain intentions and beliefs? Are there cases in nature where A wouldn't be the thing that caused B unless C had been the thing that caused D? Imagine also that there is (as there would have to be for the utterance to have "event" meaning) a mapping between objects and properties, on the one hand, and expressions on the other hand, and that that mapping depends upon tokens of that type meaning what they do. Or, to put it in less semantically rich terms, the speaker utters the word he does because of what would cause the words to be uttered under fidelity conditions. Can that explanation be divorced from the beliefs of the speaker? That would turn on the issue of whether what would cause a word to be tokened under certain conditions can be causally relevant to the tokening of the word, or whether it is only our beliefs about what would cause it to be tokened under certain conditions that can enter into the causal chain by means of which it is produced. (It depends, e.g., on whether the being white/"gray" law could depend upon the being gray/"gray" law without the intervention of our beliefs.) If the sort of causal counterfactuals established by the nexus-dependency could be present in nature, and if symbols could be tokened because of what other tokens of that type indicate, then event meaning would not essentially depend on psychological states for its production. Those, of course, are very big Ifs.

Bibliography

Anscombe, G. E. M., *An Introduction to Wittgenstein's Tractatus* (London: Hutchinson, 1959).

——, "Retractation," *Analysis*, 26 (1965), pp. 33–6.

Austin, J. L., "How to Talk: Some Simple Ways," in his *Philosophical Papers* (Oxford: Oxford University Press, 1961), pp. 181–200.

Bergmann, G., "Ineffability, Ontology and Method," *Philosophical Review*, 69 (1960), pp. 18–40. Reprinted in *Essays on Wittgenstein*, ed. E. D. Klemke (Urbana: University of Illinois Press, 1971), pp. 3–24.

Bradley, F. H., *Appearance and Reality*, 2nd edn. (London: Swan Sonnenschein, 1906).

——, *Principles of Logic*, 2nd edn. (London: Oxford Press, 1922).

Candlish, S., "The Unity of the Propositions and Russell's Theories of Judgement," in *Russell and the Origins of Analytical Philosophy*, ed. R. Monk and A. Palmer (Bristol: Thoemmes Press, 1996).

Carruthers, P., "On Concept and Object," *Theoria*, 49 (1983), part 2, pp. 49–86.

Cook Wilson, J., *Statement and Inference with Other Philosophical Papers*, 2 vols. (Oxford: Oxford University Press, 1926).

Davidson, D., "Truth and Meaning," *Synthese*, 17 (1967), pp. 304–23.

Dennett, D., "Evolution, Error, and Intentionality," in his *The Intentional Stance* (Cambridge, MA: MIT Press, 1987).

Dretske, F., "Conclusive Reasons," *Australasian Journal of Philosophy*, 49 (1971), pp. 1–22.

——, *Knowledge and the Flow of Information* (Cambridge, MA: MIT Press, 1981).

——, "The Epistemology of Belief," *Synthese*, 55 (1983), pp. 3–19.

——, "Misrepresentation," in *Belief*, ed. R. Bogdan (Oxford: Oxford University Press, 1986).

——, *Explaining Behavior: Reasons in a World of Causes* (Cambridge, MA: MIT Press, 1988).

Dummett, M., *Frege: Philosophy of Language*, 2nd edn. (Cambridge, MA: Harvard University Press, 1981).

Fodor, J., "Semantics, Wisconsin Style," *Synthese*, 59 (1984), pp. 231–50.

——, *A Theory of Content* (Cambridge, MA: MIT Press, 1990).

Frege, G., "Function and Concept" (1891), in *Translations from the Philosophical Writings of Gottlob Frege*, tr. P. Geach and M. Black (New York: Philosophical Library, 1952), pp. 21–41.

——, "On Concept and Object" (1892), in *Translations from the Philosophical Writings of Gottlob Frege*, tr. P. Geach and M. Black (New York: Philosophical Library, 1952), pp. 42–56.

——, "On Sense and Reference" (1892), in *Translations from the Philosophical Writings of Gottlob Frege*, tr. P. Geach and M. Black (New York: Philosophical Library, 1952), pp. 56–78.

——, *Begriffschrift* (1879), in *The Frege Reader*, ed. M. Beaney (Oxford: Blackwell, 1997), pp. 47–78.

——, "Comments on *Sinn* and *Bedeutung*" (1892), in *The Frege Reader*, ed. M. Beaney, (Oxford: Blackwell, 1997), pp. 172–81.

——, *The Foundation of Arithmetic* (1884), in *The Frege Reader*, ed. M. Beaney (Oxford: Blackwell, 1997), pp. 84–129.

——, "Thought" (1918), in *The Frege Reader*, ed. M. Beaney (Oxford: Blackwell, 1997), pp. 325–45.

Gaskin, Richard, "Bradley's Regress, The Copula and The Unity of the Proposition," *Philosophical Quarterly*, 45 (179) (1995), pp. 161–79.

Geach, P., *Reference and Generality* (Ithaca, NY: Cornell University Press, 1962).

Gibson, M., "Asymmetric Dependencies, Ideal Conditions, and Meaning," *Philosophical Psychology*, 9 (1996), pp. 235–59.

——, "The Unity of the Sentence and the Connection of Causes," *Philosophy and Phenomenological Research*, 58 (4) (1998), pp. 827–45.

Grice, H. P., "Meaning," *Philosophical Review*, 66 (1957), pp. 377–88.

Griffin, J., *Wittgenstein's Logical Atomism* (Seattle: University of Washington Press, 1964).

Grimm, R. H., "Names and Predicables," *Analysis*, 26 (1966), pp. 138–46.

Hylton, P., *Russell and the Origin of Analytical Philosophy* (Oxford: Clarendon Press, 1990).

Johnson, W. E., *Logic*, part 1 (Cambridge: Cambridge University Press, 1921).

Kant, I., *Critique of Pure Reason*, tr. N. Kemp Smith (New York: St. Martin's Press, 1965).

Kaplan, D., "Quantifying In," *Synthese*, 19 (1969), pp. 178–214.

Kripke, S., *Naming and Necessity* (Cambridge, MA: Harvard University Press, 1972).

Leibniz, G. W., "What Is an Idea," in *Philosophical Papers and Letters*, ed. L. E. Loemker (Dordrecht: Reidel, 1977).

Linsky, L., "The Unity of the Proposition," *Journal of the History of Philosophy*, 30 (1992), pp. 243–73.

Palmer, A., *Concept and Object: The Unity of the Proposition in Logic and Psychology* (New York: Routledge, 1988).

Pears, D., "The Relation between Wittgenstein's Picture Theory of Propositions and Russell's Theories of Judgment," *Philosophical Review*, 86 (1977), pp. 177–96.

Plato, *The Sophist*, in *The Collected Dialogues of Plato*, 15th edn., ed. E. Hamilton and H. Cairns (Princeton, NJ: Princeton University Press, 1994), tr. F. M. Cornford, pp. 957–1117.

Ramsey, F. P., "Facts and Propositions," *Aristotelian Society Supplementary*, 7 (1927), pp. 153–70. Reprinted in *The Foundations of Mathematics*, ed. R. B. Braithwaite, (Paterson, NJ: Littlefield, Adams, 1960), pp. 138–55.

——, "Universals," *Mind*, 34 (136) (1925), pp. 401–17. Reprinted in *The Foundations of Mathematics*, ed. R. B. Braithwaite (Paterson, NJ: Littlefield, Adams, 1960), pp. 112–34.

Russell, B., *Introduction to Mathematical Logic*, 2nd edn. (London: George Allen & Unwin, 1920).

——, "Knowledge by Acquaintance and Knowledge by Description," in his *Mysticism and Logic* (New York: W. W. Norton, 1929), pp. 209–32.

——, *The Principles of Mathematics*, 2nd edn. (London: George Allen & Unwin, 1937).

——, "The Philosophy of Logical Atomism" (1924), in his *Logic and Knowledge* (London: Unwin Hyman, 1956), pp. 321–44.

——, "On Denoting" (1905), in *Logic and Knowledge*, ed. R. C. Marsh (London: Unwin Hyman, 1956), pp. 103–24.

——, "On Relations of Universals and Particulars" (1911), in his *Logic and Knowledge* (London: Unwin Hyman, 1956), pp. 103–24.

——, "The Philosophy of Logical Atomism," *Monist* (1918). Reprinted in *Logic and Knowledge* (London: Unwin Hyman, 1956), pp. 175–82.

——, "On the Nature of Truth and Falsehood" (1910), in his *Philosophical Essays* (New York: Simon & Schuster, 1966), pp. 147–59.

——, *The Problems of Philosophy* (New York: H. Holt, 1912). Reprinted (Buffalo, NY, Prometheus Books, 1988).

Ryle, G., "The Theory of Meaning," *British Philosophy in Mid-Century*, ed. C. A. Mace (London: George Allen & Unwin, 1957), pp. 239–64. Reprinted in *Philosophy of Ordinary Language*, ed. C. E. Caton (Urbana: University of Illinois Press, 1963), pp. 128–53.

Sainsbury, M., "How Can we Say Something," in *Russell and the Origins of Analytical Philosophy*, ed. R. Monk and A. Palmer (Bristol: Thoemmes Press, 1996), pp. 137–51.

Sellars, W., "Naming and Saying," *Philosophy of Science*, 29 (1962), pp. 7–26. Reprinted in *Essays on Wittgenstein*, ed. E. D. Klemke (Urbana: University of Illinois Press, 1971), pp. 78–103.

Stalnaker, R., *Inquiry* (Cambridge, MA: MIT Press, 1984).

Stampe, D., "Show and Tell," in *Forms of Representation*, ed. B. Freed, A. Marras, and P. Maynard (New York: American Elsevier Publishing, 1975), pp. 221–45.

——, "Toward a Causal Theory of Linguistic Representation." Reprinted in *Contemporary Perspectives in the Philosophy of Language*, ed. P. A. French, T. E. Uehling, and H. K. Wettstein (Minneapolis: University of Minnesota Press, 1979), pp. 81–102.

——, "Verification and a Causal Account of Meaning," *Synthese*, 69 (1986), pp. 107–37.

——, "Content, Context and Explanation," in *Information, Semantics and Epistemology*, ed. E. Villanueva (Oxford: Blackwell, 1990), pp. 134–52.

Strawson, P. F., *Individuals: An Essay in Descriptive Metaphysics* (London, Methuen, 1959).

——, "The Asymmetry of Subject and Predicates," in *Language, Belief and Metaphysics*, ed. H. E. Kiefer and M. K. Munitz (Albany: State University of New York Press, 1970). Reprinted in *Logico-Linguistic Papers* (London: Methuen, 1971).

——, *Subject and Predicate in Logic and Grammar* (London: Methuen, 1974).

Wiggins, D., "On Being in the Same Place at the Same Time," *Philosophical Review*, 77 (1968), pp. 90–5.

——, "The Sense and Reference of Predicates: A Running Repair to Frege's Doctrine and a Plea for the Copula," *Philosophical Quarterly*, 34 (136) (1984), pp. 311–28.

Wittgenstein, L., *Tractatus Logico-Philosophicus*, tr. D. F. Pears and B. F. McGuiness (London: Routledge & Kegan Paul, 1961).

——, *Notebooks 1914–1916*, 2nd ed., ed. G. H. von Wright and G. E. M. Anscombe (Chicago: University of Chicago Press, 1979).

Index

BC 181 .G46 2004

Gibson, Martha I.

From naming to saying